REMAKING HISTORY

Remaking History considers the ways that historical fictions of all kinds enable a complex engagement with the past. Popular historical texts, including films, television and novels, along with cultural phenomena such as superheroes and vampires, broker relationships to 'history', while also enabling audiences to understand the ways in which the past is written, structured and ordered.

Jerome de Groot uses examples from contemporary popular culture to show the relationship between fiction and history in two key ways. Firstly, the texts pedagogically contribute to the historical imaginary and secondly, they allow reflection upon how the past is constructed as 'history'. In doing so, they provide an accessible and engaging means to critique, conceptualize and reject the processes of historical representation. The book looks at the use of the past in fiction from sources including *Mad Men*, *Downton Abbey* and Howard Brenton's *Anne Boleyn*, along with the work of directors such as Terrence Malick, Quentin Tarantino and Martin Scorsese, to show that fictional representations enable a comprehension of the fundamental strangeness of the past and the ways in which this foreign, exotic other is constructed.

Drawing from popular films, novels and TV series of recent years, and engaging with key thinkers from Marx to Derrida, *Remaking History* is a must for all students interested in the meaning that history has for fiction, and vice versa.

Jerome de Groot is Senior Lecturer at the University of Manchester. He is the author of *The Historical Novel* (2009), *Consuming History* (2008), and *Royalist Identities* (Palgrave, 2004).

REMAKING HISTORY

The past in contemporary historical fictions

Jerome de Groot

Routledge
Taylor & Francis Group

LONDON AND NEW YORK

First published 2016
by Routledge
2 Park Square, Milton Park, Abingdon, Oxon OX14 4RN

and by Routledge
711 Third Avenue, New York, NY 10017

Routledge is an imprint of the Taylor & Francis Group, an informa business

© 2016 Jerome de Groot

British Library Cataloguing-in-Publication Data
A catalogue record for this book is available from the British Library

Library of Congress Cataloging-in-Publication Data
De Groot, Jerome, 1975–
   Remaking history: the past in contemporary historical fictions /
Jerome de Groot.
   pages cm
   Includes bibliographical references and index.
   1. Historical fiction – History and criticism. 2. Literature and history.
   3. History in literature. I. Title.
   PN3441.D44 2015
   809.3′81 – dc23
   2015003903

ISBN: 978-0-415-85877-9 (hbk)
ISBN: 978-0-415-85878-6 (pbk)
ISBN: 978-1-315-69339-2 (ebk)

Typeset in Bembo and Stone Sans
by Florence Production Ltd, Stoodleigh, Devon, UK

Printed and bound in the United States of America by
Edwards Brothers Malloy on sustainably sourced paper

This one's for Ariadne

CONTENTS

FIGURES

ACKNOWLEDGEMENTS

Sande Cohen, Robert Burns, Alun Munslow, and Robert Rosenstone all commented generously on the project at various stages, and I thank them for their time, advice, and enthusiasm. Thomas Cauvin looked at the Introduction and helped greatly with its development. James Stanley, Andrew Moor, and Olivia de Groot all read chapters and made excellent suggestions for changes. I have spent much time discussing ideas with Sue Chaplin. I'd like to thank Stewart Mottram, Jennie Chapman, and Jo Metcalf, and the Department of English at the University of Hull, who kind of persuaded me to write this book after I gave a seminar there. I've given portions of this paper at seminars and conferences in University College Cork, Bishopsgate, Northumbria University, the Open University, and the University of Ulster, and I would like to thank all those who invited me to speak and listened and asked questions. I've talked about this with Kaye Mitchell, Anke Bernau, Kier Waddington, Robert Eaglestone, Christopher Vardy, Kate Byrne, Sarah Dunant, Marnie Hughes-Warrington, Emma Darwin, Chris de Groot, Lucy Munro, Ben Harker, Emily Weygang, Kate Graham, Emma Darwin, and Sally O'Reilly, so thanks to them all.

Part of the discussion about this book has taken place outside the UK, and this is something I am very excited about, but also something that often depends on the goodwill, generosity, intellectual engagement, and language skills of others. Thanks to Ian Christie and Veronika Klusáková for the great welcome and discussion at Olomouc. Thanks also to Vera Dubina and Andrei Zorin for a wonderful time in Moscow and some great insights. I should thank Yuri, Rosa, and Katya for a great afternoon in Delicatessen discussing ideas, and to Irina Prokhorova and the team at the *New Literary Observer* for stimulating times at Memorial and afterwards. Thanks also to Daniela Fleiß and Angela Schwarz at Siegen. Barbara Korte and Sylvia Paletschek were great hosts in Freiburg.

As ever, the team at Routledge has been excellent. Thanks to Eve Setch, Catherine Aitken, Paul Brotherston, and Amy Welmers. Thanks to my colleagues in the Division of English, American Studies and Creative Writing at the University of Manchester and also in SALC, particularly to Amanda Mathews, for keeping me smiling. I pay tribute, as ever, to Jeremy Maule and James Knowles, who taught me very little about popular history but a lot about thinking and writing.

I would not be able to do any of this without Sharon, and her love keeps me keeping on. The book is dedicated to my niece Ariadne/Hairy Bad Knees, with much affection and love.

PERMISSIONS

Sections of Chapter 1 are reprinted from '"Who would want to believe that, except in the service of the bleakest realism?" Historical fiction and ethics', in Emily Sutherland and Tony Gibbons (eds), *Integrity in Historical Research* (London and New York: Routledge, 2011), pp. 13–28, with permission.

Sections of Chapter 3 are reprinted from '"Perpetually dividing and suturing the past and present": *Mad Men* and the illusions of history', *Rethinking History: The Journal of Theory and Practice* 15: 2 (2011), 269–87, with permission.

The section of Chapter 3 on Sarah Waters is reprinted from '"Something new and a bit startling": Sarah Waters and the historical novel', in Kaye Mitchell (ed.), *Sarah Waters* (London: Continuum, 2013), pp. 56–70, with permission.

Sections of Chapter 4 are reprinted from 'Afterword', in Barbara Korte and Sylvia Paletschek (eds), *Popular History Now and Then* (Bielefeld: transcript, 2012), pp. 281–95, with permission.

Sections of Chapter 5 are reprinted from 'Invitation to historians', *Rethinking History: The Journal of Theory and Practice* 18: 4 (2014), 599–612, with permission.

Excerpts from *Anne Boleyn* copyright © Howard Brenton 2010, published by Nick Hern Books (www.nickhernbooks.co.uk).

INTRODUCTION

Perverting history

This book considers how the past and imaginative art are bound up in the praxis *practice*
termed historical fiction. It looks at the ways in which the past, and the
contemporary relationship to it, is represented. Further, it investigates the processes
by which historical fictions broker this relationship and articulate for a sense of
historicity and also of historiography. The relationship between 'history' and
'fiction' is a strange, complex one that requires constant attention, and *Remaking
History* seeks to demonstrate how these uncanny qualities are fundamental to the
purpose and the effect of the texts. Those creating such fictions have sometimes
discussed this aspect of their work. When justifying writing about the case of Peter
Sutcliffe, known as the Yorkshire Ripper, the novelist David Peace considered the
ethics of fictionalizing horrific events:

> Perhaps novels and their fictions are, perversely, the more 'honest' way to
> try to understand and write about the past [. . .] a novel will always, already
> be a work of fiction and thus can never claim to be the whole truth and
> nothing but the truth.[1]

Peace argues that his particular form of narrating the past – the novel – achieves
something beyond the scope or the aim of mainstream historical discourse. He
suggests that fiction is not inherently the wrong mode for an investigation of the
past. For Peace, novels are a particular way to 'try to understand and write' pastness,
modulating comprehension as well as being a process of textualizing events. Yet
the rationalist epistemological models that have become socially acceptable for
engaging with the past (those apparatuses often termed History) continue to
maintain a hold over the vocabulary of enquiry and the imagining of how to think
about past events.[2] In Peace's view fictions attain a simpler kind of truth-telling
in their fragmented manifestation, or at least strive sincerely while acknowledging

their inability to comprehend. In his striking conjunction of honesty and perversity might be found the power and the strangeness inherent in historical fictions of all kinds. The combination of a term of distortion and diversion with the seemingly true figures the disavowing, inverting move that such works often enact. In particular, the sense inherent in the word 'perversely' that historical fictions might be wrongly right, against rationality, and, as Peace suggests, a way from 'the whole truth' is extremely resonant. Fictions challenge, 'pervert', critique, and queer a normative, straightforward, linear, self-proscribing History. They are entities that are interested in mocking and undermining such a way of analysing the past, while suggesting instead a set of very strange templates for a type of understanding that does not neatly fit with perceived notions of the 'historical'.[3]

Any historical imaginary that can hold within itself *Abraham Lincoln: Vampire Slayer* (Timur Bekmambetov, 2012), Ali Smith's *How to Be Both* (2014), *Spartacus* (Starz, 2010–13), *Downton Abbey* (ITV, 2010–) and *12 Years a Slave* (Steve McQueen, 2013) is more complex than has been hitherto described.[4] These fictions might be (and have been) criticized – and often, by extension, disregarded – as excessive, unrealistic, sensationalist, experimental, pulp, cheap, or popular. Yet they also open up discursive spaces where ideas about the past, desire, time, horror, nationhood, identity, chaos, legitimacy, and historical authority are debated. Such discussion is as much configured by the excessive, unrealistic, sensationalist, pulp, cheap, popular aspect of such texts as their 'historical engagement', and these diverse elements contribute to the historical imaginary that they enable and resource. These texts allow a culture to think in new ways about what historical engagement, and the writing of the past, might actually be, and to rethink the terms of historical understanding. They contribute to the historical imaginary, both in their diegetic content and also in the modes of narrativization, knowing, and articulation that they deploy. Fundamental to the purpose of these works are just the qualities that are often disregarded – their fictive elements, that is, their 'perversity', in contrast to the rationalism expected of true historical engagement.[5]

This book, then, argues that historical fictions of all kinds – but specifically novels, films, TV shows – do work that needs to be understood and studied in more depth than hitherto.[6] Their conjunctions of honesty and perversity should be analysed and interrogated. *Remaking History* looks at anglophone film, television, and novels concerned with the past over the last decade or so, to demonstrate the still unacknowledged contribution that they make to the way that society comprehends and narrativizes the past. The book seeks to understand the kinds of epistemological position that these fictions enable and suggest. Its central contention is that these historical fictions have two key effects. First, they contribute to the historical imaginary, having an almost pedagogical aspect in allowing a culture to 'understand' past moments. Second, and most importantly for the book's purpose, they allow reflection upon the representational processes of 'history'. They provide a means to critique, conceptualize, engage with, and reject the processes of representation or narrativization. These works provide the audience with a historiographical toolkit that allows them to remark upon the discourse of 'making' history. This is not to

- Past, time, truthfulness, honesty

suggest that popular historical fictions simply mimic 'mainstream' models, but that they provide positions of their own, which can be discerned and, to an extent, described. As Marnie Hughes-Warrington has argued about historical film:

> Historical film studies is thus no longer simply about reading and analysing films [. . .] What makes a film historical, I believe, is its location in a timebound network of discussions – more or less explicit – on what history is and what it is for. On this definition any film may be historical because it is viewed as offering indexical markers – on-screen phenomena seen as capturing or connected with past phenomena – or because it suggests something about how and why histories are made.[7]

This book, then, considers fictional engagement with 'how and why histories are made'. It is uncommon still for scholarship to look seriously at the ways in which historical fictions might work, other than to analyse their *representation* of the past.[8] Yet, as will become clear, what is presented in these fictions is not 'history' but modes of knowing the past. They are ways of exploring and engaging that are fundamentally fictional, while generally using the realist mode to suggest rational truthfulness of some kind.

Historical fictions may not be Public History and are probably not History.[9] In fact, using the terms 'history' and 'historical' at all might be problematic. Yet these texts engage with tropes of pastness and, in doing so, articulate a historiographical sensibility.[10] Most importantly, they are, for the most part, identified as 'historical' or part of a set of recognized historicized aesthetic models. In some ways, research into historical fiction of this type has been hamstrung by the 'historical' descriptor. There is a presumed binary relationship between history and fiction (with 'fiction' invariably being the lesser partner).[11] Seemingly, historical fiction seeks to contribute to mainstream historical knowledge, as it represents the past in the present according to certain key rules, most often by the use of evidence, realism, and a seriousness of tone. Historical fictions are texts that suggest an experience of a 'past' that cannot and does not exist, insofar as it is fictional and the past is irretrievable. Manifestly, the term 'historical fiction' is not something definable and comprehensible. This paradoxical, contradictory phrase is unstable, while striving for clarity, a characteristic that might be descriptive of historical fictions themselves. The phrase – 'historical fiction' (or replace fiction with 'film', 'TV', 'novel', 'game', and the like) – is inherently contradictory (or a tautology, insofar as all history is fiction). Simply put, research into historical fiction has been bedevilled by an overriding concern about the *historicalness* of such work. Developing from this, the concern of this present work is to assume that historical fictions are unstable, but to think about how the fictional element of the relationship inflects the historical – not the other way around, which is often the case in studies of this kind. What do the strategies of fictionalizing – from addresses to emotion to shifts in narrative technique – suggest about modes of knowing? If it is possible to trouble the terms 'historical' and 'fiction', how might they challenge each other when yoked together? If history is fiction − which is not a new, or a particularly bold, claim − what does that mean for *fiction*, rather than history, and the fictive knowing of the past? Does fiction − with all its messiness, disorder, range, and strangeness − have a traceable historical effect of any description?

Robert Rosenstone argued this several years ago in an extremely suggestive section of his seminal *History on Film/Film on History*. Suggesting that film might be 'a new form of historical thinking', he asserts:

> The history film not only challenges traditional History, but helps return us to a kind of ground zero, a sense that we can never really know the past, but can only continually play with it, reconfigure, and try to make meaning out of the traces it has left behind.[12]

Rosenstone's claim here is radical, placing the historical film as a critique of 'traditional' forms of knowledge.[13] The historical film, in his account, explicitly challenges 'History'. It reinterprets and answers this monolithic, 'traditional History' by offering new interpretations of what 'evidence' there is. It lets an audience think differently. However, he also argues further that such texts allow the audience to *know* differently, or, at least, to become aware of the structures of knowing that are being worked through. There is something generous in this account, the way that film aids ('helps') a *reconstructed* sense of how the past and history relate to one another. These texts add to our understanding and appreciation of pastness. Historical film invokes, through a number of elements − texture, form, content − a relationship to the past, as well as a representation of that past. By foregrounding self-consciousness about the mode of creating 'history', such film does historiographical work and undertakes something valuable at the level of epistemology.

Despite its gesture to healing, Rosenstone's historiographical articulation emphasizes ambiguity and absence. There is something melancholic in this known lack of knowledge. Rosenstone's invocation of 'ground zero' here is a strange moment of uncanniness in his writing that underlines this valedictory tone. The apocalyptic sense of 'ground zero' as the location directly underneath a nuclear explosion, and, moreover, its use as a phrase in targeting and bombing warfare of all kinds, and, thence, its being representative of the increasing use of military jargon in standard discourse (along with 'recruit' and 'deploy', for instance), all point to a very deliberate placing of the phrase here. Of course, it also invokes the traumas of 9/11 and very clearly is meant to stand here as a way of considering apocalypse, revelation, the relationship of the body to the past and of the revenants of trauma. This echo of 9/11 is used to speak plainly of the revelatory, destructive quality that history film might have, something that might strip away great effacing structures and supposed false idols. Rosenstone also uses it to suggest that a kind of post-Enlightenment rhetoric of historical 'knowing' has taken 'us' away from the unknown actuality, has drawn 'us' from the starting place of the not-known.[14] The movement ('return us to') both is to the past itself (the return of the historical consciousness to a purer state of some kind) and also depends to a certain extent on a sense of temporal linearity. He illustrates a return from a fruitless journey to the source, the beginning again (the moment of 0 in accounts of past events).

Rosenstone's diction is key, and its significance is worth teasing out. He makes a binary of 'sense' and 'know', rendering the effect of the history film as something affective (sensory), in opposition to a discourse that strives for rational understanding and comprehension (knowing). Instead, he argues, 'we [. . .] continually play' with the past. Play is used in several senses here – toy, move, compete – but is primarily suggesting a kind of Derridean *jouissance*, something ludic and possibly (un)serious in an engagement with pastness, which is picked up again in the term 'trace'. Again, this is put in parallel with rationalizing terms – 'reconfigure' is particularly technocratic, a language suited to computing, electronics, or cartography. *Knowing* is contrasted with a not-knowing articulated as 'play', something that is not simply the reflected other of knowledge, but a different thing altogether. Making meaning, remodelling and reshaping, playing and shifting – for Rosenstone, this is the essence of the history film and, in particular, its implicit critique of 'traditional History'. *Knowing* the past is impossible. The history film allows this to be seen and, by utilizing emotions and imaginative affect, brings comfort of a kind and a new perspective. It presents a new way of knowing, one that is contradictory and un-rational. This perspective might be bleak, as not knowing the past renders the present differently. A very modern sense of historio-solitariness might be invoked here. This is maybe why the 9/11 reference is used – a sadness about the return to a nothingness, a fragmentation of human relationships inherent here in the undermining of this knowledge system, the violent birthing of a new world order. It also invokes a sense of the possibly traumatic relationship between historical knowledge and fictional knowledge. 'History' gives identity, agency, future, temporal order, nationhood; historical fiction might replace this with something, but its undermining of totalizing models of knowledge leaves people very much alone. Without 'History', all a society has are 'traces', made into various collages to mimic an order it cannot believe in.

Remaking History is interested in this latter element of Rosenstone's thinking. Rather than being concerned solely with how historical fictions of various types *render* pastness – their accuracy, their politics, the way that they adapt or translate – the book proposes to examine how these fictions provide ways of knowing and engaging with the past. Of necessity, owing to space but also with some polemic purpose, the book reads 'historical fictions' as in some ways homogeneous – that is, it is important to be aware of the local generic and formal detail of a text, but in some ways their action might be generalized within a wider arc of popular historiography.[15] This is a problematic assertion, but, in the chapters that follow, it becomes obvious that each and every 'text' approaches the past differently, and so any kind of generalization, even within discussions of the same 'kind' of work, will miss some of the key formal, generic, or precisely local elements. A precise typology is yet to be written and may be impossible – and, to an extent, undesirable, insofar as it would attempt to impose a template upon an anarchic, fragmented, and wilful set of texts. The point here is that it is key to look at the various ways that the past has been translated into the present (and the present into the past), in order to discern how historiographic ideas circulate and are modulated in the cultural imagination – that is, to understand their epistemological consequence. It is necessary to look on novels, or films, or plays, or games, or TV series, not as poor versions of history, nor within a binary wherein they are at the margins of a centrifugal historical culture, nor as parasites on 'proper' historical knowledge and practice, but as establishing modes of historical awareness, engagement, narrativization, and comprehension. Hayden White argued this in 1966:

> It is the same notion of objectivity that binds historians to an uncritical use of the chronological framework for their narratives. When historians try to relate their 'findings' about the 'facts' in what they call an 'artistic' manner, they uniformly eschew the techniques of literary representation which Joyce, Yeats, and Ibsen have contributed to modern culture. There have been no significant attempts at surrealistic, expressionistic, or existentialist historiography in this century (except by novelists and poets themselves) for all of the vaunted 'artistry' of the historians of modern times. It is almost as if the historians believed that the *sole possible form* of historical narration was that used in the English novel as it had developed by the late nineteenth century.[16]

White's point here is to undermine the realist mode in historical expression. His sense of the English novel as essentially a bourgeois form articulating a colonial panopticonism through its tropes of narrative authenticity and omnipresent – though diegetically absent – authorial voice is used to attack historical writing as similarly beholden to its own authority. This attack on the representational strategies of realism is essentially a desire to disestablish the normative tropes of historical discourse, and to demonstrate mainstream historiography as essentially one *structure* of knowing, among many others, that has attempted to authenticate its own centrality.[17] What is key here, though, is White's slightly off-the-cuff articulation of different types of historiography as practised by poets and novelists – 'surrealistic, expressionistic, or existentialist'. In attempting to make realistic historical narrative cede its centrality in the historical imagination, White demonstrates that multiple other types of historiographical writing and engagement exist away from the 'centre'. These historiographical others are hidden in plain sight within culture, but 'History' has rarely acknowledged them, argues White. Since he wrote this, there have been numerous challenges to the centrality of certain historical discourses, and, in particular, the idea of historical narrative has been roundly critiqued, but the imaginative historiographic imaginary he describes has been largely ignored.[18] It is the sense of the artistic or fictional historiographical model as other to mainstream history that this book explores, working this idea through various motifs in order to try to discern how and why imaginative history might work.

Considering the ethics of historicizing, the historiographer Frank Ankersmit reflects upon the strange status of the historical text:

[a] representation of the past in much the same way that a work of art is a representation of what it depicts [. . .] we have the discipline of history in order to avail ourselves of these representations of the past that may best function as a textual substitute for the actual, but absent, past.[19]

'History' creates versions of the past, 'textual substitutes' for something that is not there, absent, unfilled, chaotic, empty. These are the consolations that the 'discipline of history' provides. It is a way of putting *something* in place of a missing, errant alterity-other-past. Ankersmit's comparison to art is instructive. Much as art often works by and through pointing out its own artfulness, the lag between the real and the representation, so historical texts are fundamentally expressive of the misrecognition they entail, the disjunction between then and now. All historical texts enact a desire for truth that is leavened with a fundamental understanding that it is not there; there is nothing innately real in an encounter with it. 'History' is the attempt at reconciling the unseen other of the past with contemporary fractured identity; as in all attempts at such psychic healing of trauma, it is doomed to failure.

If 'History' is a representation of this unachievable alterity, *historiography* articulates the ways in which this illustrative process has been made to work and the rules of engagement. It is a tool enabling the comprehension – or at least some appreciation – of the discourses, concerns, and issues involved in articulating 'history' or translating pastness. Historiography analyses the discipline of history and looks at the methodologies inherent in the writing, production, and creation of historical 'knowledge'. Historiography is the set of tools that the discipline of history is articulated through, ordered, or organized by. Historiography suggests, debates, theorizes about, and presents the ways in which historians grapple with 'truth', subjectivity, ethics, and otherness in their practice and approach. Epistemology, language, indeterminism are all discussed and conceptualized, worked through, reflected upon. Historiography provides a means of describing the problems inherent in historical representation.

Ankersmit's comments, however, as with much historiographical writing, are concerned with auditing the practice of academic or professional History. Discussions about ethics, epistemology, and historiography still tend to make the figure of the historian central in undertaking a narrative/account/storytelling/rendering/translation of the past.[20] Scholarly work regularly ignores the contribution to the historical imaginary and to popular historiography of the swathe of films, television, and books representing and versioning the past. It is unusual to come across work that seeks to comprehend the historical and historiographical *work* being done by textual iterations outside the academy. Yet, in the contemporary anglophone world, the ways in which individuals encounter time, the past, 'history', and memory mostly fall outside an academic or professional framework. Indeed, in popular culture, the professional historian is at best one of a range of voices contributing to an awareness of things that happened in the past. Historical fictions engage with the processes that Ankersmit is outlining here, demonstrating a concern with the processes of historicization – that is, a historiographical sensibility. Understanding how this works is the task of *Remaking History*. The book does not seek a template or to taxonomize. Instead, it is an attempt at demonstrating the multitude of ways that the past is engaged with.

Remaking History takes into account a wide number of television series, films, and novels. In approaching the ways in which historical fictions work, the book considers several key ideas: ethics, nationalism, the body, affect, emotion, pleasure, terror, death, time, and materiality. It is broadly organized into three thematic parts. Part I (Chapters 1 and 2) focuses on *ethics, politics, and nationalism*. There is a consideration of the historical novel as a form of ethical reading of the past, and a set of arguments relating to nationalism and film. Part II (Chapters 3 and 4) analyses *haunting, ghostliness, and the undead*. The insubstantiality of the past in the present is key here, and the ways that historical fictions stage the encounter with this absence are analysed. Part III (Chapters 5 and 6), on *pleasure, affect, and performance*, approaches the physical through consideration of the uncanny power of historical fictions, their ability (and need) to provoke some kind of physical reaction in their audiences, from terror to desire.

In *Hamlet*, Hamlet, stunned at the performance of the Player King, asks 'What's Hecuba to him, or he to Hecuba,/That he should weep for her?' (*Hamlet*, II, ii, 563–4). This acknowledgement of the seen/unseen gap between past event and present performance is inherent in all historical fictions. The internalized, syncopated relationship between then and now ('or he to Hecuba'), not necessarily linear but in tension, argues that performance of pastness can have emotive, physical, bodily power and affect in the present (he weeps). Yet, while acknowledging the weft of authenticity, an audience similarly sees its falseness (Hamlet's assertion of his own 'real' emotion). The popular historical text can express a physical connection – the body of the actor, weeping – but it cannot be real. In this self-denying fictiveness, this corporeal ethereality, this ability to reconcile the abstract and the physical, might be discerned the working of popular historical fictions. The representation of the past enfranchises the viewer by showing and revealing, by staging the internal historiographic debate of each text. An audience can see the joins. Fundamental to the encounter with the historical text is the desire for a wholeness of representation that understands that the text is *fundamentally* a representation. This book attempts to understand further how and why these texts work, in order to understand this encounter more fully.

Notes

1 David Peace, 'Why the Yorkshire Ripper?', *Daily Beast*, 7 March 2010; available online at: www.thedailybeast.com/articles/2010/03/07/why-the-yorkshire-ripper.html (accessed 25 November 2014). On Peace more generally, see Katy Shaw, *David Peace: Texts and Contexts* (Brighton, UK: Sussex Academic Press, 2010).
2 On the wide-ranging discussion of the place and influence of History in culture, see, for instance: Martin Davies, *Imprisoned by History* (London and New York: Routledge, 2012); Sande Cohen, *History out of Joint* (Baltimore, MD: Johns Hopkins University Press, 2005); Marnie Hughes-Warrington, *Revisionist Histories* (London and New York: Routledge,

2012); Jorma Kalela, *Making History* (Basingstoke, UK: Palgrave, 2011); and Keith Jenkins, *At the Limits of History* (London and New York: Routledge, 2009). A good overview of recent work in History and Theory is Ludmilla Jordanova, 'What's in a Name? Historians and Theory', *English Historical Review*, 126:523 (2011), 1456–77.

3 On the relationship between culture and history, see, for instance: Raphael Samuel, *Theatres of Memory* (London: Verso, 1994); Beverley Southgate, *History Meets Fiction* (Harlow, UK: Pearson, 2009); Jerome de Groot, *Consuming History* (London and New York: Routledge, 2008); and Alexander Macfie, ed., *The Fiction of History* (London and New York: Routledge, 2014). The key debate in the UK on this relationship, particularly as it regards the idea of 'heritage', was during the late 1980s; see: Patrick Wright, *On Living in an Old Country* (London: Verso, 1985); David Lowenthal, *The Past is a Foreign Country* (Cambridge, UK: Cambridge University Press, 1985); Robert Hewison, *The Heritage Industry: Britain in a Climate of Decline* (London: Methuen, 1987); and Samuel, op. cit. Greatly useful in this area, if slightly at an angle to this work, is Frank Ankersmit, 'Truth in History and Literature', *Narrative*, 18:1 (2010), 29–50.

4 Not to mention less 'mainstream' fictive media, such as games, adverts, documentary/ docudrama, re-enactment and the like; see: de Groot, *Consuming History*. This present book does not have the capacity to cover the whole range of articulations.

5 As Gil Bartholeyns argues:

> The debate has focused on the distinction between the 'authenticity' of the past and the historicity of the representation. Yet these aspects are in no way opposed. Instead, they maintain a fundamental connection between the impossibility of representing history and the possibility of making it live.
>
> ('Representation of the Past in Films: Between Historicity and Authenticity', *Diogenes*, 48:1 (2000), 31–47)

6 This is to build on the excellent work already undertaken by Robert Rosenstone, *History on Film/Film on History* (London: Pearson Longman, 2006); Marnie Hughes-Warrington, *History Goes to the Movies* (London and New York: Routledge, 2006); Ann Gray and Erin Bell, *History on Television* (London and New York: Routledge, 2013); Andrew Higson, *English Heritage, English Cinema* (Oxford, UK: Oxford University Press, 2003); Kate Mitchell and Nicola Parsons, eds, *Reading Historical Fiction* (Basingstoke, UK: Palgrave Macmillan, 2013); David Cannadine, ed., *History and the Media* (Basingstoke, UK: Palgrave Macmillan, 2007); Amy Holdsworth, *Television, Memory and Nostalgia* (Basingstoke, UK: Palgrave Macmillan, 2011); and other books cited throughout the following chapters.

7 Marnie Hughes-Warrington, *History Goes to the Movies*, p. 191.

8 However, a great example of analysis of the praxis of popular historical texts is the work of Rebecca Schneider, *Theatre and History* (Basingstoke, UK: Palgrave Macmillan, 2012) and *Performing Remains* (New York and London: Routledge, 2012).

9 On the relationship between 'public' and 'popular' history, see: Paul Ashton and Hilda Kean, eds, *People and Their Pasts: Public History Today* (Basingstoke, UK: Palgrave Macmillan, 2009); Jerome de Groot, ed., *Public and Popular History* (London and New York: Routledge, 2012); and Stefan Berger, Chris Lorenz, and Billie Melman, eds, *Popularizing National Pasts* (London and New York: Routledge, 2012).

10 On historiography in general, see: Robert Burns, ed., *Historiography* (London and New York: Routledge, 2005); Aviezer Tucker, ed., *A Companion to the Philosophy of History and Historiography* (Abingdon, UK: Blackwell, 2009); and, more widely, Hayden White, *Metahistory* (Baltimore, MD: Johns Hopkins University Press, 1975).

11 This has been generally discussed in work relating to the historical novel; see, for instance: Richard Maxwell, *The Historical Novel in Europe, 1650–1950* (Cambridge, UK: Cambridge University Press, 2009); and Frederic Jameson, *Postmodernism, or the Cultural Logic of Late Capitalism* (London: Verso, 1991).

12 Rosenstone, *History on Film/Film on History*, pp. 163–4.

13 Rosenstone's thought is carefully analysed in Jonathan Stubbs, *Historical Film: A Critical Introduction* (London: Bloomsbury, 2013), pp. 46–52.

14 In this, he echoes Foucault's 'Nietzsche, Genealogy, History' in Donald F. Bouchard, ed., *Language, Counter-memory, Practice*, trans. Donald F. Bouchard, Sherry Simon (Ithaca, NY: Cornell University Press, 1977), pp. 139–64.

15 See Ludmilla Jordanova's discussion of historical 'genres' here: *History in Practice* (London: Bloomsbury, 2006), particularly pp. 152–5.

16 Hayden White, 'The Burden of History', *History and Theory*, 5:2 (1966), 111–34 (p. 127). On this, see: David Leeson, 'Cutting Through History: Hayden White, William S. Burroughs, and Surrealistic Battle Narration', *Left History*, 10:1 (2005), 13–43. On White and history as discourse (of which fiction is just one part), see: *Tropics of Discourse* (Baltimore, MD: Johns Hopkins University Press, 1978).

17 See White's essay on the historical novel, 'Introduction: Historical Fiction, Fictional History, and Historical Reality', *Rethinking History*, 9:2–3 (2005), 147–57.

18 See, for instance, Alun Munslow, *Narrative and History* (London and New York: Routledge, 2007), and Southgate, *History Meets Fiction*.

19 'In Praise of Subjectivity', in David Carr, Thomas R. Flynn, and Rudolf A. Makkreel, eds, *The Ethics of History* (Evanston, IL: Northwestern University Press, 2004), pp. 3–28 (p. 8).

20 See, for instance: Edith Wyschogrod, *An Ethics of Remembering: History, Heterology, and the Nameless Others* (Chicago, IL: Chicago University Press, 1998); and Howard Marchitello, ed., *What Happens to History: The Renewal of Ethics in Contemporary Thought* (London and New York: Routledge, 2000).

PART I

Ethics, politics, and nationalism

1
READING AND ETHICS

Trusting the historical novel

This chapter considers the historical novel as emblematic of historical fictions in general. It opens with a general discussion of ideas relating to the form, as a way of outlining some of the key ideas the book as a whole will grapple with. The chapter therefore uses the well-established example of the historical novel genre to demonstrate some fundamental issues relating to historical fictions more widely. In particular, it suggests that the historical novel allows the writer to meditate upon society's strange relationship with the alterity of the past. Hilary Mantel's introductory 'Note' to *The Giant, O'Brien* – a book obsessed with the telling of stories – neatly demonstrates this central conceit. In this opening explanatory comment, commonplace in the form, she outlines the explicit intellectual and ethical challenge the historical novel presents to an audience: 'This is not a true story, though it is based on one'.[1] How do readers confront the commonplace, definitional conundrum that historical fictions cleave to fact and authenticity, even as they point out their own falsehood? The narrator of Jeanette Winterson's *The Passion* puts it in similarly disarming fashion: 'I'm telling you stories. Trust me'.[2] Fiction disavows the fact and ordering associated culturally with 'history'. In Mantel's combination of self-conscious untruth (the recounting of narrative) and an appeal to trust lies the aesthetics of historical fiction, constantly striving for a 'reality' while acutely aware of fiction. The contract made with the audience is one of trust, the reader or viewer allowing the untruths that are being presented. The reader acknowledges their fictive quality while, at some level, 'believing' in the realism and authenticity of the text.

Mantel's confident assertion is part of her paratextual outlining of the 'latitude' she has taken in writing her novel ('Note', sig. A6v). It is not true, she says, but gestures towards something that is. The logic of the sentence seems to suggest that, although this is not a true story, the historical record is itself, at best, a kind of accurate narrative: 'though it is based on one [ie. a true story]'. Mantel's note is the first text that a reader encounters after a self-conscious epigraph from George Macbeth's poem *The Cleaver Garden*: 'But then,/All crib from skulls and bones who push the pen./Readers crave bodies. We're the resurrection men' (sig. A5r). Taken together, these paratextual moments frame the novel. The Macbeth citation reminds the reader that the historical novelist deals in reclaiming those who are often long dead, resurrecting bodies from the past and breathing false fictional life into them. The 'Note' points out to a reader just some of the moments at which the author has deviated from the record. The reader, then, is signalled, not once but twice, before they even read a word of fictional historical story, that this is a wrought, created, false thing that they are encountering, part of some unholy ritual of raising dusty bodies (specifically, 'skulls and bones' and 'bodies', not ghosts).

As this example shows, historical novels clearly invite the reader to reflect upon the ways in which 'history' is told to them. They have a double effect, a kind of unsettling uncanniness, which seeks to enable an awareness of the wroughtness of both 'history' and 'fiction'.[3] Historical novels present something that looks like a past that readers think they know. They are often read within a nexus of entertainment, imaginative journeying, and pedagogy, as audiences turn to them to find out about eras and understand particular periods. This means that they contribute powerfully to the historical imaginary, and, hence, it is important to understand their own historiographic positions and aesthetic strategies.[4] Historical novels participate in a semi-serious game of authenticity and research, deploying tropes of realism and mimesis, while weaving fictional narrative. The realistic heft is what is looked for in the novels – reviewers regularly emphasize the authenticity, the affective impact, of historical fiction (it smells right, it feels right, the snap and tang of the past are communicated effectively).[5] A.N. Wilson writes of Hilary Mantel: 'Here, perhaps, we touch upon what makes historical fiction successful. I have no idea whether Mantel's More is a fair picture but because her novel is so realistic, I am prepared to believe her'.[6] Belief, here, is associated with stylistic realism, predicated upon a set of representational tropes that are agreed to be authentic rather than 'fair'. [The realist aesthetic in historical fiction, as elsewhere, is innately conservative and complex.] Yet, simultaneously, the reader is aware, as is the writer, that the 'realist' work they are reading is a narrative, incomplete, unfinished, unable to communicate anything other than a contemporary construction of an unknown, untouchable, lost, dead world.[8] Fiction undermines the totalizing effects of historical representation and points out that what is known is always partial, always a representation. Sensing this, historical novelists seek solace in authenticity and fiction simultaneously – citing their extreme research, at the same time as they distance themselves from 'reality'. The historical novel, therefore, sits at a peculiar angle to its creator, who generally disavows its reality while asserting its diegetic wholeness, authenticity, and truth. As a form, it raises questions about the virtue of representation and the choices made by both author and reader in interrogating and understanding the world.

Historical novels are diverse, strange things that contain a multitude of often-contradictory ideas about memory, ethics, history, and identity. They enact an exploration of truth, authenticity, epistemology, and historiography. Keith Jenkins points out how much historiographical theory, over the past few decades, has sought to assert the textuality of representations of the past, demonstrating that works of 'history' are merely imaginative assertions: 'For texts are not cognitive, empirical, epistemological entities, but speculative, propositional invitations to imagine the past ad infinitum'.[9] In this light, the historical novel can be seen as simply one more way of conceptualizing the past, an epistemological exercise in 'imagining'.[10] Michel de Certeau, among others, thought that fiction was 'the repressed other of historical discourse'; this was, claims Hayden White, because 'historical discourse wages everything on the true, while fictional discourse is interested in the real – which it approaches by way of an effort to fill out the domain of the possible or imaginable'.[11] De Certeau famously argued that, 'the past is the fiction of the present', outlining a view of historiography that suggested its relationship to the enaction of power structures.[12] In contrast, the potentiality of the historical novel to imagine, albeit aesthetically, to speculate and construct, is the point of writing about the past: 'the human effort to represent, imagine and think the world in its totality, both actual and possible, both real and imagined, both known and only experienced' (p. 147). Fiction is able to hypothesize, to imagine, to guess. What is compelling for White about the historical novel is that it inhabits and manages the 'borderlands between a chaotic or entropic historical reality [. . .] and the orderly and domesticated versions of that reality provided by professional historians' (p. 152). The key aspect of this particular historiographical intervention is the self-consciousness that Mantel artfully deploys. By brokering a relationship between 'real' and 'fiction' that is constantly in a state of flux and, further, by pointing out the epistemological gap inherent in representing the past (in fiction or 'history') through such self-conscious (and generically fundamental) motifs, historical novels undertake sophisticated conceptual work.

Furthermore, historical novels force the reader into a temporal disjuncture. They demand a shifting of imaginative time and, most particularly, a recognition of temporal otherness. Georg Lukács argued that the historical novel reminds the reader of their historicity and the possibility of otherness, death, and age. He posits the 'invention' of a sense of historicalness, a feeling post-revolution of the continuation and development of history as something non-static: 'Hence the concrete possibilities for men to comprehend their own existence as something historically conditioned, for them to see in history something which deeply affects their daily lives and immediately concerns them'.[13] Nietzsche appreciated Scott for the same reasons, as Richard Maxwell illustrates: 'he is historian because he is subject to history, and capable of externalizing his subjection'.[14] Lukács demonstrated that the historical novel inaugurates a revolutionary possibility through the imposition of a sense of pastness that might hold within it a sense of futurity. In its reminder of the individual as part of something that might be called history/past/timeliness/historicity, and in its creation of a dynamic timeline and imaginative space of potentiality within the representation of history, the historical novel fragments and fractures the reader's relationship with that history. The historicity that is inaugurated is not linear, but

[right margin, handwritten]
④ Historical fiction is itself liminal... situated between truth and untruth, between the real and the imagined...

dynamic and simultaneous. In a recent overview of the historical novel as a 'widespread [. . .] mutation', Perry Anderson outlines Frederic Jameson's account of the form. For Jameson, the 'exaggerated inventions of a fabulous and non-existent past (and future)' exhibited by the historical novel is intended to:

> rattle at the bars of our extinct sense of history, unsettle the emptiness of our temporal historicity, and try convulsively to reawaken the dormant existential sense of time by way of the strong medicine of lies and impossible fables, the electro-shock of repeated doses of the unreal and the unbelievable.[15]

Hence, historical novels can critique the hegemonic structure of a totalizing, explaining history. They challenge a deeply ideological sense of temporal identity, challenging hegemonic structures of knowing the now. The strategies inherent in knowing, enacting, and constructing official versions of history are laid bare by the effects of historical novels which attempt to hold within them the actuality and the authority of history, but always, always know, deep down, that they are fabrications. The past as presented in historical novels is an enactment, a recreation, a performance of pastness; it is a mimicking of a dominant discourse that enables the consideration of other multiplicities of identity and behaviour. In many ways, the popular historical text, whether it be film or television or book, is the other of the archive, the dissident, illegitimate reflection of the official, with playful inversion and misrecognition inherent in its being. Where the archive or the library is memory, the popular text is mismemory and misquotation.

The translation of the past into a recognizable, readable present demands a set of formal procedures and aesthetic assumptions that are particularly disconcerting, accruing around the illusion of authenticity. To use thoughts on linguistic translation, this involves 'the appearance . . . that the translation is not in fact a translation, but the "original"'.[16] Somehow, the historical novel must look like it is the original. This is the authentic fallacy. The illusion of this translation is key to the effect of the historical novel. Realism in historical novels – and historical fictions more generally – consists of aesthetic strategies designed to persuade an audience of the veracity of the representation. The fictions cleave to a particular set of evidentiary tropes gathered from governing discourses of authenticity. The past is filtered and reordered for a readership in the present by the gatekeeper novelist. Translation is inherently violent, and bringing the past into the present through these fictional means is problematic.[17] The ethics of translating and transporting the past into the now are complex, and meditated upon by historical novelists. The explanation of, the discussion of, the representation of, the other that is the past leads the writer into strange areas, and the provocation to the historical novelist is how to balance, understand, and conceptualize this; how to demonstrate, in their presentation of the past, that they understand the alienness and unknowability of that past.[18]

The essential relativism and reflection that link historical fiction and ontological temporal experience are expressed thoughtfully by John Fowles in his 1986 book *A Maggot*:

[She cries] the small tears of one who knows herself without choice. Her time has little power of seeing people other than they are in outward; which applies even to how they see themselves, labelled and categorized by circumstance and fate.[19]

At first glance, this seems to argue for historical relativism – the audience are not like them – of the kind that Fowles deploys regularly to rebut Marxist views of history in his earlier *The French Lieutenant's Woman* (1969). Yet the affective moment here (the emotional, resonant echo of pastness) is counterpointed by Fowles's assertion of mutual incomprehension, when he continues:

To us such a world would seem abominably prescribed, with personal destiny fixed to an intolerable degree, totalitarian in its essence; while to its chained humans our present lives would seem incredibly fluid, mobile, rich in free will [. . .] and above all anarchically, if not insanely, driven by self-esteem and self-interest.

(p. 55)

They were, the reader is, neither is correct; both are simply nodes in the river of history – which has the appearance of continual flow in one direction, but has great fluidity, eddies of strangeness, and huge inertia at points. The past is obscene, but so is the present, and, in this moment of disavowal, Fowles interrogates the historicity of the reader, challenging them to realize that they are part of a chaos that society attempts to frame as 'history'.

Another key moment of self-consciousness in Fowles's text comes much later, where he is attempting again to account for historical difference:

We should do better to imagine a world where, once again, a sense of self barely exists; or most often where it does, is repressed; where most are still like John Lee, more characters written by someone else than free individuals in our comprehension of the adjective and the noun.

(p. 392)

Fowles reaches for the metaphor of textuality to try to explain a life without interiority in the modern sense. What is different is identity, and, particularly, the way in which our modern lives are fundamentally equated to language ('free individuals' = adjective + noun). Modern people have become archivized, able only to express themselves – and, strikingly, their freedom – through words, rather than more bodily, less cerebral (or selfish) existence. That said, Fowles illustrates the loss of – the absence of – self by using language ('repressed') that plays with modern articulations. This is a moment of address to the reader, a stern injunction regarding the ways in which they might understand, not just the text, but also the context of the text, or the world of the text. The modern reader – whoever that is, wherever they are – is to understand by not understanding, or by seeking to depress or repress their own sense of what a person should be or how they should act.

Hilary Mantel argues that, in writing about the past, the novelist spends much time avoiding the rawness that it contains, suggestive of the sublimity of history:

> A relation of past events brings you up against events and mentalities that, should you choose to describe them, would bring you to the borders of what your readers could bear. The danger you have to negotiate is not the dimpled coyness of the past – it is its obscenity.[20]

So, the past is obscene, something inexpressible and incomprehensible to modern sensibilities. Mantel's insight about ameliorating the unrecognizable otherness of the past – the 'obscenity' of history that cannot be spoken, that might be controlled or smoothed over by the art of the novelist – highlights an interesting point in conceptualization of the relationship between history and fiction. The past is a foreign country, literally other, and full of horror and problematic chaos. The novelist and the historian both seek to disavow this horror and negotiate a relationship between then and now. However, this simply points out more clearly the otherness of the past.

This 'obscenity' is akin to the way that postmodern historiographers have characterized the sublimity of history: that is, that which is chaotic and terrifying and that works, in tandem with echoes of the traumatic rupturing from that past through the imposition of language and signification on the subject, to disavow identity of any real, true, innate kind.[21] Amy Elias outlines the effect that the encounter with the historical sublime has on the novelist:

> The postmodern turn on history, at base an assertion of the sublimity of History, is from this view a desire for meaning that paradoxically insists on an incomplete answer to 'Why?' It is an ongoing negotiation with the chaos of history that continually strives towards completion and fulfilment, towards final knowledge, and is continually thrown back from the barrier of language and culture. Thus what I call 'metahistorical romance' to some extent repeats the contemporary debate about history in historiography.[22]

That is, the historical novel reflects the concerns of a philosophy of history that seeks to outline the fragmented, the incomplete, the deferred, and the lack at the centre of History and historical discourse. The movement enacted is towards the completeness of the past, while constantly being undermined by the knowledge of the impossibility of this encounter. The historical novel plays a role in communicating the indeterminacy and unknowability of history to the reader and through culture to society as a whole. The alterity of the historical novel and its ability to 'open up new life narratives and alternative relations to time and space' (despite – simultaneous with – its often innate conservatism) – brings it, therefore, within the compass of the suite of texts, ideas, theories, and positions that have been thought to destabilize discourses of dominance.[23] The historical novel demonstrates the sublimity of history because it subverts the legitimacy of mainstream ways of thinking about the past. The historical novel enacts the 'ongoing negotiation with the chaos of history' within popular culture and enables an awareness in the readership of the fragmentary, tentative, fragile nature of their relationship with the past.

Yet Mantel also sees the action of writing about the past (or remembering it) as somehow regenerative or like a kind of imaginative resurrection. While visiting Ralph Sadleir's Tudor house, she is overcome with emotion in an extraordinary moment of uncanniness:

> It was then that the shock of the past reached out and jabbed me in the ribs. They were as alive as I am; why can't I touch them? Grieved, I had to stuff my fingers in my mouth, fish out my handkerchief, and do what a novelist has to do: unfreeze antique feeling, unlock the emotion stored and packed tight in paper, brick and stone.[24]

Mantel has an affective response to the physical evidence of the past, and it upsets her. She figures historical fiction here as something that allows a kind of grieving, indeed, is an aspect of her mourning. It translates her sadness and allows her to communicate her emotions. Rather than rationalize her response – to try to control her tears – she blocks them and gets on with her 'work'. The 'shock of the past' is the comprehension of herself in the 'now' (in history) and, hence, the proleptic understanding of her own death. Mantel strives to ignore this by translating the experience into prose, controlling it through fiction. 'History' has given her 'paper, brick and stone', but the historical novelist resists this typological definition, looking to find that which has been stored and packed away by that superficial controlling structure. On the one hand, then, this event seems to clarify the difference between a textual (physically structuring) History and the 'emotion' (sense, empathy, comprehension) communicated somehow by the novelist. Mantel and the others cited here create a binary between History and historical fiction, suggesting that their practice disrupts the rational, taxonomizing structure of a totalizing – but empty – way of translating the past into the present. At the same time, Mantel also demonstrates how historical fiction itself describes and controls her own affective response to the past. She is forced to comprehend her own historicity, but her action as a translator of the emotion of the past turns her away from that feeling. She uses her professional, workmanlike approach as a way of ignoring the trauma of her encounter with the rawness of history, the 'shock of the past'. Historical fiction, then, might be a way of both acknowledging the powerful emotions experienced in the past – a way of communicating a more embodied, material, human pastness – while similarly attempting to smooth over this 'shock', to disavow the effect and affect that the past might have upon those in the present if not properly, formally controlled. The historical novel works to render history present and, hence, to flatten time, to make the past contemporary.

This transhistorical impetus ensures that a reader might not necessarily see their historicity in the way that Mantel did – it might be smoothed out, the past othered into a consoling fiction, but, through those representational strategies, understood and comprehended, disciplined and controlled.

Crucially, Mantel the novelist here seeks out the affective in the material – the 'emotion stored and packed tight in paper, brick and stone'. The emotional resonance of the material elements of the past is an elegant way of thinking about the actions of a historical fiction, and yet Mantel is clearly only 'unlocking', rather than creating; she acts as a conduit (and translator). The past is there as a spectre, unseen but not disappeared. The emotions that are part of the fabric of the past are as much 'history' as the writings, walls, or gardens of the house; the novelist accesses the past through this, though, adding the heft of flesh to the bodily frame of history. Furthermore, what history (in the shape of the heritage site, the text of the museum) tells us is that the past is dead – leading Mantel to grieve – and this is the 'shock of the past'. In Mantel's reading, then, what the historical novelist does is to overcome this – not to disavow it, or ignore or repress it, but to allow for some kind of affective relationship between then and now that 'normal' history cannot accomplish. The traumatic moment of historical understanding – the recognition of death and disappearance as marking out the past and our relation to it – is constantly attended to and only partially reconciled or repressed through the comforting actions of fiction (all types of fiction, including the ones that societies tell themselves, disguised as 'history'). Historical fiction inflects the historical or archival record through consideration of the personal, the individual, the unwritten, the unseen, the unheard and unsaid.

Mantel highlights something about the oxymoronic corporeal spectrality of the encounter with the past: physical and conceptual, ghostly and frozen. This sense of the actuality and the materiality of the past, somehow linked with place, but nostalgically, mournfully, tragically distanced from us – a sense of frail mortality and chronological specificity, a self-conscious historicity – suggests that the encounter with the past is what makes us human, and the desire to somehow raise the dead is what brings us to historical fiction. As Alessandro Manzoni argues, the historical novelist offers 'not just the bare bones of history, but something richer, more complete. In a way you want him to put the flesh back on the skeleton that is history'.[25] The historical novel reinserts the human and the bodily back into the historical narrative. Manzoni, though, argues further: it makes the past richer and more complete, rendering what was unsaid said, and what was not seen visible; the historical novelist, though, caters to the whims of the reader – 'you want him to put the flesh back' on to the dry, unbodily structure of the past that history has given us. J.G. Farrell similarly argues that, 'History leaves so much out [. . .] everything to do with the senses, for instance. And it leaves out the most important thing of all: the detail of what being alive is like'.[26] For Farrell, historical fictions can create an affective and empathic connection that 'History' cannot. History is a cold description compared with the richness and human detail of a fiction; in Farrell's conceptualization, historical fiction has something profoundly authentic to say about

↑ memory

the past through its concern with what 'History' might consider lost and irrelevant ephemera – sensual impression. The historical novel reinserts the human back into the past, through touch and body and emotion, placing the reader there and making the past richer and more comprehensible as a consequence. This articulation of the historical fiction writer's craft suggests both a physical translocation and also what Manzoni argued differentiated them from historians, the ability to conjure the physical. This sense of the material and the resurrectionary is key to understanding fictional writing about the past, as is the sense of richness and completion that the historical novel brings: a kind of satisfaction that replaces the tentative fragility of historical discourse. Readers enjoy historical novels: that is why they sell.

Similarly, the affective relationship of the participant to the past demonstrates that readers desire completion and coherence, while understanding their impossibility. They ask, 'Why can't I touch them?', demanding resolution and the ability to circumvent or cross the abyss between then and now. But, despite their privileged access to the emotional booty of the past, historical novelists cannot cross the gap, cannot touch the dead. Instead, they present rewrites of an imagined past, creating an affective relationship or engagement with a past that didn't exist, that never existed, that could not – de facto, fundamentally, by default – have happened. It is a past in suspension, somehow – it is possible, but impossible, probable, but never the case. The tension between the bones of fact and the fictional flesh can be problematic, as Leon Garfield argues: 'Often you have to suppress what you actually know, and do it in a way that doesn't seem as though you're doing it, and you can only do that, I find, by being very subjective in your writing'.[27] In this, the historical novel writer acknowledges the innate fictionality of what they are doing and how it suffuses everything, even the so-called 'facts'. This kind of fiction is predicated upon an absence, a gap, which is deferred, but nonetheless acknowledged constantly. In its turn, this unspoken – or relatively unindicated – truism about historical fiction overlaps into fiction more generally, as something that has an emptiness about it. Historical writing is a spectral projection on to the past, something that addresses the gaps at the heart of epistemology, but simply covers them up with more comforting absences. Rewriting pastness, intervening in the fictive struggle to remember, the translation and revoicing of history in uncanny and ultimately queer ways: these are what the historical novelist participates in. The memory act of writing historical fiction is sincere but not possible and, in its self-defeating moment, presents a doubling of history, a 'playing' of historicalness for emotive, affective appreciation (and to keep a readership from fearing death). Mantel points to the crucial, emotional power of history over the individual, something that most historians find problematic. Deploying the potential affect of the past on and in the present is what historical novelists do, rather than investigating its effects, which they leave to historians.

Finally, historical fictions reflect upon the haunting of the present by the past. They enact a kind of haunting. They voice ghosts within the now, echoes and revenants. Importantly, those ghosts and echoes are imagined rather than 'real', part of an aesthetic economy rather than materially real. These voices are fictional.

The emptiness of signifying systems, of language itself...

The always already absent...
→ Like the overlays of cities, past and present

The intervention of the fictional past into the 'actual' present is a dislocating move, disrupting the now. Historical 'sensibility' might be defined as the empathic, material relationship to the past that such fictions can provoke, the encounter with ghosts that are not real, the affective engagement with a fictional past. Historical 'sensibility' might describe the brokering of binaries by texts – the reconciling of sense/intellect, physical/rational, emotion/thought through the working of the imagination and the aesthetically embodied engagement with fiction.

To bring these theoretical issues into practical focus, this chapter moves on to consider several key novels. The sections argue that historical fiction enables a reader to reflect upon the nature of historical representation itself, highlighting the ways in which the past is communicated to the present. The historical novel also enables a consideration of ethics, form, and historiographical engagement. The chapter, therefore, seeks to demonstrate the central contention of this book; that is, that historical texts undertake historiographical work. As Hsu-Ming Teo has written, 'If historical fiction is not always history [. . .] it is always historiography'.[28] The chapter comes early in the book as it demonstrates how historical texts conceptualize and attempt to control the way in which they are engaged with, comprehended, and understood. The chapter looks at two key literary fiction writers – Hilary Mantel and Ian McEwan – before working through similar models in more pulpy, conservative, mass-market fiction. In particular, the chapter considers the double effect of such writing – shifting between authenticity and fiction – and the ethical consequences for popular historiography of the novel form. So, these texts debate the reader's engagement with the past by meditating upon memory, narrative, fiction, lying, truth, and realism. The self-consciousness of the historical novel, demonstrated in the example from *The Giant, O'Brien*, suggests precise modes of reading. Furthermore, in Ian McEwan's *Atonement*, the reader is shown the conscious way a text manipulates the reader in order to present a particular version of the past. It is key, then, to pay attention to the moments when popular historical fiction dramatizes textual reception itself. Therefore, the remainder of the chapter looks at reading, the figuration of the reader (and author), and the construction of evidence and the archive. These books represent historiographical interventions at the same time as they stage moments of reading and engaging with the past, imagining responses and creating imaginative communities. These paratexual and diegetic moments of the novels show how historical texts conceptualize and attempt to articulate and construct an imagined reader, a community of engagement. They help the reader know how to use the text. At the same time, the gaps in knowledge foregrounded by the novel form provoke a discussion of ethics in rendering the past in the present. Consideration of this allows the chapter to draw conclusions about the potentiality of the text to provide a historiographic intervention.

Wolf Hall and the 'double effect' of historical fiction

These issues relating to obscenity, haunting, fictive doubleness, and the iterations of memory, in addition to a keen sense of the ways in which the novel might

'Historical sensibility' could be described as being liminal...

Reconciliation of opposites...

meditate upon the actions and representations of 'history', are uppermost through-out Mantel's most celebrated work. Her 2009 multiple-prize-winning novel, *Wolf Hall*, negotiates these particular ideas in a very self-conscious fashion. *Wolf Hall* tracks several key years in the life of Thomas Cromwell (specifically 1521–35), narrating events, both domestic and national, from his own particular point of view, in a deeply complex, third-person narrative style.[29] The treatment of ghosts, affect, repetition, memory, and a personal and deeply felt relationship with the past demonstrates a narrative self-consciousness about the historical fictional mode. *Wolf Hall* is a very self-aware book, written by an author who has thought deeply about the problems inherent in writing historical novels, and the issues it raises are clearly applicable to the genre as a whole. Particularly, this is the ability of the novel form to broker the relationship between 'fact' and 'fiction' and to ensure that the reader is aware of (but simultaneously unmindful of) the 'double effect' it creates.

The sense of imaginative possibility and doubleness in narrative construction is key to historical fiction and outlined in Mantel's articulation of her relationship with her readership in the 'Author's note' to her 1992 novel *A Place of Greater Safety*. Initially, she points out the indeterminability of the past: 'This is a novel about the French Revolution. Almost all the characters in it are real people and it is closely tied to historical facts – as far as those facts are agreed, which isn't really very far'.[30] Her work, then, is an intervention into a debate that has very few 'agreed' terms of reference. Following Keith Jenkins, these are imaginative iterations and speculations. She continues:

> I am very conscious that a novel is a cooperative effort, a joint venture between writer and reader. I purvey my own version of events, but facts change according to your viewpoint. Of course, my characters did not have the blessing of hindsight; they lived from day to day, as best they could. I am not trying to persuade my reader to view events in a particular way, or to draw any particular lessons from them. I have tried to write a novel that gives the reader scope to change opinions, change sympathies: a book that one can think and live inside.
>
> (p. x)

This sense of a collaborative approach, of enabling a reader to be self-aware and participant in the fiction, is the key historiographical intervention the genre makes. Meaning is created between novelist and reader, and, hence, any 'output' historiographically will be considered some kind of collaboration. Mantel's comments here instruct the reader to suspect the text. To her, the novel is not an act of persuasion or pedagogy, but a space for debate and thought that comments upon the action of constructing a historical narrative.

Wolf Hall meditates on how fiction and reality might be combined into a narrative, and the effect this might have on a reader or an audience. The relationship between art and 'life' and the dynamic between a (possibly) idealized memory and the 'true' reality are outlined in Cromwell's description of the Thomas More family portrait:

Entering the house, you meet the family hanging up. You see them painted life-size before you meet them in the flesh; and More, conscious of the double effect it makes, pauses, to let you survey them, to take them in [. . .] Master Holbein has grouped them under his gaze, and fixed them for ever: as long as no moth consumes, no flame or mould or blight.[31]

The More family portrait does not exist (a sketch is all that survives), and so the final sentence here is an in-joke, a reference to the seeming (but illusory) power of fictions to outlive their subject. The picture, a piece of evidence in a historical account, despite being a work of art, is rerendered within this fictional narrative. The 'double effect' is an uncanny, almost uncomfortable, moment, as the 'real' and the 'wrought' stand together in the same room. The image is clearly, consciously made ('grouped', 'fixed'), but also mimicking reality ('life-size'); the portrait is the double of the real, breathing family. It reflects them, but the viewer is evidently aware of the disjunction between real and painted. The portrait is of a past moment that doubles, echoes, mimics the bodies of the family in the 'now'; it contributes to their meaning and, taken together, has an effect and an affect, moves the viewer in some way. Mantel's (and Cromwell's) uncanniness, here and throughout the novel, is pre-Freud – ghosts, doubles, echoes, all 'live', but do not necessarily work to disorientate or even to invade the now and confuse it. They are flat, renderings with little perspective. The 'double effect' of historical fiction – the recognition of something that once existed and its difference from the artistic rendering – is used precisely to indicate chronological and temporal difference. This history does not mingle in the now and disrupt it, but is a flat, uninflected recollection. In this vein, Mantel meditates upon the strange act of creating 'historical fiction' and what it might mean.

The character of Thomas More is one of the most revisionist things about the text.[32] More is a vicious, ruthless, hideous figure here, not the saintly martyr of common imagination. A clear contrast is made throughout between Cromwell (generally seen in historical fiction as the more Machiavellian figure) and More, enacting the revisionism at the heart of the book, keen to resurrect Cromwell's character from the opprobrium of popular history.[33] More is the foolish but nasty dreamer, missing the point; Cromwell is the realist, interested in statehood, nation, accounts (through them, a kind of modernity), and a seemingly recognizable secular sensibility. In many ways, *Wolf Hall* uses religion to communicate the obscenity of the past, focusing in its later sections on oppression and martyrdom. Cromwell recounts at length the burning of a Loller woman (p. 355). Yet the account is itself a memory, one that viscerally affects him (p. 352). He remains at the body, interested in why the bones will not burn, until the Loller's friends arrive to pray for her. One anoints Cromwell's hand with 'a smear of mud and grit, fat and ash' (p. 357). He is marked by this violence, unable to comprehend it properly – either the reason for it or the faith needed to suffer so for one's faith. The account concludes with Cromwell's self-consciousness:

> Now, when he thinks back on this, he wonders at his own faulty memory. He has never forgotten the woman, whose last remnants he carried away as a greasy smudge on his own skin, but why is it that his life as a child doesn't seem to fit, one bit with the next?
>
> (p. 357)

Cromwell's childhood memory casts the person recollecting as an uncomprehending witness, one marked by the past but unable to understand it, both revolted by, and inured to, the violence inherent in that past. He remembers key emotive scenes, but has no sense of an overview or coherent development; his own 'history' is fragmented, awkward, something that returns to him unbidden sometimes. So, diegetically, the novel foregrounds reflection upon the past, while rendering the 'historical' a violent, strange, and unfamiliar place.

Wolf Hall opens with a 'Cast of characters', followed by a set of family trees ('The Tudors', pp. ix–xiii, and 'The Yorkist Claimants', pp. xiv–xv). Each character is described, in terms of both their position or employment and their situation (geographically or in familial terms). Although many of them are 'real', they are here presented to the reader as a 'cast', a set of characters presenting an entertainment, mere ciphers or representations or lifelike echoes of 'reality'. The family trees present textual evidence for relationships, seemingly demonstrating a formulaic and inflexible, 'true' past. These paratexts yoke a theatrical performative element to dynastic politics. As in *The Giant, O'Brien*, such elements are crucial to the way that the book is framed, and they present a pedagogical intervention. The paratexts combine the obviously fictional with the seemingly factual. They suggest the way the book might be used, and its meta-historiographic intervention. There are also two epigraphs, one from Vitruvius's description of theatrical architecture in *De Architectura* and one cast list from the poet John Skelton's political morality play *Magnificence* (*c*.1520). Taken as a whole, then, the paratexts present to the reader numerous key conceptual templates for interpreting what follows: truth and evidence, the combination of performance and aristocratic setting, advice writing, early modern and Renaissance classicism, and the inflexible positivism of the 'family' tree and its relation to Tudor political life. The Vitruvius epigraph demonstrates a clear self-consciousness about genre. It concerns the correct stage dressing for 'three kinds of scenes, one called the tragic, second the comic, third the satyric' (p. xvii). This is how each type of literary production might be framed, made to look (visually) correct. The epigraph recalls Cromwell's narrative concern with the arrangement of rooms and scenes (not least, his interest in the Thomas More family portrait), suggesting his own stage-managing of events, but it also suggests the reader consider the ways that the tropes of genre are being deployed. Particularly, Vitruvius is interested in tragedy, which is contrasted to the 'ordinary dwellings' of comedy (p. xvii). Tragedy is something that is obviously wrought, 'delineated with columns, pediments, statues and other objects suited to kings' (p. xvii), populated with artefacts to signify gravitas. What follows, as the novel, is a combination of comic and tragic, a text obsessed with making the grand and

[Handwritten marginalia, right margin top:] Freudian return of the repressed, also the idea that Cromwell's violent, traumatic childhood shapes his worldview & makes him sympathetic to modern readers is very Freudian

[Handwritten marginalia, circled:] ✗ ①

[Handwritten marginalia, right margin bottom:] Mantel knows that modern readers will be moved by & will instinctively understand how childhood trauma forms his character

[Handwritten marginalia, bottom of page, illegible]

Who said humans are meaning-making machines? It's not just in historical fiction that people blend fact and fiction—it's the essential way we make sense of our lives...

what has often been reified as excessive and glorious into something familiar and domestic, something that is recognizable.

Wolf Hall domesticates Cromwell and Henry, reminding the reader that they were real, solid human beings by returning to the details of normality and the minutiae of everyday life. This most public of historical events is also, simultaneously, exceptionally private. This relationship between public life and the domestic is one of the reasons for the keen interest in the Boleyn years by novelists.[34] Throughout Wolf Hall, the public actions of figures are read through their private characters and thoughts. This is history that returns the body of the historical subject to the story, history from behind the scenes; it is interested in the way that:

> The fate of peoples is made like this, two men in small rooms. Forget the coronations, the conclaves of cardinals, the pomp and processions. This is how the world changes: a counter pushed across a table, a pen stroke that alters the force of a phrase, a woman's sigh as she passes and leaves on the air a trail of orange flower or rosewater; her hand pulling close the bed curtain, the discreet sigh of flesh against flesh.
>
> (p. 61)

History, here, is in the detail, the unseen minutiae of normal life. It combines the textual with the bodily material, physical objects (counters) with smells. Linear, narrative moments ('the pomp and processions') are mere window-dressing for the real significance of human relationships that can, ultimately, rarely be redis-covered – they can only be reimagined. As Colin Burrow argued in his review of the novel:

> Mantel's chief method is to pick out tableaux vivants from the historical record – which she has worked over with great care – and then to suggest that they have an inward aspect which is completely unlike the version presented in history books. The result is less a historical novel than an alternative history novel. It constructs a story about the inner life of Cromwell which runs in parallel to scenes and pictures that we thought we knew. She works particularly well with witnesses like Cavendish, who are both extremely vivid and slightly unreliable. Such sources enable her to suggest that history, even when witnessed first-hand, can mingle fact and mythology: that gossip, misunderstanding, anecdote and deliberate distortion play a part in the processes of living as well as in the process of recording.[35]

human beings aren't objective recording devices

This self-conscious conjunction of 'history' and the novelization of history, the rendering of the work of historicizing obvious to the reader, is key to the novel's 'double effect'. It presents us with a familiar history, a set of characters and stories and events that are almost excessively well known. Simultaneously, Mantel allows the unseen, the unheard, the unclaimed to permeate. This might be characterized as a relationship between 'history' and 'the historical' as representational modes.

to bring alive through imagination the gaps in the historical record.... malleability of history

Persuasion:
Christabel LaMotte wrote a poem about Melusina. —

Chapter II of Part Two is entitled 'An Occult History of Britain. 1521–29' and covers a range of legends, myths, and suggestions. Although Cromwell is a rationalist, concerned with exorcizing the foolishness of superstition, he recognizes the importance of symbols, stories, and legendary narratives (as in Wolsey's description of Melusine and the fact that Eleanor Talbot was descended from a swan; pp. 95–6). Occult means unseen, under the surface, behind comprehension, out of human understanding – the idea of 'occult history' invokes myth and mystic ways of thinking about the world (suggesting, further, something unseen that controls or might shape and order events). Yet occult also means secret and hitherto unseen, something that might be revealed by the right person (in this way, David Peace writes 'occulted' histories of the 1970s and 1980s).[36] The opening of 'An Occult History' discusses Brutus, Aeneas, the giants of old England, before moving to the diegetic contemporary and the rueful reflection that all these narratives might be complicated by the domestic, the emotional, the bodily, the female: 'Beneath every history, another history' (p. 66). This is the 'occulted' story of Britain, the story that is not told because it is not comprehensible by mere dry, evidence-based 'history'. The past is a layer or collage of stories, and what the astute reader of the past does is to focus on particular elements in order to comprehend the present. The story of this woman, who is irrelevant to the grand progression of kings and heroes, will become crucial. Dynastic positivism will be broken by the interjection of a woman's body, and the rejection of another's. Wolsey will need to understand the personal history of Boleyn in order to (while failing to) attempt to comprehend and shape the future. There is always another 'history' underneath, waiting to be shown. Mantel's style here is able to consider the future and the past simultaneously – before moving to a kind of present: 'The lady appeared at court at the Christmas of 1521, dancing in a yellow dress. She was – what? – about twenty years old' (p. 66). This combining of exactitude with seeming and interrogative vagueness articulates the mode of the historical novel, embedding the dancing body of Boleyn into the narrative factuality of date, age, situation, time. The interrelationship between 'real' history and 'fictional', between fact and body, enables this uninflected 'double effect', something that works unconsciously at a level beneath assertion, constantly alerting the reader to the speciousness of what they are reading.

Mantel's novel is obsessed with ghosts, echoes, and the seemingly physical remnants of the past in the present. This is characteristic of the historical novel form's desire to conceptualize its own engagement with a variety of non–official pasts. For Mantel, the encounter with the past is often intertwined with ontological unreality of one kind or another: 'He will remember his first sight of the open sea: a grey wrinkled vastness, like the residue of a dream'. Cromwell regularly sees figures from the past, converses with those from his memory (his father, his dead wife, and so on). On All Hallows Day 1529, his grief takes over:

> Now it threatens to capsize him. He doesn't believe that the dead come back; but that doesn't stop him from feeling the brush of their fingertips, wingtips, against his shoulder. Since last night they have been less individual forms

something about all this is reminding me of the slipping signifier: is it applicable? ~ Not really…

and faces than a solid aggregated mass, their flesh slapping and jostling together, their texture dense like sea creatures, their faces sick with an undersea sheen.

(pp. 154–5)

The dead seemingly return to challenge his rational contemporaneity. He attempts to ignore them, the physical consciousness of them. This section articulates a particular relationship to pastness. Although ghosts do not exist in rational modernity, the audience is aware of their presence in the action of reading this novel about dead people. Those in the past are indistinct until given articulation of a kind by a novelist, brought into focus. Such an awareness of the past also has an affective, emotional iteration. Cromwell holds his wife's prayer book in his hand, and weeps.[37] The novel attempts to explain, through this stylistic work, the mediation and shift from a society in which ghosts, haunting, mystical moments of the dead were commonplace through to a post-Restoration Protestant rationality that sceptically ignored the idea of such things as purgatory and concentrated on what could inductively be proven. At this level, then, the gestures towards ghosts and the spirit world in the novel are thematically and historiographically crucial, showing the movement from one sensibility to another. This interest in pre-modern hauntings and ghosts reflects recent literary and scholarly work in the field.[38] Yet the invocation of the ghostly and the haunting of the past in the present also demands a self-consciousness on the part of the reader about the ways in which they themselves engage with, understand (or misunderstand), and recognize the past. Dramatizing the relationship between the affect of memory and the rationality of telling the past is key to the novel's own effect upon its readership. Again, it is possible to discern this type of novel seeking to construct its readership and conceptualizing the way that they might engage with the past or reflect upon their ways of encountering past events.

The novel also focuses on the relationships between fathers and sons, on the materiality of ancestry, lineage, and wills. At the moment that Cromwell realizes he has not made his will, he is accosted: 'He takes Rafe's arm. On his left side, a hand touches his: fingers without flesh. A ghost walks: Arthur, studious and pale. King Henry, he thinks, you raised him; now you put him down' (p. 147). These are studiously not the ghostly revenants of Gothic writing, echoes of transgressions and misdeeds, but an attempt at communicating a historical sensibility. Yet, at the same time, the return of the dead throughout *Wolf Hall* comments upon the novel's own re-presentation or re-animation of these figures, both achingly normal and similarly other and haunting. Again, the motif enacted by the paratexts – the combination of echoes or revenants in figures performed and the factuality of dynastic outline – seems a keynote of the text. This is the 'double effect', the jolting, uncanny conjunction of real and fictional. Once the will has been made (and transcribed in full; p. 148), its legality is made strange by the knowledge that it will echo in a disembodied fashion throughout subsequent centuries; it will stand (as a 'testament', as a witness, as part of textual evidence) for the absent Cromwell, give him voice. Yet it is transcribed in a fictional context and made 'double' by the way the character 'Cromwell' considers and interprets it.

The ghosts that Cromwell encounters are, seemingly, a consequence of the way in which he remembers. In Italy, he learns to create a memory house. This kind of memory system, with peculiar images imagined in familiar settings, was very common in medieval and early modern society.[39] The reference gives the representation of Cromwell's memory a kind of historical heft (it is generally historically accurate as a practice), as well as demonstrating the way in which his very rational memorial technique means he creates fictional, artistic representations in his head. It means that Cromwell sees memories, suggests that the ghosts he encounters are merely part of his rational memorial system, rather than an actual haunting. This is a self-conscious moment again, betraying a concern with highlighting how memory works, how recall can be constructed through systems. Ghosts, according to Cromwell's, are simply unconsciously recalled remnants of memory, almost an automatic reaction to a place. His diegetic contemporary consciousness of a place is filled with memories, but these are flat, administrative memories somehow, without emotion necessarily, simple aides-memoires constructed by his rational mind. Memory here is replaced with recollection, the ability to know something; it becomes a rationalizing system for ordering and comprehending (and, for Cromwell, for mastering) the chaotic world. It does not have real, affective meaning in the present.

Cromwell is the ultimate administrator, constantly seeking order through organization (particularly of domestic arrangements, of households). He sees figures and administration as beautifully utilitarian: 'The page of an accounts book is there for your use, like a love poem. It's not there for you to nod and then dismiss it; it's there to open your heart to possibility' (p. 365). His function is to bring order where there was superstition and chaos, something that he achieves domestically and nationally. Hence, his facility with languages, a mastery over structures that describe and contain the world. His version of memory might seem particularly alien to a contemporary reader. It constructs the past as a series of images that are to be arranged – albeit in a weird, fictional cavalcade – for the humanistic, pedagogic purpose of furthering his own cause, for bettering himself. Yet Cromwell's memory system, which allows him to recall all but the vagaries of life, often ensures that these memories are emotionally problematic and disrupt his rational view of the world. The memory system is referred to during his emotional outburst in front of Cavendish, again combining the practical technique of recollection with ghostliness: 'But he is crying again. The ghosts are gathering, he feels cold, his position is irretrievable. In Italy he learned a memory system, so he can remember everything: every stage of how he got here' (p. 156). Although Cromwell attempts to control the past, to ensure that it simply does his bidding and becomes another expedient set of knowledge for him (like language), its unbidden invasion into the present leads to an emotional response. His kind of memory, so intense it means that no location is empty of ghosts, seems monstrous: 'he can remember *everything*' (my emphasis), a kind of fable-like curse on the ultimate technocratic Renaissance man applying the scientific techniques of recall to control and order the world. What is needed is some kind of filter; otherwise, the chaos of the past threatens to flood the fragile present and destroy it utterly.

Funes, The Memorious – Borges

Historical fiction and ethics

In writing about her novelistic practice, Hilary Mantel considers the ways in which history and fiction relate in terms of their shared uncertainty:

> The past is not dead ground, and to traverse it is not a sterile exercise. History is always changing behind us, and the past changes a little every time we retell it. The most scrupulous historian is an unreliable narrator [. . .] Once this is understood, the trade of the historical novelist doesn't seem so reprehensible or dubious; the only requirement is for conjecture to be plausible and grounded in the best facts one can get.[40]

Mantel explicitly equates the historian and the novelist, both deploying epistemological models to communicate something about the past, both as important as each other.[41] The key is the idea of the 'plausible' and how this works on a readership. The relationship between 'plausible' and 'grounded' is the crucial aspect, inherently unstable and unique in every instance. The relationship between then and now is subtly dynamic, reliant on a shifting set of relationships. The way in which the past is understood and represented is as much reliant on the here and now as on historical events. Mantel's careful choice of the word 'trade' professionalizes the writer of historical fiction, grounds them in a rational-world pursuit. Given that these comments come in her first published essay after her first Booker Prize victory, Mantel very clearly aligns the writer of historical fiction – the wordsmith, tradesperson – within an economic nexus with novel as commodity. The raw materials of the past are turned into fiction through the labour of the writer, and all that was solid melts into air. What Mantel points out, quite fundamentally, is that the writer of historical fiction continually works with unclean (non-sterile) materials, and they have volatility and an affective impact that must be considered carefully. The choices inherent in writing about the past are unavoidably ethical in nature, from the mode of composition to the ways in which characters speak, but, in making such choices, the historical novelist merely echoes the moral and ethical decisions undertaken by all those who would tell 'history'.

As has been suggested, the historical mode in most cultural representation, and particularly the novel form, is realist: that is, it is written in a style that addresses a kind of imagined authenticity.[42] The style and tone are generally buttressed by a series of statements and paratextual apparatuses that support the 'realism' and therefore address a kind of truth that the texts make. Yet historical novelists, as James Forrester admits, 'lie deliberately about the past', and in doing so they engage in an ethical discussion with their readers about the nature of representation and the relationship between aesthetics, formal conventions, historiography, and 'truth'.[43] Books that explicitly represent the past fictionally are therefore forced to negotiate a very complex set of aesthetic, ethical, and representational parameters, while accounting for authenticity and understanding the strangeness and physical foreignness that constitute the fundamental definition of the alterity called the past. The representation of the otherness of the past necessitates a writing practice that is keenly attuned to the moral, ethical, historiographical, and political issues that are at stake. The unknowability of the past challenges the reader, and the writer, to deal with the consequences of attempting to order that which eschews such control. The historical novel also asks that a reader confront the affective horror of that past. Historiographical theory relating to ethics and epistemology often places the historian central in rendering the past in the present.[44] Yet to write historical fiction, this section will argue, is to engage in an ethical mediation and demands an aesthetic and epistemological sophistication that is often missed by critics of the genre. This ethical complexity in fictionalizing history is recognized by Peter Middleton and Tim Woods: 'The distance between epistemology and ontology, or historical knowledge and literary fiction could be negotiated only by some kind of moral practice, although a morality of tradition or universalising precepts is insufficient for the textual conditions of late modernity'.[45] Echoing J. Hillis Miller's attempt at reconciling the ethical work of literature, they argue that the line between fiction and fact demands an ethics of representation, albeit one that might be corrupted or problematized by the conditions of postmodernity.[46] Representing the past demands a 'kind of moral practice', that is, an approach that understands the relationship between knowledge and experience, between the rational and the bodily. Through their ambivalent term 'negotiated', Middleton and Woods suggest the attenuated way in which historical fictions both point a direction and engage in some form of dialogue. They suggest a 'moral practice' in writing about the past, in brokering the relationship between 'epistemology and ontology'.

When questioned about ethics, authenticity, and their duty to history, writers of historical fiction demonstrate a range of responses and diversity of opinion. The genre-wide phenomenon of the 'historical note', discussed throughout this chapter, demonstrates that they all have a position on the issues. The 'historical note' and its paratextual kin illustrate the writers' need to situate their ethical standpoint and to outline how they relate to history, their sense of responsibility to the past, and how they articulate something fictive out of source material that cleaves to a kind of truth. Sarah Waters argues:

> I don't think novels should misrepresent history, unless it's for some obvious serious or playful purpose (though this suggests that we can represent history accurately – something I'm not sure we can do; in fact, I've always been fascinated by the ways in which historical fiction continually reinvents the past). I think we have a duty to take history seriously – not simply to use it as a backdrop or for the purposes of nostalgia. This, for me, means writing a fiction with, hopefully, something meaningful to say about the social and cultural forces at work in the period I'm writing about.[47]

Waters, here, makes several key assertions. First, she, like most of her peers, seeks not to misrepresent. This implies that history itself – the set of ideas, sources, evidence, and narratives that 'tell' the past – is not already a misrepresentation. That said, she acutely points to the fact that the disconnection inherent in fiction

– that novelists can't 'represent history accurately' – creates a space for reinvention. Her points about nostalgia and the seriousness of the craft of historical fiction demonstrate a clear engagement and a politicized desire to lay bare the workings of the past. She demonstrates a concern that historical fictions have purpose and political heft. In Waters' view, historical novelists have a very active duty to history, but, similarly, they have a political and moral duty to the present, through the choices they make in representing the past. This impetus to represent the past as dynamic and affective, while eschewing nostalgia, argues an understanding of the historical novelist's project as something that has virtue and value, and, most importantly, ethical significance.

One of the most important recent examples of the historical novel's engagement with a 'moral practice' and the questionable ethics of writing about the past, *Atonement* (2001) is Ian McEwan's second historical novel after *The Innocent* (1990).[48] It is a very self-conscious intervention into the genre. The novel is stylistically indebted to a range of writers, from Virginia Woolf to Elizabeth Bowen, and, in its two sections, it inhabits classic locales of the later twentieth-century English fictive historical tradition – namely the country house and the Second World War.[49] It is also a novel that is self-aware enough to play games with the readers and, in so doing, highlights some of the really problematic – but fundamental – issues accruing around historical fiction and the ethics of representing the past.[50] It demonstrates another way a text might engage with its readership and attempt to steer engagement. *Atonement* enables an understanding of the mechanics of fictionally representing the past as much as it is a case study of how novels themselves engage with their readers.

Most problematically, *Atonement* entered into debates regarding ethics and the past through the controversies associated with McEwan's alleged plagiarism. McEwan was accused by various newspapers of borrowing too liberally from one of his source texts, Lucilla Andrews' memoir *No Time for Romance* from 1977, a book he acknowledged in his concluding historical note. McEwan, in a defence of his use of Andrews' book, articulated a very austere line on authenticity and, in doing so, underlined a particular sense of the novelist's duty to the past:

> The writer of a historical novel may resent his dependence on the written record, on memoirs and eyewitness accounts, in other words on other writers, but there is no escape: Dunkirk or a wartime hospital can be novelistically realized, but they cannot be re-invented.[51]

Everything is textual in McEwan's version of the ways in which the past is written as fiction; the words of those who were there become the groundwork for the contemporary writer. The reaction to the accusations that McEwan should have made his debt to Andrews more explicit ranged from editorials defending the right of the historical novelist to use the work of others ('That, I find myself thinking, is what novelists do when they choose to take on historical subject matter: research is the name for this work') to various letters from eminent writers around the world.[52] The novelist Thomas Pynchon wrote to *The Daily Telegraph*:

[Handwritten marginal notes, left side:] Each writer is like both its strength & its ↑ a very specific consciousness – that of the story to life. Each writer is like both its strength & its — facts pass through a very specific consciousness – that of the author – who provides the perspective of characters, in the flesh, bringing the story to life. This is the narrative. This is to us today. ④ Maybe the key to historical fiction is that history, i.e. facts pass through a very specific consciousness – that of the author – who provides the perspective of characters, in the flesh, bringing the story to life. A sieve bringing their own concerns & visions & arguments to the narrative; i.e., how problematic Margaret Mitchell's take on the South is to us today. This is both its strength & its weakness.

Unless we were actually there, we must turn to people who were, or to letters, contemporary reporting, the Internet until, with luck, we can begin to make a few things of our own up. To discover in the course of research some engaging detail we know can be put into a story where it will do some good can hardly be classed as a felonious act – it is simply what we do.[53]

What this case and these writers' passionate interventions point out is that writing historical novels is not the same, fundamentally, as writing contemporary novels, and that there are numerous historiographical, ethical, and aesthetic issues involved in the undertaking. Historical novels are judged in a different way, too, and read differently, directly because of the form's invocation of these issues. The protagonist of *Atonement* claims that, 'No one will care what events and which individuals were misrepresented to make a novel', but she is evidently incorrect in her assumption.[54]

Atonement takes place during the 1930s and the 1940s and concerns the Tallis family and, in particular, the actions of the youngest daughter, Briony. In 1934, England is sweltering in the heat of a long, dry summer. Briony Tallis, a dreamy, bookish 13-year-old with a penchant for writing and acting in her own plays and psychodramas, sees her sister and Robbie Turner, son of the housekeeper, during a moment of sexual tension and, through a series of errors, becomes convinced that Robbie has raped her sister. Robbie, mainly on the malicious and false testimony of Briony, is convicted of sexual assault on another girl and imprisoned. He is released into the army and meets Briony again, during the war, when she seeks out her sister to apologize and attempt to make right what she has done. He is angry with her but tasks her to record, in letter and oath, her revised story. The revision of the record must be undertaken textually and legally. The letter that she will write will allow her forgiveness, as she calmly reflects: 'She knew what was required of her. Not simply a letter, but a new draft, an atonement, and she was ready to begin' (p. 349). Her action of righting the wrongs of the past will allow her to reconcile herself to the present.

Or, rather, that is what she tells the reader. The novel then moves to a short coda in which it becomes clear that Briony is a novelist, and the novel has been her own act of textual, fictional atonement. Not only is she a novelist, she is a writer of historical fiction. Briony visits the Imperial War Museum for the last time to say her farewells, as she has been writing a novel of the war. In fact, she has written her last novel, a revision of a drafted book she wrote in 1940 to outline what actually happened that night in 1935, revising it through her life, but never able to finish or publish it for legal reasons:

> I put it all there as a matter of historical record. But as a matter of legal reality, so various editors have told me over the years, my forensic memoir could never be published while my fellow criminals were alive.

> (p. 370)

She claims that her work is 'a matter of historical record', a document that – in its intersection with the law – has the status of a deposition. The law makes something false, despite its 'truth'. The law here creates inaccuracy in the historical record – or, rather, protects the lies that have been told – but also articulates what the historical novelist is allowed to write about, and what they are not. As Cormack argues, 'If it is postmodern, it is not postmodernism of the playful celebratory type. At the end of the novel both Briony Tallis, our narrator, and we, her readers, are profoundly troubled by the uncertainties we face'.[55]

In atoning for her sins – confessing in print – Briony also seeks to make things better for those whom she betrayed. Therefore, although the crime itself is truthfully represented – if that is possible, from such a dissembling, problematic narrator – what follows is fiction. Rather than account for what actually happens to her sister and Robbie, she writes an account – the account that the reader has just been reading – rooted in historical accuracy ('the letters the lovers wrote are in the archives of the War Museum') but completely fantastical:

> The preceding drafts were pitiless. But now I can no longer think what purpose would be served if, say, I tried to persuade my reader, by direct or indirect means, that Robbie Turner died of septicaemia at Bray Dunes on 1 June 1940, or that Cecilia was killed in September [1940].
>
> (p. 370)

Briony's comments here, although self-serving, bring up numerous ethical issues associated with historical fiction. She points out the movement of the historical novel to romance, towards reconciliation and conclusion; in effect, to order in the face of the fragmentary nature of knowledge about the past:

> How could that constitute an ending? What sense or hope or satisfaction could a reader draw from such an account? Who would want to believe that they never met again, never fulfilled their love? Who would want to believe that, except in the service of the bleakest realism?
>
> (p. 371)

In particular, the historical novelist fudges the actuality of death, substituting instead a comforting fiction that draws the sting of the past, disavows its trauma. Although the form is realist, it might seem to eschew the 'bleakest realism', that is, to see the sublimity of the past or to comprehend the unfeeling chaos of history. Attempting to narrativize (adding an 'ending') is associated here with a 'sense of hope or satisfaction'. Turning away from a kind of reality – the actuality of the past – is something a reader is presumed to wish for; it is what the form demands. But, furthermore, the past itself is bleak and real, something that the contemporary reader may wish to avoid. The reality of the past is found in the pitiless archive; the novel is an attempt at ignoring that actuality.

[handwritten margin note: In contrast are novels like Finn and The Underground Railroad, which grapple with the brutality of the past...]

In Briony's formulation, the historical novelist imposes order upon the chaos of the past, turning horror into narrative. In doing so, they make choices to change, manipulate, or misrepresent, to a greater or lesser extent, while attempting to ground their account in reality. The dynamic here is awkward, to say the least – being able to reconcile this need to augment and sculpt the past in ways that it refuses to be directed with a commitment to representing that past somehow truthfully argues a fundamental dissonance at the heart of historical fiction. Every single historical novel is an ethical negotiation on the part of the author, and each writer more or less acknowledges this. However, this negotiation and the very action of choosing how to represent the past, the values at stake in articulating that past, and the continual knowledge that the past is never going to be fully, accurately realized – these are the concerns of the historian as much as of the novelist, and the ethical struggles of historical fiction in representing the past in themselves articulate a historiographical verity.

Briony dates her manuscript 'London 1999', and the final section of the novel is dated '1999'; given the book's publication in 2001, there is a minor doubling of historical narrative here, a similar effect to that of Sebastian Faulks's *Birdsong* (1993), which has sections from 1910–18 and 1979. What seems to be the 'contemporary' or the 'now' of the novel is not, further warping the view of the reader. Briony's testimony is already historical, past, and its effects – if it has any – are neutralized further by this fact. The coda itself is followed by McEwan's 'Acknowledgements', which begin with him thanking the Imperial War Museum and also recording his indebtedness to several books, principally *No Time for Romance*, by Lucilla Andrews. The rawness of this – the moment of the fictional historical novelist concluding their fictional history, followed by the actual historical novelist – adds the compounding effect of the paratextual elements.[56] More than most historical novels, this one presses the nose of the reader in its own artificiality, but, in doing so, it merely points out the fact that all historical fictions are tissues of lies that misrepresent and misappropriate.

Briony has vascular dementia – a disorder affecting the memory – which means that:

> The little failures of memory that dog us all beyond a certain point will become more noticeable, more debilitating, until the time will come when I won't notice them because I will have lost the ability to comprehend anything at all.
>
> (p. 354)

Consciousness – life – is dependent on memory and the ability to keep it in place and order, to sustain its relationship to the present. Without this, Briony expects to become 'just a dim old biddy in a chair, knowing nothing, expecting nothing' (p. 354). Memory is everything in neurological terms – language, selfhood, and consciousness. Without it to create the dynamic then–now and to provide language, the body is an empty shell, with no purpose or agency. She will no longer be in history, but will step outside it into meaninglessness, 'fading into unknowing' (p. 355).

The novel presents a challenge to two types of 'official', textualized history – that of the archive (particularly the physical repository of the Imperial War Museum library) and the story of national self-creation; that is, the war itself as remembered in the United Kingdom (and, particularly, the memorialization of the war rendered in novels and dramatic re-enactments).[57] Briony's atonement for her lies or misrepresentation is to lie further, and to turn from the shocking realist chaos of history to the comfort of fiction. Yet this rendering of narrative order on to horror simply leads to a moment in the text of rupture and further epistemic violence, insofar as the ordering structure of the text–reader relationship is broken. Briony's admission that she makes things up – most obviously, the things that the reader has been reading – forces that reader to recognize the entire novel as a tissue of lies. Yet these are lies in the service of salving the conscience of the author – atoning for what she has done. Briony admits that she consciously changes the facts to make her interpretation, her preferred version of the 'truth' – self-evidently not such – fit the storyline. Briony has been using the services of a witness to give authority to her writing. Her contact, a former soldier, corrects her language and her terminology: 'I love these little things, this pointillist approach to verisimilitude, the correction of detail that cumulatively gives such satisfaction' (p. 359). Briony's language here is instructive – 'verisimilitude' rather than realism or authenticity or truth – the representation of pastness is what she attains through this collage of fact. That said, she reflects later on that, 'If I really cared so much about facts, I should have written a different kind of book' (p. 360).

Hermione Lee, writing in *The Observer*, considered the coda in some depth for its literary qualities, although – along with most commentators – she used this to reflect upon McEwan's generic accomplishment:

> If fiction is a controlling play, a way of ordering the universe in which the writer is away in her – or his – thoughts, then is it a form of escapism, lacking all moral force? Is it just another form of false witness, and so always 'unforgivable'? And are some forms of fiction – modernist, middle-class, limited to personal relations – more unforgivable than others?[58]

Lee asks some quite profound questions here, but articulates them within an overarching disciplinary context. She is considering 'forms of fiction', but, to push her thoughts further, McEwan demonstrates, not only how the novelist controls the chaos of the universe, but, furthermore, how fiction in the present orders, disciplines, and rewrites the fragmentations and actual traumas (rape, war) of history. What is 'unforgivable' about the novel is that it is not history, it cannot tell the truth – it is always bearing 'false witness'. What McEwan's novel encapsulates, then, is this central truth of fiction. It is a lie that sits at an awkward and morally problematic angle to history. All novels lie, but historical novels lie about facts, or at least about events that a culture or society considers had an actuality

[handwritten margin note: But can this be generalized to all fiction? McEwan creates Briony, she's not a historical figure so he's the one who's created this problematic, unreliable narrator.]

and a 'truth' to them. If fiction is about lying – Lee's 'escapism' – then the historical novel, with its apparatus and self-conciousness, is at least more honest than most in presenting the reader with the tools of critique. Historical fiction, in its notes and footnotes and afterwords and general paratextual commentary, points to its own wroughtness, its own partiality as an account of the past. Historical novels do not make a claim to completeness. Yet, at the same time, through their emotive force, interactivity, dissembling, and implication of the authentic fallacy, they continually pull the wool over the eyes of the audience.

War, blood, guts: Combat and violence in mass-market novels

In *Ace, King, Knave*, Maria McCann introduces her thirty-nine-book 'Select Bibliography' with the lines, 'To acknowledge one's sources is not to present oneself as a historian.'[59] She then argues in her 'Acknowledgements' that, 'Historical errors and deliberate distortions are of course my own responsibility' (p. 497). In the tension between these assertions, it is possible to discern the workings of the historical novel's peculiar epistemology. What is at stake here is how a historical intervention might be defined. McCann is outside the academy, albeit writing something that requires sources. However, she freely admits to perverting 'truth', but does not say where and how. Her 'deliberate distortions' sit with historical errors as part of the responsibility of the author. On the one hand, she cleaves to an academic discourse regarding citation and building 'truth' through revising the work of others.[60] On the other, she points to the clear fabrication she is undertaking, but also to the possibility that some 'mistakes' might simply be errors, and that such is the way of making history.

This concluding section moves to consider how the chapter's central ideas – popular historiography (achieved in many ways through paratextual elements), ethics, reading, and a meditation upon realism and authenticity – work in more populist historical fictions. In particular, the section looks at Ben Kane's *Spartacus: The Gladiator*, published in 2012.[61] Kane's book is part of a large number of anglophone, mass-market novels aimed at a male readership, specifically dealing with combat and adventure in the past. In the same way that romance fiction needs a wish-fulfilment element, whereby the reader associates themselves with the protagonist, these military, historical novels seem to allow a particular readership to feel what it is like to be in the heat of combat, communicating to them something of the experience of the savage historical other.[62] The novels therefore have much in common with the recent publishing phenomenon of army and combat novels, such as those written by Andy McNab. The past in these historical novels is a place where things are easier, more straightforward, and ordered by rules such as virtue and honour, but also less modern, less rational, and significantly more violent. The contention of this chapter is that all historical novels and fictions engage in the meditations upon representing the past discussed so far. The shift to looking at these mass-market texts is to demonstrate that the range of historical novels contribute to the popular historiographical imagination. Additionally, these present texts might be seen as somehow 'conservative' and, hence, be set in contrast to the more interrogative literary texts so far considered. What kind of 'radical' revisionist historiography might these muscular, male, reactionary, violent texts present us with? Their revisionist move is to suggest the savagery and chaos of the past. That past is a place of violence and combat, with the story of one figure a route through this complexity. On the one hand, they suggest an understanding that a linear narrative history is purposeless, sharing a sense within historical fiction, traceable to Tolstoy, that war is incomprehensible as a whole and only approachable via the experience of the individual. 'War' comes to stand for 'history' as a collection of events that are unnavigable in any real or purposeful sense, only to be experienced and survived. On the other hand, these novels attempt to impose some kind of order on this chaos through their narratives, their style, and their paratexts.

There is a strong heritage for such male-orientated, military, historical writing, from C.S. Forester's Hornblower books (1937–67) through to Bernard Cornwell's Sharpe novels (1981–2007), but these series have grown exponentially in the past decade and have become increasingly violent and sensational. The books dramatize combat in a variety of historical locales, concentrating in the main on moments of war. Rome is the most popular setting, allowing a combination of violent warfare and a recognizable social order. Similarly, the Crusades, the English Civil War, the Napoleonic wars, and the Norman conquest are well represented. Each specific period brings a kind of context and set of tropes; each also allows for a meditation upon the circumstances of warfare. They also clearly reflect concerns about the contemporary world. Simon Scarrow's *Sword and Scimitar* dramatizes 'the great battle of our age. The decisive test of arms between our faith and the false faith of Islam', for instance.[63] These books are sold by mass-market publishers, are bestsellers around the anglophone world, and are extremely popular. The authors are also prolific, sometimes producing two books a year. The books are often published as part of series involving popular characters, and this shift to serialization over the past decade demonstrates a change in reader demand. The ten books examined in this section were published within months of one another between late 2011 and early 2012, providing a snapshot of a mass-market industry often not remarked upon by scholars.

The novels are detailed, explicit, and very violent. Sometimes, this violence is witnessed, and its effects are represented, as in this blunt section from Michael Arnold's *Hunter's Rage*:

> Stryker gazed at the carnage left behind and was put in mind of the shambles at Smithfield. Twisted, bleeding, and unrecognizable, strewn in haphazard array among lumps of torn muscle and gelatinous entrails. But this butchery had been done by gunpowder, and the stench of scorched flesh hung ripe and nauseating in the air.[64]

The gaze of the protagonist considers the gore of the past (literally what was 'left behind'). This gaze frames it, attempts to understand and comprehend, but is unable to. War has made these bodies 'unrecognizable', disordered and fragmented. Stryker looks on something that is uncategorizable. It is common in these texts to find these brief moments of reflection, framing instants when the reader is invited to reflect upon their own gaze, looking on the formlessness of the past and the violence enacted upon unknown bodies. The reader is forced to contemplate the ethics of representing this past, and their choice in reading about it. This realism literally cleaves to violent action and suggests a readership comfortable with violence enacted upon historical bodies. As an approach, it asks the reader to consider the ethics of representing the past. Thus, authenticity, the practice of reading, and an ethical discussion combine here powerfully.

Part of the aesthetic and historiographic purpose of these novels comes from their precise style, particularly when describing combat or the preparation for it:

> He was already dressed. Tunic, padded jerkin, mail shirt, studded sandals. Baldric over his shoulder, sica in its scabbard by his left side. A leather belt with a sheathed dagger on it. He reached down to the stool by his bedding and picked up his Phrygian helmet.[65]

Kane's style here is characteristic of an aesthetic strategy that is itself historiographic. The precision and brevity of the writing are counterpointed by the detail. The punchiness of the style communicates something serious and authentic, without the frippery of description. This is muscular, lean writing that seeks to disavow literariness. The detail and the information communicated are all; the narrative is pared down to that which is necessary. The ferocity of the books and their gory concentration on the mechanics of fighting communicate a historical sensibility. This is an aesthetics that depends upon the authenticity of violence, in the diegesis and in the prose itself. Violence somehow equates to an authentic action, something transhistorical and comprehensible. The precision of violence, movement, and narrative are intertwined:

> Driving his shield into his opponent's, he swung a wicked blow at his head. The traveller, rocking back slightly from the impact of the strike, ducked his head out of the way. Reaching around with his sica, he sliced the big man's left hamstring in two.
>
> (p. 5)

Every sentence in this section contains a movement with associated violent action. The final sentence enacts a staccato move that is then ended with the death of the attacking bandit:

> A piercing scream rent the air, and the bandit collapsed in a heap. He had enough sense to raise his pelte, but the traveller smashed it out of the way with his shield and skewered him through the neck. The thug died choking on his own blood.
>
> (p. 5)

The development of the section, therefore, depends on a literal narrative thrust. This, associated with the third-person, present-tense immediacy and urgency of tone, allows the prose to be continually in the moment and moving forwards relentlessly. Violent action, narrative movement, and prose style are associated, therefore, with a type of authenticity that itself presupposes something about the historical accuracy of the writing and the fiction.

Kane's Spartacus is a self-aware historical subject, with insight, agency, and mobility. In this, he is similar to the heroes of all these texts, able to comprehend their situations in a way others cannot:

> The men might not have the martial background you describe, Castus. They aren't as well equipped as the Romans either. But what they do have [. . .] is the burning desire to be free! They won't suffer the ignominy of being enslaved again. Am I not right?
>
> (p. 364)

This notion of insurrection, of being freed through the purity of combat (even if death is imminent), is key to the appeal of these books. Their heroes are defined through their relationship to violence and their physical ability, rather than by a state or social relationships. They desire a kind of wild freedom and are often famous rebels or acting during moments of revolution and uprising. Yet Kane also ensures that Spartacus is othered, through his religion and his desire to die as a warrior. This is part of his heroism: 'I'm a warrior who stands and fights, not a yellow-livered coward who skulks off when times get hard, leaving the weak to fend for themselves' (p. 284). He is savage but attractive, incomprehensible to a modern sensibility, but somehow communicated via the medium of the imaginative fiction.

Spartacus: The Gladiator cleaves so closely to a type of historical authenticity that it has a nine-page glossary at the back, explaining key terms and phrases and describing locations. There are also several maps. Maps, glossary, and author's note provide a framework for interpretation of the text, a part of the contract between reader and author: 'As always I have stuck to historical detail whenever possible in this tale. Where I deviated from it, I will explain why' (p. 396). Given that he also admits the dearth of material on the decisive battles that Spartacus fought (which make up the bulk of the narrative), this authenticity claim is somewhat disingenuous. The 'historical note' is a key part of the apparatus of any historical novel, as has been argued throughout this chapter. In these combat books, it becomes central to demonstrating the aesthetic purpose and focus of the text. In particular, it signposts the way in which the text might be used and highlights problems regarding how knowledge is to be considered in relation to it. Lindsey Davis argues, 'Writing about this period is tricky, since, apart from a few fixed events, it is notoriously difficult to plot dates with certainty; I made the best sense of it I could. Novelists have to choose.'[66] Her self-awareness here is characteristic of the 'historical note' sub-genre, linked always with an explication of what is real and what is not (and why choices were made). Conn Iggulden's comments in *Conqueror* illustrate the common combination of imaginative and factual: 'I should add that there is no evidence that Guyuk was homosexual. I needed to explain how he fell out with Batu on the return from Russia – a detail missing from the historical record.'[67] The 'historical note' allows this shift between what is 'known' and what is not; it similarly allows the author to articulate something quite profound about the difference between fiction and history. Angus Donald points out the clear purpose of the 'historical note': 'But the point of this note is to help the reader understand which parts of my book are based on historical fact, and which parts are not'.[68]

The apparatuses for these novels are extensive and outline their historiographical intervention. Michael Arnold's *Hunter's Rage* has extensive historical notes, maps, and web links to re-enactment societies; Iggulden's *Conqueror* has a historical note, family trees, list of characters, glossary of terms, and maps; Robert Lyndon's *Hawk Quest* has a note on languages, chronologies, information about prices of falcons, an extract from the Exeter Book, and a map.[69] Anthony Riches's *Empire: The Leopard Sword* goes further, with a fifteen-page apparatus including a historical note, an explanation of the cult of Mithras, and a description of the Roman Army in 182 AD.[70] Bernard Cornwell's *1356* has a historical note arguing that, 'the battle has receded from common memory [. . .] Yet Poitiers deserves a place among England's most significant military achievements'.[71] The novel is, therefore, both educating and reminding 'common memory'. Its explicit historiographical intervention is not into the academy but into the popular imagination. Cornwell continues to outline the detail of the battle, although he concedes that much is unknown about it. Then, he outlines a series of historical source books, claiming, 'I could not have written the novel without the help of several books [. . .] I owe thanks to all those historians' (pp. 432–3). Novels are built on the historical research of others but have their own intervention to make, and this is made clear, often through the device of the paratextual note.

Gerard Genette has argued influentially about the paratextual elements of a novel:

> It is an 'undefined zone' between the inside and the outside, a zone without any hard and fast boundary on either the inward side (turned toward the text) or the outward side (turned toward the world's discourse about the text), an edge, as Philippe Lejeune put it, 'a fringe of the printed text which in reality controls one's whole reading of the text.' Indeed, this fringe, always the conveyor of a commentary that is authorial or more or less legitimated by the author, constitutes a zone between text and off-text, a zone not only of transition but also of transaction: a privileged place of a pragmatics and a strategy, of an influence on the public, an influence that – whether well or poorly understood and achieved – is at the service of a better reception for the text and a more pertinent reading of it (more pertinent, of course, in the eyes of the author and his allies).[72]

Paratexts, in this reading, contribute to the impression of the text, 'contributing to a better reception' for the novel in a subtle and complex fashion. The 'historical note' is just such an influential moment, suggesting research integrity and an ethical engagement with the precious truth of the past. It would be unethical not to have a 'historical note', in terms of not only ignoring foundational scholarship but also failing to point out the fictive quality of the writing and any additions or elisions made. The 'historical note' inflects the novel in a similar fashion to the way that informational epilogues or epigraphs work in film and television. They situate the text in a continuum of a 'truth', but at an angle to this, something different. They are a way of ordering the text and, inherently, its version of the past. They point out the difference between 'truth' and the fictive representation. Genette's point about 'transaction' is key – the 'historical note' is part of the contract made between reader and writer, an agreement allowing the author to write their fiction. They contribute to the 'contract' between reader and writer that establishes and articulates genre.[73] The 'historical note' is the entity that defines the historical novel, contributing a professionalized sheen to the author's activity in writing such a book (research, engagement with debate, awareness of archives). In the case of the novels considered here, the paratexts construct a reader who is aware of the ethical decisions made in narrating the past and is prepared, under certain conditions, to allow the author the latitude they need.

This chapter began with Hilary Mantel's 'Historical Note' and her attempt, through that extra-diegetic textual incursion into the imagination of the reader, to frame and order the way that the novel might be read. Paratexts such as these allow us to understand the intentions of the historical novel, to discern how, as a representative form, it seeks to work. They highlight the ethical conundrum in composing fiction about the past. Moreover, they demonstrate, as a microcosm of the action of historical novels more generally, a set of epistemological problems related to representing the past. The novels by McEwan and Mantel do not seek to present a coherent understanding. Instead, they dramatize the multiple ways in which the past might work in the present and be brought to life. They point out how stories, memories, histories, and fictions are elaborately woven for a multi-plicity of purposes. They suggest an epistemological scepticism, and a need for an ethics of engagement. In the mass-market fiction, the motivation is towards authenticity, provoking a kind of aesthetics of 'truthfulness'. Yet, in their paratextual excess, these texts highlight the complex interface between 'fact' and 'fiction' and the way that the historical novel might navigate between each pole. These latter novels show how historical fictions might attempt to close down debate regarding truthfulness, while being painfully aware of their own fictive qualities. Popular historical texts are constantly concerned with their address to truth (through 'authenticity' in representation), their realism, their ethical position, and the way that they might be read. As these novels show, each individual interrogation of the past is achieved through a variety of means. The popular historical text has a sense of its own ethical purpose and position, an awareness of its intervention into historiographical debates, and yet a keen understanding of the potential of fiction to achieve something ineffably beyond the scope of mainstream historical enquiry. The next chapter moves to consider how this potential might be made the basis of a critique of particular national and historical positions.

Notes

1 *The Giant, O'Brien* (New York: Picador, 1998), 'Note', sig. A6r.
2 *The Passsion* (London: Vintage, 2001), p. 5.
3 On the development of the historical novel form, see the following: Richard Maxwell, *The Historical Novel in Europe, 1650–1950* (Cambridge, UK: Cambridge University Press, 2009); Diana Wallace, *The Woman's Historical Novel* (Basingstoke, UK: Palgrave, 2005); Helen Hughes, *The Historical Romance* (London and New York: Routledge, 1993); S.L. Johnson, *Historical Fiction: A Guide to the Genre* (Westport, CT, and Oxford, UK: Libraries Unlimited, 2005); Avrom Fleishman, *The English Historical Novel: Walter Scott to Virginia Woolf* (Baltimore, MD: Johns Hopkins University Press, 1971); Harry Shaw, *The Forms of Historical Fiction: Sir Walter Scott and his Successors* (Ithaca, NY: Cornell University Press, 1983); Jerome de Groot, *The Historical Novel* (London and New York: Routledge, 2009); Franco Moretti, *The Bourgeois: Between History and Literature* (London: Verso, 2013).
4 See Fredric Jameson, *Antinomies of Realism* (London and New York: Verso, 2013).
5 An almost boilerplate review of *Rebels and Traitors* (2009), for instance: 'Lindsey Davis succeeded in producing a thoroughly researched, well-written history of the English Civil War, infused with a lively fictional storyline and totally believable characters', Kathy Stevenson, 'Historical Fiction', *Daily Mail*, 2 October 2009; available online at: www.dailymail.co.uk/home/books/article-1217654/Historical-fiction.html (accessed 6 September 2014).
6 'The Best is History', *Financial Times*, 13 August 2010; available online at: www.ft.com/cms/s/2/0c06fa58-a668-11df-8767-00144feabdc0.html (accessed 3 December 2014).
7 Frederic Jameson, 'Antinomies of the Realism–Modernism Debate', *Modern Language Quarterly*, 73:3 (2012), 475–85.
8 For an overview of recent work on the historical novel as something challenging and strange since its inception in the eighteenth century, see the essays in Kate Mitchell and Nicola Parsons, eds, *Reading Historical Fiction* (Basingstoke, UK: Palgrave Macmillan, 2013).
9 *Refiguring History* (London and New York: Routledge, 2003), p. 49.
10 The form has often been seen as a way of reconceptualizing a contemporary engagement with a particular period or a way of challenging epistemology; see Patricia Waugh, *Metafiction* (London: Routledge, 1984); Frederic Jameson, *Postmodernism, or, The Cultural Logic of Late Capitalism* (Durham, NC: Duke University Press, 1991); Linda Hutcheon, *A Poetics of Postmodernism* (London: Routledge, 1988); and Kate Mitchell, *History and Cultural Memory in Neo-Victorian Fiction* (Basingstoke, UK: Palgrave, 2010).
11 Hayden White, 'Historical Fiction, Fictional History, and Historical Reality', *Rethinking History*, 9:2–3 (2005), 147–57 (p. 147). On White and historiography, see Paul A. Roth, 'Hayden White and the Aesthetics of Historiography', *History of the Human Sciences*, 5 (1992), 17–35.
12 *The Writing of History*, trans. Tom Conley (New York: Columbia University Press, 1988), p. 10. He continues to meditate upon the binary between scientific discourse and narrative fiction that 'History' must avoid:

> History would fall to ruins without the key to the vault of its entire architecture: that is, without the connection between the act that it promotes and the society that it reflects; the rupture that is constantly debated between a past and a present; the double status of the object that is a 'realistic effect' in the text and the unspoken element implied by the closure of the discourse. If history leaves its proper place – the limit that it posits and receives – it is broken asunder, to become nothing more than a fiction (the narrative of what happened) or an epistemological reflection (the elucidation of its own working laws).
>
> (p. 44)

13 *The Historical Novel*, trans. Hannah Mitchell (Lincoln, NE: University of Nebraska Press, 1983), p. 24.
14 Maxwell, *The Historical Novel in Europe*, p. 60.

15 Quoted in 'From Progress to Catastrophe: Perry Anderson on the historical novel', *London Review of Books*, 33:15 (2011), 24–8 (p. 27). Jameson has since developed and, to a certain extent, rejected his own arguments here; see *Antinomies of Realism* (London: Verso Books, 2013).

16 Lawrence Venuti, *The Translator's Invisibility: A History of Translation* (London: Taylor and Francis, 2008), p. 1. Walter Benjamin argues that, 'The task of the translator consists in finding that intended effect upon the language into which he is translating which produces in it the echo of the original', 'The Task of the Translator' in Lawrence Venuti, ed., *The Translation Studies Reader* (London and New York: Routledge, 2000), pp. 15–23 (p. 18).

17 On the violence of translation, see Gayatri Chakravorty Spivak, 'The Politics of Translation' in Venuti, *The Translation Studies Reader*, pp. 397–417.

18 On the otherness and alterity of the past, see Jacques Derrida, *Specters of Marx*, trans. Peggy Kamuf (New York and London: Routledge, 1994), discussed at length in later chapters.

19 John Fowles, *A Maggot* (London: Vintage, 1996), p. 55.

20 'Booker Winner Hilary Mantel on Dealing with History in Fiction', *The Guardian*, *Saturday Review*, 17 October 2009, p. 3.

21 For the sublime and history, see particularly the interesting discussion in Frank Ankersmit, *Sublime Historical Experience* (Stanford, CA: Stanford University Press, 2005), who argues that:

> Sublime historical experience is the experience of a past breaking away from the present. The past is then born from the historian's traumatic experience of having encountered a new world and from the awareness of irreparably having lost a previous world forever.
>
> (p. 265)

See also his 'Historiography and Postmodernism', *History and Theory*, 28 (1989), 137–53.

22 Amy Elias, 'Metahistorical Romance, the Historical Sublime, and Dialogic History', *Rethinking History*, 9:2/3 (2005), 159–72 (p. 163). See also her *Sublime Desire: History and Post-1960s Fiction* (Baltimore, MD, and London: The Johns Hopkins University Press, 2001).

23 Judith Halberstam, *In a Queer Time and Place* (New York: New York University Press, 2005), p. 2.

24 'Author, Author: Unfreezing Antique Feeling', *The Guardian*, *Saturday Review*, 15 August 2009, p. 3.

25 *On The Historical Novel*, trans. Sandra Bermann (Lincoln, NE: University of Nebraska Press, 1984), pp. 67–8.

26 Cited in Sam Jordison, 'Looking Back at the Lost Booker', *The Guardian*, Books blog, 15 April 2010; available online at: www.guardian.co.uk/books/booksblog/2010/apr/15/booker-prize-fiction (accessed 20 August 2014).

27 Roni Natov, 'Reimagining the Past: An Interview with Leon Garfield', *The Lion and the Unicorn*, 15:1 (1991), 89–115 (p. 91).

28 'Historical Fiction and Fictions of History', *Rethinking History*, 15:2 (2011), 297–313 (p. 312).

29 The sequel, *Bring up the Bodies*, won the Booker Prize in 2012, and a final novel will be published in 2015. The novels have been adapted for television (BBC, 2015) and the stage (RSC, 2013) and are a good example of multimedia/multiplatform historical fictions. See Göran Boltin, 'Digitization, Multiplatform Texts, and Audience Reception', *Popular Communication*, 8:1 (2010), 72–83.

30 *A Place of Greater Safety* (New York: Picador, 1992), p. ix.

31 *Wolf Hall* (London: Fourth Estate, 2009), p. 227.

32 See de Groot, *The Historical Novel*, pp. 69–78.

33 Self-consciously alluded to when Cromwell looks at his own Holbein portrait and remembers that Mark Smeaton said, 'I looked like a murderer' (Mantel, *Wolf Hall*, p. 527).

34 See de Groot, *The Historical Novel*, pp. 69–78.

35 Colin Burrow, 'How to Twist a Knife', *London Review of Books*, 31:8 (2009), 3–5 (p. 4).

36 See Katy Shaw, *David Peace: Texts and Contexts* (Brighton, UK: Sussex Academic Press, 2010). See also the discussion of nationalism in Chapter 2.

37 Colin Burrow points out that this is how Mantel undermines a famous scene in Cromwell's 'known' biography, as George Cavendish's report of Cromwell weeping is generally thought to show him as a 'hypocritical reformer playing at penitence among the ruins of his prospects'; in contrast, 'Mantel finds hidden within the tableau of Cromwell weeping in the window a private, alternative history of personal grief and embarrassment' ('How to Twist a Knife', p. 3).

38 There has been an extensive literature on early modern ghosts and hauntings over the past two decades, particularly since the publication of Keith Thomas's influential *Religion and the Decline of Magic* (London: Weidenfeld & Nicholson, 1971). See, for instance, Tom Rist and Andrew Gordon, eds, *The Arts of Remembrance in Early Modern England: Memorial Cultures of the Post Reformation* (Farnham, UK: Ashgate, 2013) and Kathryn A. Edwards, 'The History of Ghosts in Early Modern Europe: Recent Research and Future Trajectories', *History Compass*, 10:4 (2012), 353–66. Edwards argues, 'most research on ghosts has appeared in the last fifteen years' (p. 354).

39 See, for instance, Mary Carruthers, *The Book of Memory* (Cambridge, UK: Cambridge University Press, 1992).

40 'Booker Winner Hilary Mantel on Dealing with History in Fiction', *The Guardian*, p. 3.

41 This section is largely reprinted from '"Who Would Want to Believe That, Except in the Service of the Bleakest Realism?" Historical Fiction and Ethics' in Emily Sutherland and Tony Gibbons, eds, *Integrity in Historical Research* (London and New York: Routledge, 2011), pp. 13–28.

42 In this, it participates in the kind of textual historical performance discussed by Roland Barthes in 'The Discourse of History', trans. Stephen Bann, *Comparative Criticism*, 3 (1981), 7–20. See Stephen Bann, *The Inventions of History: Essays on the Representation of the Past* (Manchester, UK: Manchester University Press, 1990). Michel de Certeau discusses Barthes's interest in the artifice of historiographical discourse: 'The *signified* of historical discourse is made from ideological or imaginary structures; but they are affected by a referent outside the discourse that is inaccessible in itself', *The Writing of History*, p. 42.

43 'To Lie Deliberately About the Past', *Financial Times*, 13 August 2010; available online at: www.ft.com/cms/s/2/0c06fa58-a668-11df-8767-00144feabdc0.html (accessed 3 December 2014). He also makes this point in 'The Lying Art of Historical Fiction', *The Guardian*, 6 August 2010; available online at: www.guardian.co.uk/books/books blog/2010/aug/06/lying-historical-fiction (accessed 10 August 2010).

44 See, for instance, Edith Wyschogrod, *An Ethics of Remembering: History, Heterology, and the Nameless Others* (Chicago, IL: Chicago University Press, 1998), and Howard Marchitello, ed., *What Happens to History: The Renewal of Ethics in Contemporary Thought* (London and New York: Routledge, 2000).

45 *Literatures of Memory* (Manchester, UK: Manchester University Press, 2000), p. 78.

46 See J. Hillis Miller, *The Ethics of Reading: Kant, De Man, Eliot, Trollope, James and Benjamin* (New York: Colombia University Press, 1989).

47 Email to author, 31 October 2006.

48 See also the controversy surrounding Jonathan Littell's novel *The Kindly Ones* (*Les Bienveillantes*), a war novel told from the point of view of a former SS officer, published in French in 2007. This episode is more about how history might be told, rather than the ethics of representation, but some of the concerns are similar, and it is clear that the Second World War, for various reasons, is a focal point for considerations of historiographical issues in fictional terms. See Sara Nelson, 'Will Controversial Holocaust Novel Find an Audience?', *Wall Street Journal*, 4 March 2009; available online at: www.wsj.com/articles/SB123617512234329265 (accessed 8 December 2014).

49 See Andrew Higson, 'Re-presenting the National Past: Nostalgia and the Heritage Film' in Lester Friedman, ed., *Fires Were Started* (London: Wallflower, 2006), pp. 91–109, his *English Heritage, English Cinema* (Oxford, UK: Oxford University Press, 2003), and de Groot, *The Historical Novel*, pp. 214–5.

50 See Alastair Cormack, 'Postmodernism and the Ethics of Fiction in Atonement' in Sebastian Groes, ed., *Ian McEwan: Critical Perspectives* (London and New York: Continuum, 2009), pp. 70–83, and Dominic Head, *Ian McEwan* (Manchester, UK: Manchester University Press, 2007), pp. 156–77. McEwan's stylistic debts are examined in Earl G. Ingersoll, 'Intertexuality in L.P. Hartley's *The Go-Between* and Ian McEwan's *Atonement*', *Forum of Modern Language Studies*, 90:3 (2004), 241–58.

51 Ian McEwan, 'An Inspiration, Yes. Did I Copy From Another Author? No', *The Guardian*, 27 November 2006; available online at: www.guardian.co.uk/uk/2006/nov/27/books comment.topstories3 (accessed 25 June 2010).

52 Erica Wagner, 'Plagiarism? No, It's Called Research', *The Times*, 27 November 2006; available online at: www.thetimes.co.uk/tto/law/article2214331.ece (accessed 2 May 2015).

53 Quoted in Nigel Reynolds, 'The Borrowers', *The Telegraph*, 5 December 2006; available online at: www.telegraph.co.uk/news/uknews/1536064/The-borrowers-why-McEwan-is-no-plagiarist.html (accessed 10 August 2010).

54 *Atonement* (London: Vintage, 2002), p. 371.

55 Cormack, 'Postmodernism and the Ethics of Fiction', p. 76.

56 See Belén Vidal, *Figuring the Past: Period Film and the Mannerist Aesthetic* (Amsterdam: Amsterdam University Press, 2012), pp. 194–6.

57 See Emma Hanna, *The Great War on the Small Screen* (Edinburgh, UK: Edinburgh University Press, 2009), for an overview of the problematic influence of televisual representation on the popular cultural imagination.

58 'If Your Memories Serve You Well . . .', *The Observer*, 23 September 2001; available online at: www.guardian.co.uk/books/2001/sep/23/fiction.bookerprize2001 (accessed 14 June 2010).

59 *Ace, King, Knave* (London: Faber & Faber, 2013), pp. 495–6.

60 Revisionism in history is not uncontroversial: see Marnie Hughes-Warrington, *Revisionist Histories* (London and New York: Routledge, 2013).

61 *Spartacus: The Gladiator* (London: Random House, 2012).

62 See Gillian Beer, *The Romance* (London: Methuen, 1970); Janice Radway, *Reading the Romance* (Chapel Hill, NC: University of North Carolina Press, 1984); and Lisa Fletcher, *Historical Romance Fiction* (Aldershot, UK: Ashgate, 2008).

63 Simon Scarrow, *Sword and Scimitar* (London: Headline, 2012), p. 94.

64 Michael Arnold, *Hunter's Rage* (London: John Murray, 2012), p. 120.

65 *Spartacus: Rebellion* (London: Random House, 2012), p. 341. This latter is the sequel to *Spartacus: Gladiator*, published in the same year.

66 *Master and God* (London: Hodder & Stoughton, 2012), p. 485.

67 *Conqueror* (London: HarperCollins, 2011), p. 527.

68 *Warlord* (London: Sphere, 2012), p. 446.

69 *Hunter's Rage*, pp. 463–8; *Conqueror*, pp. 527–37; *Hawk Quest* (London: Sphere, 2012), sig. A2r–6v.

70 *Empire: The Leopard Sword* (London: Hodder and Stoughton, 2012), pp. 364–79.

71 *1356* (London: HarperCollins, 2012), pp. 425–33 (pp. 425–6).

72 *Paratexts: Thresholds of Interpretation* (Cambridge, UK: Cambridge University Press, 1987; reprinted 1997), p. 2. Literary paratexts are discussed in D.C. Greetham, ed., *The Margins of the Text* (Ann Arbor, MI: University of Michigan Press, 1997), and Beth A. McCoy, 'Race and the (Para)Textual Condition', *PMLA*, 121:1 (2006), 156–69. Cinematic paratexts and extratextual elements are discussed at length in Jonathan Gray's *Show Sold Separately: Promos, Spoilers, and Other Media Paratexts* (New York: New York University Press, 2010), and Werner Wolf and Walter Bernhart, eds, *Framing Borders in Literature and Other Media* (New York: Rodopi, 2006).

73 As Frederic Jameson argues, 'Genres are essentially contracts between a writer and his readers [. . .] they are literary institutions, which like other institutions of social life are based on tacit agreements or contracts', 'Magical Narratives: Romance as Genre', *New Literary History*, 7:1 (1975), 135–63 (p. 135).

2

CHALLENGING NATIONAL HISTORIES

Much scholarship on cinema and television over the past 20 years has been concerned with their relationship to nation. As part of the mechanics of nation-making and dissemination, and also of the establishment of dominant cultures globally, cinema and television have been analysed for their ability to contribute to and dissent from the construction of identity.[1] Film and television are key contributors to national identity and also to debates about nationalism. Their engagement with the national past, particularly within anglophone epistemological and historiographical traditions, is complex and diverse. They are increasingly being considered in a cosmopolitan framework, too, as something that works both nationally and internationally.[2] Indeed, the 'national' framework is often criticized as being far too prescriptive and limiting, and as ignoring the complex transnational work that cinema and, increasingly, television undertake. In their engagement with the past, moreover, contemporary film and television open up an ethical discussion of nationalism and identity. Accordingly, this chapter looks at a range of anglophone film and television texts to demonstrate how historical fictions enact a critique of the mythos of nationalism and narrowly constrained imagined community. Consideration of the ways that cultures present the past in fiction allows a meditation upon how the creation of myths and dreams of national identity – Benedict Anderson's 'imagined communities' – might be interrogated.[3] Historical fictions are a potent way to articulate national myths and nationalistic events; they have been used for centuries to secure and communicate the idea of self-governing nationhood.[4]

Nations are imagined in relation to a historical identity. They depend on origin, beginnings, myths of conception, and, therefore, a linear model of temporality (there to here). The identity of nationhood is predicated upon a relationship with pre-sumed events of a 'shared' past. Yet, as Homi K. Bhabha writes, 'despite the certainty with which historians speak of the "origins" of the nation as a sign of the "modernity" of society, the cultural temporality of the nation inscribes a much more transitional social reality'.[5] Historical fictions allow for this consideration of the nation as something complex and protean, continually in flux and negotiated. Ato Quayson derives from Bhabha the idea of 'subjunctive historiography' – 'that which, even though seeming to be steadfastly engaging with the past, is actually providing models of agency for the present'.[6] Historical fictions provide an interzone space for this kind of conceptualization.[7] Dipesh Chakrabarty furthermore aligns Western historiographical practice with 'modernization', outlining a concept of colonialism through historicizing:

> So long as one operates within the discourse of 'history' produced at the institutional site of the university, it is not possible simply to walk out of the deep collusion between 'history' and the modernizing narrative(s) of citizenship, bourgeois public and private, and the nation–state. 'History' as a knowledge system is firmly embedded in institutional practices that invoke the nation–state at every step.[8]

For Chakrabarty – drawing upon subaltern studies – being forced into models of temporality and modernity through the imposition of Western historiographical models simply serves to replicate oppressive power structures. Through a range of case studies, therefore, this chapter considers how national identity and nationalism might be discussed, critiqued, underlined, and reimagined in historical fictions. The texts analysed suggest ways of resisting organizing, oppressive temporality and strive for newer configurations. As Chakrabarty argues, it is key to eschew the 'discourse of "history"' (p. 41) in order to avoid replicating oppressive structures through the imposition of epistemology. Historical fictions, as hybrids and outside the academic historical mainstream, often provide an alternative, marginal voice. They are outside certain types of organizing discourse and 'other' to particular structural approaches to the past. They can, therefore, imagine differently – either to attempt to engender anew, or to show the ways nationhood works, or how it oppresses and destroys.

Andrew Higson argues that national cinema is, like national identity, 'subject to ceaseless negotiations'.[9] The historical fictions considered in this chapter are part of these negotiations, providing audiences with complex discussions of nationhood in order to develop the concept. In the explicit engagements with national identity and history that form the basis of this part can be seen the process by which film and television might articulate a set of historiographical arguments critiquing and undermining assertions of nation. This chapter argues that the popular historical text is both nationally specific *and* nationless (insofar as it appears from the ether of history). It is both colonized and colonizer, playing out a fantasy of control over the otherness of the past, while being the representational product of that past. It allows a subversion of, or an attack upon, nation–state myth-making. Furthermore, the popular historical text can queer the nation's story and critique it. As such, it participates in a historiographical debate, actively engaging with discussions of origin, identity, and nationhood. The chapter works through nationhood by first looking at origins and the post-colonial (Ireland) and then moving to the explicit historiographical positioning of the Western. A section on British nationalism and nationalist politics in the *This Is England* texts is then followed by a final meditation upon the illusions of nation as critiqued by the American TV series *Mad Men*.

Discussion and origins: *Jimmy's Hall*

English director Ken Loach claimed, when accepting the 2006 Cannes Palme d'Or for *The Wind That Shakes the Barley*, that, 'Our film is a little step in the British confronting their imperialist history. Maybe if we tell the truth about the past we can tell the truth about the present'.[10] Set in Ireland during the War of Independence (1919–21) and the subsequent Civil War (1921–3), it is a clearly politicized attempt at educating. The film is as much about Britain as Ireland, and Loach's comments demonstrate a key concern with truth-telling. He argues that a clear view of the past enables a better understanding of the present. His filmmaking purpose, in considering historical subjects, is to correct, to revise, and to enable a clearer comprehension of the contemporary.[11]

Loach has been heavily criticized for the various elisions and controversial assertions that he makes in *Barley*. Roy Porter argues that the subject matter makes it problematic: 'while it may be difficult to reflect history accurately, it is an even more daunting task to convey a contested historiography'.[12] Loach's films about Ireland make a conscious attempt to intervene in particular arguments and demonstrate the way that polemic historical film might contribute to debate about identity, nation, and memory. In particular, his contributions to the historiography of the incipient nation, struggling to define itself at the end of the colonial period, open a discussion about self-determination and nation self-fashioning. Characteristically for Loach, this involves actual, diegetic debate on-screen. Hence, a consideration of his most recent historical film allows this section to illustrate the way that historical fictions might provide a space for reconceptualization and reconsideration, for imagining different and new connections. The film engages in the discussion about the relationship between history, memory, colonialization, the nation state, and identity suggested by Chakrabarty.

Jimmy's Hall (Ken Loach, 2014) relates the little-known story of the only Irishman to be deported from Ireland, Jimmy Gralton. Having originally emigrated to the USA, he returns to the west of Ireland in 1932 to reopen a hall originally built by the community in the immediate aftermath of the War of Independence. A bravura opening montage of contemporary footage plots the shift from the glory of New York (skyscrapers, bright theatres) to the starving horror of the Depression. This montage itself presents a revisionist account of the American Dream and the Irish involvement in it. Jimmy's movement back to Ireland from the USA recounts a rejection of the glamour of capitalism (see the later discussion in this chapter of the political impact of montage in historical film).[13] When reopened, 'Jimmy's Hall' becomes a utopic space of possibility, somewhere built by the workers for the workers, transcending class hierarchy, and presenting the possibility of a new future for the youth of the young nation. The youth are the ones who want Jimmy to open the hall again so that they can dance and shrug off the oppressive influence of family, social hierarchy, church, and state. They wish to define a new set of identities, based in the utopic space of the hall and expressed through dancing itself. Dancing becomes a mode of social resistance – something explored in films from *Footloose* (Herbert Ross, 1984) to *Moulin Rouge!* (Baz Luhrmann, 2001). The body in motion – propelled by a semi-formalized musical template and time signature – provides a way of stepping outside oppressive structures. Here, it becomes a way of transgressing the organizing principles of nation. This activity quickly attracts opposition from local churchmen and landowners, and Jimmy's left-wing actions lead to political opposition and the burning down of the hall.

Despite what might seem the individualistic heroism of the central character (emphasized through the title), the film takes pains to demonstrate that his actions arise from the will of the community. A key central scene entails a lengthy discussion about a particular action to take to support an evicted tenant. There are lengthy contributions from the entire community. This is a similar scene to the celebrated and even longer political discussion in Loach's Spanish Civil War film *Land and Freedom* (1995); there are also scenes like this in *Barley*. Discussion is the way that a political position is arrived at, rather than a thrusting individualism. The mode of the film is collectivist, in contrast to the state's desire to punish the individual. Rather than a celebration of the one, the hall is the expression of the many, built and run by the community to enrich everyone. This discursive scene provides the film's key polemic, historiographic intervention, suggesting the importance of discussion and debate in action, of collective and social engagement, rather than the importance of one heroic figure. Actions must be understood socially, and a film must attempt to provide an analysis of this as much as outline a narrative.

In providing an alternative way of organizing and living, and being a focus for resistance, Jimmy becomes 'stateless' and is deported. He is rejected by his nation. He is arrested for deportation outside his mother's house, the place he was born, and the film reflects here upon the difference between identity and nationhood. Jimmy is Irish, but he is forcibly removed from Ireland; he is othered by the state, because of the alternative he represents. This is fundamentally about property and, hence, the material configuration of the nation. The danger he represents is the forcible rejection of land ownership. The key political action he undertakes is to return a tenant farmer to his cottage after the estate had summarily evicted him. The cottages are contrasted with the huge mansions of the landlords, a motif echoing and critiquing standard costume drama obsession with country houses.

Ruth Barton argues that many historical films about Ireland:

> perform a public function of enabling their viewers to work through the legacy of Irish history in its more traumatic formulations. At the same time, such works satisfy expectations that Ireland is a country absorbed by its past and many of them rehearse the signifiers of Irishness that outside audiences expect from Irish fictions.[14]

In this, she demonstrates the problems inherent in rendering specifically Irish history, in films ranging from *Michael Collins* (Neil Jordan, 1996) to *The Magdalene Sisters* (Peter Mullan, 2002). Barton argues for the contribution of *Michael Collins* to political debates about nationhood: 'the film was to become only one of a number of competing interventions in a contest to establish a dominant narrative of Irish history' (p. 142). In contrast to these films, which themselves do contribute to a discussion and critique of a national identity inflected through historical awareness, *Jimmy's Hall* offers a debate about the how the future might be worked out. The film is a kind of proleptic history, figuring a road that was then not travelled. Both this film and *Barley* suggest an alternative history that never happened, a path for the republic that was never taken. In the early years of the newly post-colonial nation, many ways of ordering the state were suggested. Jimmy's social experiment suggests a way forward that is violently rejected by those with vested interests. It achieves something of a parable status, therefore, in many ways eschewing its historical actuality to meditate upon the way that states work to eject the views and needs of the workers. Hence, this is a deeply historiographical film, presenting, not so much a revisionist history, as an account of the death of potential. In this it chimes with *Barley* and also Loach's earlier film about the violent death of idealistic possibility in 1930s Spain, *Land and Freedom*. The state constantly steals the future from the workers, imposing hierarchy and the order of property. The utopian thinking of the films – literalized in the free space of Jimmy's hall – is crushed, and the future of possibility is denied. The films show the development of a nation-state, from the fight for freedom to the working through of social relations in the early stages of the new country. Loach suggests that nationalism is easy when there is a target – the colonial oppressors – but that, when the state begins to define itself, things become much more complex. *Jimmy's Hall* is a film about what might have happened and the problems inherent in creating a nation that needs to eject difference.

Disrupting pioneer myths: The Western

The chapter now moves on to more 'mythic' representations of collectively imagined nation creation. Westerns have, through their history, been read as engagements with nationalism and meditations upon the ethics of nationhood.[15] The Western is freighted with nationalist meaning, but equally continually undermines such myths and demonstrates the constructed aspect of such an imagined community. André Bazin's influential argument regarding Westerns runs that they somehow step out of the past, aesthetically creating something new: 'For the relations between the facts of history and the western are not immediate and direct, but dialectic'.[16] Bazin argues that the myth-making effect of the Western is to take the historical out of 'history' and to turn it into epic: 'The Civil War is part of nineteenth century history, the western has turned it into the Trojan War of the most modern of epics. The migration to the West is our Odyssey' (p. 148).

This mythologizing of the form is problematic, suggesting the genre somehow transcends historical representation. Much scholarly work on contemporary

Westerns, in contrast, has pointed out their allegorical function and the ways in which they present a sophisticated historiographical account.[17] Indeed, the Western has increasingly been seen as a key genre for meditating upon political understanding through historiographical commentary.[18] Bazin's comments on the Western demonstrate an attempt at taking it as a genre out of historiography, ascribing it something more, but, in the main, the gritty undermining of myth is exactly what many contemporary Westerns have been interested in doing. In contemporary film, the Western evidently presents a version of the past and reflects upon the terms, aesthetics, ethics, and visual vocabulary for turning these versions into 'history'. This is not new. The myth-making of the Western form is continually undermined by the films themselves, from the political expediency of storytelling in *The Man Who Shot Liberty Valance* (John Ford, 1962) to the death of heroism in *Unforgiven* (Clint Eastwood, 1992). American Westerns are habitually melancholic, mourning an idealized world that is continually demonstrated, by the films themselves, never to have existed. They are genres that constantly revise, while also reflecting upon the historiographical process of revision and history formation.[19]

True Grit (Ethan Coen, 2010), for instance, is a self-conscious remake, a reworking of an iconic 1969 John Wayne film that itself was a version of a novel. Hence, it has a quality of echo, encouraging an understanding of the West as a place already haunted in the cultural imagination. The dead are regularly present in the movie, as several opening scenes in an undertaker's demonstrate (although death is also a financial burden, and the opening scene contains an argument over the cost of a coffin). The final words of the film, spoken over a grave, are 'time just gets away from us', and the film's self-conscious elegiac mode is clear here in this coda. The film is entirely a memory, notwithstanding the coda, told at 25 years' distance from the events. Therefore, from its beginning, the movie reflects upon the shaping of the past in the present through memory. A long scene in a courtroom (another staple of the genre) demonstrates the way that memory, testimony, witness account, and fact might be quite different things. This self-conscious overlaying of narrative memorial styles ironizes the tropes of the Western, but in a way that recognizes that they have always been undermined. The Coens' characteristic ironic mode here meets a genre that is already conscious of its myths.

True Grit is a revenge narrative, as 14-year-old Mattie Ross engages drunken US Marshal Rooster Cogburn to find her father's killer. She witnesses a public hanging and reflects upon how she wants to see these men hanged, but she is obliged to use bounty hunters, as the criminals have escaped to lawless areas. The film is, therefore, interested in the intertwining of justice, vigilantism, and memory, suggesting that the incipient nation-state represented in the Western requires the violent ejection of criminal acts and an ability to reach beyond the borders of the 'civilized' for retribution. It also contains the literal silencing of the Native American, as a man condemned to hang is hooded before he can speak his final words. In comparison with the verbosity of the main protagonists, the Native American is rendered silent and put to death.

The film reflects upon how the West was already a performance, as, in the framing narrative, Ross is to meet Cogburn at a Wild West show that he is performing in. This self-reflective showmanship is a feature of Westerns, even creeping into Gothic Victoriana such as *Penny Dreadful* (Sky, 2014). In *Unforgiven*, for instance, the gunfighter English Bob travels with his biographer. This is also worked through in the Western TV show *Deadwood*'s concern with the production of 'truth' in the town's newspaper, *The Deadwood Pioneer* (HBO, 2004–6). The ideas of the gunman and the pioneer in the West were already being constructed in the contemporary imagination; *True Grit* reflects upon this performed identity of vigilante justice and the way that the 'show' occludes the violent reality. The coda, then, set 25 years after the action of the film, demonstrates how the story of the past is quickly taken over for commercial gain, inserted into popular culture in a sensationalist fashion. The genre's gritty violence, then, is regularly, diegetically contrasted with the carnival or circus 'West' in the popular imagination, and this contrast is a motif for the way that the Western might work in relation to an audience's historical understanding. The Western has become a fundamentally revisionist genre – indeed, it probably always has been – and this is signalled through its diegetic rejection of easy populist narratives such as are found in such showmanship. The form unpicks its own narrative clarity, pointing out the inconsistencies in characters' actions and regularly having the imposition of law be problematic or corrupt. This revisionism is embedded in the genre's approach and is inextricably linked with its suspicion of narrativizing the past.

True Grit is the Coen brothers' companion piece to *No Country for Old Men* (2007), a neo-Western based on the novel by Cormac McCarthy (2005). Both book and film are engaged in updating the Western, thinking about how the key issues inherent in such films might be worked through in a more contemporary setting (both are set in 1980). In particular, both are interested in the loss of heroism and the pioneer spirit, as the compromised characters in the film suggest the end of a particular way of representing the West. This 'West' is dead, but still buttresses a sense of nationhood, leaving a country striving for identity with only a violent present and future in prospect. Tommy Lee Jones's cowardly Sheriff Ed Tom Bell begins the film in voice-over, reminiscing about lawmen who refused to carry guns:

> I always liked to hear about the old-timers [. . .] You can't help but compare yourself against the old-timers. Can't help but wonder how they'd have operated these times [. . .] The crime you see now, its even hard to take its measure'.[20]

These opening words situate the film itself as responding to its forebears, suggesting it represents a grimmer world full of senseless crime. The words also suggest a kind of nostalgia for the 'old-timers', when things were more comprehensible or knowable. From the beginning, then, the film's engagement with the Western form reworks and redefines it in order to present a much more compromised and problematic vision of the 'country' it represents.[21] The new West is poor, violent, bleak, and empty; its lawmen are poor at their jobs, and there is a set of threats undermining its ordering, from the unrelentingly murderous other represented by the villain Chigurh to drug cartels smuggling into Texas from Mexico. The nation is leaky and ill defined, paranoid and violent. The borderlands now are places of seedy motels, bad deals, and violence. There is no heroism, and what violence is enacted is in the service of motiveless evil or petty greed. However, in a key late scene, Bell visits his Uncle Ellis and tells him 'I feel overmatched'. Ellis's response is to suggest things have always been violent, and that any sense of a new horror is an illusion. He tells a story of frontier violence in 1909, suggesting that the West has not changed, and its inherent violence is something the myth of nationhood attempts to occlude: 'What you got ain't nothing new. This country's hard on people. You can't stop what's coming. It ain't all waiting on you. That's vanity'. Similarly, the Western has always been a genre engaged in undermining the myths of nation. *No Country for Old Men* reinvests the genre with a kind of dread and articulates a fundamental bleakness in contemporary versions of the West, something that is also echoed in Andrew Dominik's elegiac *The Assassination of Jesse James by the Coward Robert Ford* (2007; also adapted from a novel by Ron Hansen).

The Coens' measured approach – updating and undermining the mythos of the West and the bases of American nationhood – is mirrored in *Brokeback Mountain* (Ang Lee, 2005). Lee's film is based on a historical short story by Annie Proulx. The literariness of these reimaginings of the West is important. The reworking of the myth of the West in novel and short story demonstrates the migration of historiographical engagement across media, as well as showing that the revisionism of each text is part of a wider cultural shift.[22] *Brokeback Mountain* recounts a loving relationship between two men working as sheep-herders in the mountains of Wyoming in 1963. They continue to see each other over decades, while also getting married and having families. The explicitness of the sexual relationship between them challenges the heteronormative model of aggressive masculine achievement or sacrifice as represented by the 'cowboy'.[23] One of the men wants to become a rodeo rider, the ultimate pointless expression of cowboy culture (and another nod to the 'performance' of the West). The nation has 'ordered' the pioneer into a caricature buttressing heterosexuality. The film suggests a range of different narratives should be available for writing the West. In contrast to this, though, is the horrific violence of heterosexual culture towards sexual difference. Ennis talks about a couple from his hometown: 'I tell ya there . . . there were these two old guys ranched up together, down home. Earl and Rich. And they was the joke of town, even though they were pretty tough ol' birds'.[24] Their difference is tolerated, for a while: 'Anyway they . . . they found Earl dead in an irrigation ditch. Took a tire iron to 'im. Spurred him up, drug him 'round by his dick 'till it pulled off'. This violence is the reassertion of the centrality of heterosexuality, part of an aggressively familial or genealogical model of identity. The children are forced to see the consequences of stepping out of line by their father:

| Jack Twist: | You seen this? |
| Ennis Del Mar: | I wasn't . . . nine years old. My daddy, he made sure me and my brother seen it. Hell for all I know, he done the job. |

The exchange reminds us that the way that the men desire provokes violence in the ordered state that they live in. The country is configured for those who act in a particular way, not those whose sexual identities are fluid. The violence of the cowboy in this moment is heterosexual, where often it is colonial, but it is masculine. The national identity that the West underpins is here dependent on the aggressive expulsion of otherness. The ejection of difference here can be overlain on other narratives' interest in the fate of Native Americans or Mexicans, violently othered and aggressively dispatched. In an excessive alternative, *Django Unchained* (Quentin Tarantino, 2013) figures the idealized vengeance of the slave turned cowboy, committing gory ultraviolence upon the plantation owners. *Django* posits that the only reaction to the forgetting of certain narratives is to violently reimpose them and to destroy (literally, by burning down) the house of violence. Yet this is fantastical and seen to be only generically, not historically, possible. The particular plantation might be destroyed, but slavery endured.

Meek's Cutoff (Kelly Reichardt, 2010) similarly takes a revisionist approach to the violent pioneering myths of the West. An avowedly feminist film, it combines formal anti-theatricality with austere content to provide an alternative version to the thrusting heroic narratives of male Western stories. The film presents an anti-romanticized version of events that demonstrate the disaster of settling. Most of all, it is a film about stoicism and hardship, about gaining nothing and ending in failure. In 1845, a small group of settler colonizers take an ill-advised shortcut from the Oregon Trail, led by a guide called Stephen Meek. Meek tells tall tales of Indians and bear attacks and claims to know his way, although the settlers quickly assume that they are lost and he is hoping for a lucky break, rather than leading. He tells a particularly explicit story of the massacre of a group of Blackfoot in Missouri. The group captures a Native American whom they attempt to persuade to lead them to water, and this captive situation allows the film to consider encounter, ethics, and fear. Meek seeks the death of the Native American – 'you have no idea of what you're dealing with' – but the group allows him to live, despite their suspicions.[25] The encounter with the Native American allows the film to open up a consideration of ethics and strangeness. He speaks Cayuse, and there is no communication – even sign language – between the two races. His words are not subtitled, and so the modern audience is similarly uncomprehending of him. At one point, a character aggressively asserts a kind of modernity as a way of dismissing him: 'You can't even imagine the things we've done. The cities we've built'. The mutual incomprehension is clear, and the relationship between the colonizers and their sometime guide is enigmatic.

The film is shot in 1:37:1 Academy ratio, the square-frame standard image for 35-mm films from 1932–58. It means that the film is consciously pre-widescreen (a technique introduced in 1953), literally projecting archaically. In this, it joins several contemporary historical films that use the ratio for a retro feel, such as *The Grand Budapest Hotel* (Wes Anderson, 2014), *The Artist* (Michel Hazanavicius, 2011), and *Wuthering Heights* (Andrea Arnold, 2011). The rejection of standard widescreen practice is a way of presenting an alternative to an all-encompassing, broad, and particularly epic kind of movie-making. Widescreen allowed a glorious vision in movies throughout the 1950s and 1960s (seen spectacularly in *How the West Was Won* (John Ford, Henry Hathaway, George Marshall, Richard Thorpe, 1962). Inherent in *Meek's Cutoff*'s form, then, at a fundamentally visual level, is a desire to undercut visual excess and the glorious wonder of a particular format with something that is different, if not more 'real'. An audience is forced to rethink the way that it watches film, made uncomfortable by the 'new'/old square format and, therefore, reminded of the ways that cinema – particularly 'epic' storytelling cinema – uses its visual framing to create a kind of 'real' that is entirely false. At its basic level, then, the film is revisionist and points out the limits of a particular kind of aesthetic historiography. The film proffers an alternative account and suggests that the way in which narratives of pastness are constructed might be critiqued.

The aspect ratio also works aesthetically, forcing a focus upon particular images in the centre of the frame, rather than a consideration of the sweeping vistas. This is particularly demonstrable in the night scenes, where one light source is focused upon – a lamp or a fire – and nothing else is discernible. Dialogue lets the audience know that there are people in the frame, but they are dark. The images framed like this focus attention on the point in the middle of the frame, forcing an audience to consider how the minutiae of the day-to-day lives are being rendered for it. There is no sense in the film of before, after, or a more sweeping 'narrative' of historical events. Stories are told by Meek and considered 'foolish, or actually evil', in that his tall tales have brought them to this 'terrible place'. In particular key sequences, including the final shot, the focusing upon detail is emphasized. At the conclusion of the film, the Native American walks away, framed even more by a circular shape made by the boughs of a tree. Any attempt at a wider understanding of events – Meek's stories, his 'route' that does not exist – is suspected, where what is known and material must be cleaved to.

This suspicion is part of a rejection of male mythologizing of the West and, by extension, the USA. The title, *Meek's Cutoff*, mocks the self-aggrandizing naming of topography. Meek himself proposes jokily to name some mountains after one of the young boys in the group. The attempt at cartographically comprehending, disciplining, and owning a land through naming is part of the aggressive colonizing of the West. Rather than the grandeur of Monument Valley, this film, as with a similarly feminist-centric revisionist Western, *The Homesman* (Tommy Lee Jones, 2014), concentrates on salt lakes, treeless prairie, and scrubland, with the mountains only just visible, far in the distance. The very geography of the country illustrates the contested political territory of each film's approach. The feminist purpose of *Meek's Cutoff* is part of its revisioning of the past. The film works to reinsert women into the narrative of the West, while simultaneously allowing a critique of masculine versions of the past. The film provides a new, feminist way of thinking about the West, a critique of masculine/colonizing historiographical representation. As Chakrabarty argued, it is necessary to step out of epistemological bounds to comprehend in a new way and to reconfigure identity. *Meek's Cutoff* attempts to articulate this possibility.

The aspect ratio here also articulates the actual restricted view of the women as they look from under their bonnets, unable to gain a wider perspective and, hence, forced to focus on the detail (see Figure 2.1). This is a laconic comment both on the lack of the 'gaze' of the female director (there are not many, particularly of Westerns) and also on the 'gaze' of the audience, sharing the restrictions of the women. They are literally marginalized, without agency, sidelined, and even their view is restricted. The women, who are cut out of any decision-making – literally excluded and a long way from the conversation, asking each other, 'What are they saying?' – do, however, influence the key moments, in particular defending the Native American with arms when Meek attempts to kill him. They provide an alternative to the male-directed violence and colonizing impulse. This account, then, remakes the West in a very different way and encourages a suspicion of particular past tropes. It rejects 'origin' myths entirely and organizational structures, including narrativization, violence, and cartography.

FIGURE 2.1 *Meek's Cutoff* (Kelly Reichardt, 2010)

Source: Evenstar Films/The Kobal Collection

The film emphasizes that this is the 'reality' of the West – thirst, darkness, hardship, sun, hunger, and illness. The regular night scenes are hard to comprehend, given the near total darkness around the lamps. The film is considerate of the actuality of time, the materiality of actions, and this ponderous quality communicates effectively the harshness of the environment. It also undermines heroism effectively, as, for instance, in a scene in which a rifle is laboriously loaded, primed, and fired twice – a sequence that takes around 2 minutes. There is no quick action here, just trudging. The film's particular brand of realism, then, is designed to communicate the weight of things, the hardness of the journey, and the purposeless wandering, rather than focused pioneering. This 'realism' is part of a feminist revisionism that puts women back into history, reminding viewers of their general marginalization in most Westerns. It also emphasizes that the values often celebrated by the Western genre – a kind of martial heroism, the imposition of law through violence, the establishment of order in the West (and, hence, the subjugation of peoples, colonialism, and the establishment of a society based on particular values) – are those of a dominant patriarchal culture. This kind of revisionist film, then, rather than articulating a (pre)history of modern capitalist nationhood in which the West is the virgin land forced into a successfully productive nation, seeks instead to critique an attempt at such a narrative.[26] The film ends enigmatically, with the settlers deciding to push on, despite the death of one of their number. They *may* have found water, but whether they have is unclear. Most of all, the film communicates failure and a lack of direction, an aimlessness rather than a glory. It by no means ignores the efforts of the pioneers to subdue the hard country, but it also asks why exactly they were there, how they destroyed the habitats of the indigenous peoples. Other revisionist Westerns, such as *Open Range* (Kevin Costner, 2003) and *Appaloosa* (Ed Harris, 2008), similarly challenge the myth of the nation-state and its incipient violent, genocidal, or colonial impulse. It is not simply an American discourse: John Hurt's racist character in the Australia-set Western *The Proposition* (John Hillcoat, 2008) dismisses Darwinian views regarding aboriginal peoples with, 'We are white men, sir, not beasts'.

The Western, then, is an essential form in contributing to nationalist caricature. However, from its inception, it has been a genre that has sought to undermine this easy representation. Interwoven in the aesthetic of the key 'American' genre, then, is a historiographical critique. Westerns unpick their own narrativization, pointing out the difference between 'truth' and perception. They are constantly revising what is known, challenging easy modes of representation. They are clearly historiographical, insofar as they tell a story of origin, but their engagement with the past is complex. Their epistemology is primarily about 'authenticity' (expressed, for instance, in the various meanings of the title *True Grit*), but this is designed to suggest something unspeakable or even unknowable about the experience of the West. They are a reflection upon, while simultaneously being, the way that cultural forms might express a kind of nationalism or contribute to the imagined community of nation. Their constant concern with the production of 'truth' – through news, storytelling, witnessing, carnival performance – bespeaks a suspicion of aestheticizing experience. They constantly refer to a nostalgia for the past, while sharply disavowing it. These films present various modes of engagement with past events, from memory to reperformance. Hence, they are extremely sophisticated historiographical texts, both telling a story and suggesting that the way the story is presented is deeply problematic. They are also part of a revisionary impulse in historical representation that seeks to redress particular concerns. This revisionism is largely the disavowal of nationalism. Working through the reinsertion of key figures – women, Native Americans, African Americans – this revisionist impulse implicitly critiques previous accounts of the past and seeks to correct them. This is both diegetic (through the reinsertion of stories, the redress of marginalization) and conceptual (through the critiquing of the way that form and genre might conspire to write out particular experience). They allow an audience to conceptualize historical revisionism simultaneously with a challenge to national myth-making. Westerns are not myths at all, but complex historiographical entities enabling the unpicking of foundational stories and histories.

This Is England

This section develops the discussion regarding ways that historical fictions can reflect upon and challenge ways of thinking about nation by considering aggressive political nationalism itself as a sentiment.[27] Remembering the 1980s has become a key site of contestation regarding contemporary British identity.[28] Particularly, the recollection of the recent past has become problematic in relation to understanding the legacies of Thatcherism and, more generally, neo-liberal policies around the world. The representation of the nation in versions of the 1980s is increasingly, and invariably, caught up in contentions relating to social policy, deindustrialization, and the loss of a particular type of community-based identity. Through a discussion of a suite of texts that explicitly articulate that they are snapshots of England, this section demonstrates the historiographical intervention historical fiction can make. These films also reflect themselves upon the illusions of nationalism and, particularly, how it can turn quickly into extremism.

The success of *This Is England* (*TiE*; 2006), Shane Meadows's semi-auto-biographical feature film about skinheads, led to a TV mini-series for Channel 4 (*TiE* '86 (2010), *TiE* '88 (2011), and *TiE* '90, to be screened in 2015). Each episode begins with a montage of images, both political and cultural, concluding with the statement 'This is England' (appended '86 and '88 in later manifestations). There is a sense of declaration about this, even of a manifesto, and this direct address is part of the sequence's candid and open political agenda.[29] It is also an address to a particular constructed nationhood – England, not Britain. The films instantly present a visual archive, a rendering of the past metonymically, which is then subverted by the authentic actuality of the narrative. These collages also mock the idealized visual memory texts represented by the wave of nostalgia documentaries such as *I Heart 1980s*.[30] Meadows's use of montage is actively politicized, and the opening of *TiE* '88 concludes with this cut:

> *Margaret Thatcher:* Britain was known for suffering from the British disease.
> Now we're known for having the British cure.
> [Contemporary text image: BUY NOW PAY LATER][31]

The soundtrack at this point is The Smiths' 'What Difference Does It Make?', sung over images of riots, consumable goods (early mobile phones, Porsches), the Lockerbie bomb, protest marches, floods, famine, Northern Ireland, as well as 'cultural' moments (Eddie 'the Eagle', Charles and Diana, football), and Harry Enfield's character 'Loadsamoney'. The inference is clear – cheap credit and consumable goods are the flipside of global instability and conflict. The unremembered '80s are the real thing, the bits in between the neo-liberal flash. Similarly, the political implications of attacking credit in the wake of the 2008 financial crisis are evident: nothing has changed, and this past is still wrecking the present.[32] Meadows uses montage to demonstrate how collective memory is constructed and, from the very beginning, to reflect formally upon the construction of a false-narrative version of the national past. These opening montages are formally counterpointed with sequences at the conclusion of each episode where music plays over slow-motion shots of the characters and some narrative development (most problematically when Lol kills her abusive father at the end of *TiE '86*, Episode 3). The two types of montage therefore provide alternative models of knowing pastness. This is either through the idealized 'image' or through the 'real' of everyday life. The final montage of *TiE '88* intercuts Lol having her stomach pumped with images from the past series and film, as well as archive footage of famine and riot. At this point, the personal and the political merge, traumatized by the ghostly haunting of Lol's abusive father, who also appears in these visions. Seemingly, at this point, the past is something that can actively cause psychological harm, that can haunt; it is to be feared and avoided. The 1980s, therefore, haunt the present.

The original film, *TiE*, is unflinching in its portrayal of bleak working-class life in 1983. It follows a group of friends living in the skinhead subculture and, in particular, the return of one racist member after a term in prison (Combo, played by Stephen Graham). As the critic Peter Bradshaw argued about the film on its release, the group is emblematic of a 'fatherless culture, literally and figuratively orphaned by the times'.[33] One of Meadows's techniques is to use an 'actual' historical event – the Falklands War – as an intertext within the film. Footage from the conflict bookends *TiE*, with the final, violent confrontation intercut with images of victorious British troops and Argentine soldiers collecting their dead and injured. At points, sequences of the violent, mainly male, society of the film ejecting difference by beating up or terrorizing ethnic minorities are intercut with a segment from a speech by Margaret Thatcher emphasizing the sovereignty of the Falkland Islands and their ownership by the Queen.

The Falklands War is as revolting to the film's sensibility as the raw, violent, nationalist racism of the skinhead minority. The film slowly reveals its own historiographical position, arguing that the war was somehow an expression of a wider politicized violence, most obviously expressed in the bleak, dehumanizing urban landscapes of the north of England. It is revisionist as a text, insofar as it seeks to undermine a particular heroic martial narrative. It seeks to make an active intervention into historiography, aligning political violence with nationalism.[34] In doing so, it joins a suite of texts that align Thatcherism with violence towards the working class: for instance, *The Full Monty* (Peter Cattaneo, 1997), *Brassed Off* (Mark Herman, 1996), *Pride* (Matthew Warchus, 2014), David Peace's *GB84* (2004), and *Billy Elliot* (Stephen Daldry, 2000).[35]

As discussed above, *TiE* opens with a montage of clichéd early 1980s images – Margaret Thatcher, riots, aerobics, strikes, Duran Duran – before the final images from the Falklands of injured men segue into a photo of Shaun's (Thomas Turgoose) recently killed father in uniform. Thatcher is speaking on a radio alarm that he turns off, physically closing off the diegesis of the film from the outside political life. Shaun's dead father is more important to him than 'history', and the lives of those who feature in the film are not affected, or touched, seemingly, by wider events. Yet the material consequences of political decisions are everywhere, and the film inhabits the wilderness of bleak, post-industrial Britain. England is a wasteland of empty buildings, unemployment, abandoned futures, and suburban dullness. The film is about the physicality of historical difference and the bodily reality, insofar as it is expressed and articulated in the bodies of those involved, of economic decisions. At its most extreme, the body of Shaun's father, these political actions lead to the death of the subject.

The logical expression of this corrupted and deceived England is nationalism, a voice of hate and frustration, screaming in pain. 'We are the true voice of the people of this country', says a National Front recruitment officer, and this is correct insofar as the hate and ignorance that deceive several of the characters are emblematic, expressive of their economic circumstance. They are trapped, unemployable and ignorable. Encouraged by a violent state to hate and to look for blame, and to express in violence and theft their unhappiness, the youth turn to racism: 'There's three and a half million unemployed, three and a half million who can't find work cause they're taking them all, cause of fucking cheap labour, cheap and easy labour'.[36] This makes them feel like they are:

Trumpissimo...

> fucking cheap and easy, which makes us cheap and easy, three and a half million its not a fucking joke, and that Thatcher, sits there in her ivory tower, sends us off on a phoney war. The Falklands, the fucking Falklands, what the fuck's the Falklands?

The film therefore suggests something sophisticated about rendering the texture and reality of the past and, in particular, an innovative way of conceptualizing the consequences of 'historical' events as inscribed upon the bodies of the past. The social history of the 1980s is not illustrated by consideration of key events or important people; instead, the ideologies and violences of that period are best understood by looking at their consequences. Meadows's film understands that the violence in society is an expression of something more complex than individual hatred. The seething resentment of an entire class, together with the inherent violence that ensues, is a result of the aggression and destruction that have been enacted upon that section of society. Lol attacks a district nurse in *TiE '88*:

> I envy you. You've probably got a nice life, and you probably had a nice upbringing, and you've probably got a nice husband, and you've probably got very well behaved children. I can see what you've got, and you can see what I've got.[37]

The class resentment and envy articulated here underlie the entire text. Lol's later apology renders this even more problematic, as it is evident that her anger is a result of contemporary problems (the loss of a community of support, the lack of social care) and the long-term effects of traumatic events in her past. The working-class characters are beset by problems in the then and now, an uncaring state and the consequences of an unpleasant upbringing. One will get them if another does not, and this sense of being historically isolated, rendered impotent, not just by present circumstances, but by a long-standing set of events from the past, is part of the film's deeply pessimistic view of England. On one level, the film suggests that the past is uncomfortable and violent – certainly, the innate racism of the characters seems unfeasible in a contemporary context. Yet it also demonstrates, historiographically, that comprehending the past through iconic moments or images – Thatcher, music, cultural icons – cannot in any way allow viewers to grasp its reality. The fetishizing of the 1980s through these thumbnails, these metonymic echoes, ignores the physical, grinding reality. The heft of real life, something painful and difficult, is explored in this film, an attempt at rendering the past somehow, not through a consideration of the icon, the image, but through the social reality.

The Falklands intertext returns in the TV mini-series *TiE '86* (2010), with Shaun (now sleeping rough) remembering images of the war and Thatcher's speech on the sinking of the *Belgrano*. Again, the violence of the wider socio-economic situation is intertwined with the actions of the state, and those who are the victims of it are unaware but suffering. The episode continues on diegetically contemporary Remembrance Sunday, with Shaun sitting on a war memorial for some time, and his mother receiving commemorative official flowers from two members of her dead husband's regiment. National commemoration is intercut with the experience of the individual, the reality of grief, and the consequences of fiscally conservative economic policy and the imperviousness of the state to the suffering of its citizens. The official memorial suggests community exists, somehow – imagined or otherwise – but any sense of this is disavowed by the series, which emphasizes that the only communities are marginalized, rarely engaging with the mainstream. Communities that should support or protect – families, particularly – are fragmented, often full of violence.

The other historical intertexts in the series are football World Cups. These are not mere markers, as the way in which football is represented is clearly related to

[handwritten margin note: Irony of racist nationalism is that the people they hate and blame have been screwed over by society just as they have been.]

the text's engagement with nationalism.[38] *TiE '86*, in Episode 4, articulates this clearly by opening with the news reporting the lead up to the England–Argentina game, the first competition between the nations since the Falklands conflict. The report discusses the way that the game was seen as an extension of the war in the English media (a banner reading 'Falklands 2' hangs in the pub where the group watches the game). The neo-colonial nationalist sentiment of the Falklands Conflict is seen to pervade society; it is an inescapable part of this pastness. More troublingly, Episode 3 intercuts crowds in pubs watching England's World Cup game against Poland with a graphic rape scene. Meadows invests nationalist sentiment with an echoed violence, an inherent aggression. The scene coincides with the return of the racist Combo to the narrative, again highlighting the combination of violence, nationalism, and Englishness. The sounds of the rape are played over slow-motion scenes of fans rejoicing. The rapist is presented as a violent expresser of the character of a bleak, horrific nation. At the same time, he is the physical rendering of the violent state, inflicting violence on the bodies of the vulnerable. There are no jobs, no houses; drugs and violence (particularly towards members of your own family) are the obvious means of escape.

The intercutting of the rape scene with the football, however, also asks the viewer to see that this is representation and fiction; that the 'real' pain and affective horror that are experienced while watching this are a reaction to something non-real. This moment of empathy and horror is something extraordinary, then. Meadows's film asks the audience to emotionally invest in something not real, evidently made, and to acknowledge that in the moment of horror and affective reality. It asks the audience to acknowledge the ethical implications of watching a rendering of the past and of their position to this 'history' (this was discussed in Chapter 1). Further, given that the entire set of texts are about the physical, economic, and psychological violence enacted upon England, the film asks that the audience comprehend this in a way that is beyond 'history' or narrative. The emotive and visceral response to these scenes enables a historical empathy to be engendered – one that is false, of course, or that rests on a false assumption of the relationship to the past.

At the conclusion of the first episode of *TiE '86*, a montage scene links Lol, contemplatively smoking outside a hospital, with her abusive father, sitting in a car. Both of them smoke as the sequence deploys slow motion and a wrenching soundtrack song ('Man Of The World', by Fleetwood Mac). The scene dramatizes contemplation, memory, confusion, and anxiety and links the two characters through their smoking. Smoke is used to create texture in the scene and to add a level of unknowing, indistinctness (see the discussion in Chapter 3). This type of montage is characteristic of the series – the concluding sequence that is used in each of the episodes. As a formal device, it allows reflection, the linking together of stories, the stitching of a narrative. It also demonstrates the wroughtness of all narrative, the fictive quality that the show has up to then hidden through eschewing all evident meta-textual techniques. Lol has smoked at points when she is isolated from the community, when grieving, and when reflecting. Although the series has many characters who smoke in the background, much of Lol's smoking is foregrounded, focused upon. She herself is particularized by it. Yet what links Lol and her father more physically is abuse: the smoking link highlighting, not nostalgia and melancholy, but the phantasmagoric, ghostly after-image of trauma:

> *Nurse:* You've been so traumatised, and because of that you've not been able to deal with it properly
> *Lol:* I'll never be at peace. I've so many secrets buried in me.[39]

In the later *TiE* '88, Lol's father returns as a ghost from beyond the grave, a revenant undermining her, haunting and troubling, leading her to attempt suicide. The indistinctness of their link is the desire not to remember, but being unable to forget, wreathed in ghostly memories. The past is painful, it decays and destroys the self in the present; it needs to somehow be dealt with. The series dramatizes the vengeful return of the victim to confront and kill their abusers. The impetus to finally allow the past to return in order to strive to find peace by destroying it is what is dramatized here. Lol falls apart as a consequence, her sense of identity fracturing – 'I don't feel like myself', she tells her nurse.[40]

The rape, and an attempted incestuous assault in *TiE* '86, Episode 4 – an attack that ends in murder – both happen in the same house, the same room. This disruption of the house is a staple of post-Thatcherite working-class drama, as seen, for instance, in David Eldridge's play *In Basildon* (Royal Court, 2012), where disease and abuse enter the home. The supposed sanctity and centrality of the house in English culture had been riffed on earlier in *TiE* '86 in a comic plot involving an attempt by Woody (Joe Gilgun) to convert an infested flat into a home. The houses in the films are crumbling, bleak expressions of nothingness, demonstrative of the economic straits of those who live in them and the strictures of their class.

Margaret Thatcher's various governments persistently strove to increase the number of people owning property. The Conservative Party argued that private ownership of houses would be the 'foundation stone of a capital-owning democracy' in its 1987 election manifesto.[41] Its ideological interest in the 'right to buy' had been evident from the early 1980s, and the party increasingly associated it with political enfranchisement and democracy.[42] Ownership was liberating and would effect widespread social and economic change, it was argued.

Woody's bungling attempts to get a house demonstrate the reality of this change to most of those in the working classes, forced to move into crumbling, decaying, condemned buildings. The built environmental fabric of the nation is emblematic, even expressive, of the wider society as a whole. The rendering of the vandalized, burnt-out interior of Woody's flat recalls the early scene in *TiE* when the gang destroy abandoned houses, romping through the skeletons of progress. More darkly, the house is a repository of horror and violence, a place of abuse. Far from being the place of liberation, it allows for a physical rendering of the economic violence being imposed upon the working class. The fabric of society is literally torn apart, and this is seen in the disintegration of the built environment. The home is not a place of nostalgic sentiment or safety, but a place of horror; the promises

FIGURE 2.2 *This Is England '88*, Episode 1 (Shane Meadows, 2011)

of 'freedom' associated with home ownership are not delivered upon or even offered to the people who need them. Instead, what the home represents is neither a place of sanctuary nor an escape into democracy, but an enclosure of fear. If the house is England, as it has so often been figured, it is, here, dark and horrific, filled with terror and darkness.

The house, which in the costume drama is representative of stability, an Englishness that abides, a structure articulating a particular identity, is in this series a place of violence and grief.[43] A fundamental aspect of the costume or period drama is this focus on the house (see discussions in Chapters 1 and 5).[44] The central focus of the heritage film on the house is part of its alleged conservative ideology.[45] Most obvious 'heritage' in England is physical, insofar as the historic built environment is something that infuses the day-to-day with a sense of pastness.[46] There is a clear link between 'heritage' and physicality, between the memorial of the past and the social discourse of that memory. Certainly, films as high profile as *Atonement* (Joe Wright, 2010), *Gosford Park* (Robert Altman, 2001), and *The Remains of the Day* (James Ivory, 1992) demonstrate an obsession with the country house. Recent heritage television, from adaptation (*Bleak House*, 2007) to drama such as *Upstairs, Downstairs* (BBC, 2010–12) and *Downton Abbey* (ITV, 2010–) articulate the house as the key space of nostalgic memory and of established class taxonomy (see Chapter 5).[47] A comparative intertext might be Loach's *The Wind That Shakes the Barley*, in which the Englishman's country house is a plantation building, a symbol of the usurpation of Ireland. Julianne Pidduck has argued that the manipulation and articulation of, and engagement with, 'historical' space means that the costume drama 'becomes a site of struggle', particularly in a more radical version of the past.[48] The space of the past in this reading allows for complication rather than conservatism. The houses in *TiE* are a response to mainstream period drama, rejecting their heritage sentimentality and their vision of Englishness as represented in the security of the home. The comfortable narrative of English nationhood expressed through the house is here overturned. The residents of these houses are scared and haunted.

The domestic space in Meadows's *England* texts – often shot from outside initially, before the move inside – is crumbling, decaying, neither safe nor idealized. Meadows's version of domestic space – indeed, the entire rendering of the interiors and the exteriors – allows for a meditation upon the contemporary inheritance of architecture. Unflinchingly, he presents the locale of the working class, without fetishization. Similarly to directors such as Ken Loach and Mike Leigh, he focuses on the ordinary and the day-to-day.[49] Houses are falling down, disintegrating; external locations are graffiti-covered interspaces between 'real' locations (roads, wasteland, empty sites). The texts illustrate the unyielding architecture of poverty. Importantly, though, Meadows's engagement with physical space is a disavowal of the fictions of nation and historical identity that the costume drama genre might seem to offer. The Englishness that such nostalgic representation offers is a cliché, a dangerous and diverting story. It is the national self-definition through a sense of the ideal of the past that Combo undertakes with his racist speech in *TiE*: 'That's what this nation has been built on, proud men. Proud fucking warriors. Two thousand years this tiny fucking island has been raped and pillaged by people who come here and wanted a piece of it'. He continues, parroting history and perverting nationalist sentiment into something physical and material:

> Two fucking world wars men have laid down their lives for this, for this, and for what, so we can stick our fucking flag in the ground and say this is England, and this is England [points to his heart], and this is England [points to his head], and for what?

Rhetorically, the answer is clear:

> So we can just open the fucking floodgates and let them all come, say 'yeah, come in [. . .] there's a corner, why don't you build a shop, better still why don't you build a shop and then build a church, follow your own fucking religions, do what you want.

The reference to the flag and the physical space encompassed by it articulates a sense of shared, imaginative material community ('a piece of it'). More importantly, Combo defines his version of Englishness through what the nation 'has been built on'. It has physical heft, actual foundations, that are part of the past of the nation but sustain its present. He refers to the memorialization of combat, the way in which this feeds a sense of national identity through conflict and a story of national sacrifice.[50] There is a clear sense of shared, 'imagined' community through an engagement with a presumed past. Englishness is being supplanted physically – through the building of structures that are foreign – and this is expressed economically and materially: 'there's single fucking parents out there who can't get a fucking flat'. The obvious material comparison is made and used as justification:

> and they're being given to these, and I'm going to say it people cause you're going to have to hear it, are being given to these fucking Pakis, right, who've got 50 and fucking 60 in a flat on their own, right, we're giving it to them.

English houses are being filled with alien invaders; the homes that should emblematize the inheritance of national identity, the genealogy of selfhood, are instead being given away. Combo's speech is incoherent and hateful. The text suggests that the kinds of comfort, self-identification, and collective national definition that physical structures might effect are fundamentally problematic. Nationalism is racist, inherently violent, part of the state's interpellation of the individual. It is fundamentally historical, insofar as it articulates a sense of belonging that relates to an imagined community that has a past, a shared history, and, therefore, a purposeful present. The dangers of nostalgia are that the real, hard lessons of that past might be ignored and instead interpreted in such a way as to strive to eject difference, violently reject anything that is not known.

The text suggests that histories of nationhood, or with the nation at their centre, are problematic; furthermore, such narratives are a combination of political

FIGURE 2.3 Stephen Graham in *This Is England* (Shane Meadows, 2006)

Source: Film4/UK Film Council/The Kobal Collection/Rogers, Dean

propaganda and cultural comfort (hence, the opening montage sequence). The conservative fictions of heritage, with their flattening of class difference, ignoring of ideology, and comfortable conservative visions of an idealized past, are answered by Meadows's cold-eyed viewing of the violence that the state engenders in its people.[51] *TiE* is an answer to the more conservative costume drama, insofar as it demonstrates the falsity of a type of memorializing, of a fetishization of the past. It troubles nostalgic renderings of history, treating with great suspicion the historical genre. This past is not easy, nor part of a leisure space that might be desired; it is grim, violent, and moving.

Mad Men and the illusions of History

To conclude, this chapter considers the American TV series *Mad Men* and the alternative spaces that popular history opens up for consideration of national identity.[52] This section argues that popular history can challenge models of nationhood and national identity, even while appearing to underline and celebrate them. It shows the complicated status of the nation in historical fictions. As has been argued, historical identity is often still conceptualized as 'national' in popular culture. Consider the following exchange from early in the first season of the American gangster series *The Sopranos* (HBO, 1999–2007):

> *Ariel:* You ever heard of the Masada? For two years, 900 Jews held their own against 15,000 Roman soldiers. They chose death before enslavement. The Romans? Where are they now?
>
> *Tony Soprano:* You're looking at them, asshole.[53]

The exchange demonstrates the historical specificity of religious identity as opposed to national historical identity – Ariel defines his suffering in relation to his Jewish heritage, taking comfort in a seemingly ageless stoicism (and this is a quality that has endured when other things have not). Religious identity in some creeds supposes simultaneity. Christianity, for instance, invokes a relationship with the living God as well as the historically specific Christ (as demonstrated most cogently in the year markers AD and BC). Jewish identity, however, has a greater sense of ancestry, of precedence, of inheritance of particular qualities. It is also associated often with statelessness, or a lack of a precise nationhood. That said, Ariel doesn't see the Italian–American Soprano as related to the Romans. The joke is that the power structures of 73 CE are still in place – nothing has changed, despite massive geopolitical and historical shifts. Yet, at the same time, the *truism* is that the Romans, the Greeks, the Anglo-Saxons are all part of History, and that history is othered from the present to such an extent that it is no longer relevant to contemporary states or nations. The quality of being Roman is not something that, in the popular historical imagination, might attach to Italian–Americans; it is so long in the past – 'Where are they now?' – as to be abstract rather than a concrete inheritance. They, simply, don't exist any more. In many ways, this is the grinding irony of the scene, the joke – not that Tony Soprano is *actually* Roman owing to his Italian ancestry, but that he is somehow 'being' Roman, performing a historical persecution of sorts. He might be anyone, re-enacting the pain visited upon the Jews; the historical irony of his ethnic identity complicates this, but does not augment it. Furthermore, the sequence comments on the problems inherent in resting upon historical identities – the sustaining of unequal power structures, rather than the development of new ways of thinking about ethnicity, identity, and nationhood. Here, the past is other, the past is familiar, the past somehow works now and enables the reconstruction of ethnic and national sympathy. The past is a national characteristic that can be claimed. Ariel presents a kind of constancy of pastness, a relationship to history that is simultaneous somehow; deeply felt as part of religious and racial identity; stoic and defiant, giving succour to the pain of the present. Soprano demonstrates a way of being past that – although echoing ethnic identity – doesn't actually depend upon it, a way that is dependent on action. In the process, the exchange neatly characterizes two ways of thinking about one's past.

The Sopranos as a series is deeply interested in the ways in which history works in the popular imagination. Initially, from a metatextual point of view, the show itself is structurally compelled to either gainsay or reject its own representational forebears. Accordingly, one of the key things it does is rewrite the gangster clichés of a swathe of movies. However, it is always in dialogue with them, as the advertising tagline, 'Family redefined', reveals. Diegetically, Tony Soprano is regularly shown watching *The History Channel* while working out. His interest in such documentary channels is both part of his attempt at bettering himself and an index of his spectacular normality. Day-to-day working-class and blue-collar American life is shot through with an engagement with the past through documentary. Finally, the key arc of the first series of *The Sopranos* is psychoanalysis, and, in his tortured exploration of how the past has invaded his present, Tony Soprano stands as an everyman figure. The show dramatizes how everybody lives in a here–now–then, a shifting temporality of consciousness that is framed, imposed, forced into our minds through the fact that, as Tony's psychoanalyst says, 'we are the only animals that know we are going to die'.[54] Not only this, but humans are the only animals who had to invent a way of engaging with or negotiating death. The ways in which death/past/memory integrate, reconcile, and crystallize are articulated throughout culture as a way of attempting to understand, and history itself is simply part of this invented, comforting process.

The Sopranos shows how the past can work in contemporary popular culture, insofar as it shows how a programme or a cultural artefact might enact questions and concerns relating to a kind of historical knowledge or model of pastness through strategies outside the ken or scope of other types of historical representation. This example shows how it is important to trace the ways in which 'pastness' works in non-overtly historical cultural artefacts – revenants, flashbacks, remnants, recognitions, time travel, time-slip, memory, echoes, repetitions, and spectral presences. A historical imaginary might be as shaped by these more esoteric processes of pastness as by the trappings of that which is recognizably and evidentially 'historic'. Comprehending the structures of spectrality seen here in *The Sopranos* provides crucial insight into the workings of history as Raphael Samuel's 'social form of knowledge', insofar as it affords a perspective on the ways in which historical epistemes might function. This kind of example shows how the past works phenomenologically, and how culture continually rehearses numerous rhetorical and methodological approaches to that which has already happened – a kind of popular historiography that encompasses 'historical' and 'pastness'. What popular texts can show us are, first, the manifestations and 'returns' of the past in the present, and, second, the models and structures whereby that past might be relationally translated into the present. Identity within the present is a process of negotiation between now and then, a continual working through and reconcilement between the two, an ongoing process of reclamation of now; the other of the past at once rejected and embraced, recoiled from and run toward, translated and transported.

The Sopranos has been forensically examined for its various engagements with Amerian national identity, from its use of Western tropes to the position of women within the series.[55] The show, as Jay Parini argues, is keen on 'drawing attention to the fault lines in family and community life' and, as such, acts as a critique.[56] Genre is inextricably bound up in national identity, as the post-war American gangster film, from *White Heat* (Raoul Walsh, 1949) through *Chinatown* (Roman Polanski, 1974) to *Goodfellas* (Martin Scorsese, 1990), shows as much as the earlier discussions in this chapter about Westerns. The contestation of national stories and the challenging of narratives are central to much historical fiction. Yet America is also the pre-eminent country in the world for representations of various particular pasts that work towards the focal point of now, a rejecting of the 'old ways' for the compelling modernity of the self-in-nowness. Consider the revisionist, iconoclastic attack on American identity undertaken in James Ellroy's *American Tabloid*:

> America was never innocent. We popped our cherry on the boat over and looked back with no regrets. You can't ascribe our fall from grace to any single event or set of circumstances. You can't lose what you lacked at conception.

Maintaining the fiction of this innocence is dependent on a particular type of memory, that created in order to maintain a particular kind of oppression through culture:

> Mass-market nostalgia gets you hopped up for a past that never existed. Hagiography sanctifies shuck-and-jive politicians and reinvents their expedient gestures as moments of great moral weight. Our continuing narrative line is blurred past truth and hindsight. Only a reckless verisimilitude can set that line straight.[57]

Ellroy attacks all idealized versions of the American past in fiction and film, a past that 'never existed'. He argues against destructive realism, the illusory 'reckless verisimilitude' that never looks below the shiny surface. It is not possible to look into the past to learn truth, but it is possible to understand the chaos and grimness that is the present. Ellroy continues, 'It's time to demythologize an era and build a new myth [. . .] to embrace bad men and the price they paid to secretly define their time' (p. 5). This cynicism regarding nationalist representation of the past is particularly centrally represented in the recent series *Mad Men* (HBO, 2007–). Set in 1950s New York on Madison Avenue (hence, *Mad* Men), the series explores the various lives of members of an advertising agency. In particular, it focuses on Don Draper, brilliant but flawed, and in possession of a dirty secret in that he stole his identity during the Korean War. Sold around the world, the show articulates a particular type of challenge to post-war American national identity, meditating upon the illusions of capitalism, the empty dream of wholeness, and how nostalgia for a particular past might be cynically used for profit. Aesthetically, it is rich, beautiful, but essentially empty, a quality meditation upon style and sheen that seemingly eschews narrative direction in order to render the past more richly detailed.[58]

Reviewers initially noted the visceral jolt that historical difference forced upon the audience:

> Wow, what a place. All morality has been sucked out, and replaced with Lucky Strike smoke. Everyone, without exception, is smoking – and sharp-talking, back-stabbing, shagging, drinking, and being sexist and racist. Sleep with everyone, trust no one, make a lot of money, smoke – that seems to be how these guys operated.[59]

Sam Wollaston senses the shock of the old, the jag of misrecognition that disavows nostalgia and replaces it with something much more useful, a kind of fascination with difference. The series revels in its props of pastness, as seen in its use of cigarettes (see Chapter 3).[60] Much media debate around the show has focused upon its misogyny, racism, and homophobia, and there have even been calls for it to carry anti-smoking disclaimers. In choosing to emphasize the difference through focusing on the differences, *Mad Men* offers a revisionary view of the immediate past. This work has been called the 'critical nostalgia' of the show.[61] The show's issues regarding physical historical difference became focused in its presentation of a central female character who challenged contemporary body image. Actor Christina Hendricks gained a lot of media attention for being a size 14. The series foregrounded her as attractive and assured, but she certainly does not conform to a contemporary body shape and has commented herself on this fact.[62] She is physically historical, her body actively inscribing the difference of then and now (in aesthetic and cultural discourse, rather than reality, highlighting the gap between the two in popular representation).

Through its consideration of marketing and advertising, the series considers how product is sold. In particular, it is keen to demonstrate how the 'dream' of the commodity is something constructed, made into a narrative, in order to boost sales. The Series 1 finale features an audacious *coup de metathéâtre*, when Draper pitches for the Kodak slide projector account: 'Technology is a glittering lure, but there's the rare occasion when the public can be engaged on a level beyond flash. They have a sentimental bond with the product'. Rather than simply sell new, the past can be utilized:

> Teddy taught me the most important idea in advertising is 'new', it creates an itch, you simply put your product in there as a kind of calamine lotion. But he also talked about a deeper bond with the product, nostalgia. It's delicate, but potent.

Draper suggests that 'nostalgia' can be used to create a solid bond between public and product, deploying this as a way of ensuring a stronger set of sales for a commodity, but also placing that thing as central to people's identity, bound up with their sense of self. The lights go down, and a slideshow begins, with images of Draper and his family, saying 'in Greek nostalgia literally means "the pain from an old wound"', it's a twinge in your heart far more powerful than memory alone'. He renames the technology as part of this process, combining marketing with emotional response ('This device isn't a spaceship, it's a time machine') and claiming:

> It goes backwards, forwards; it takes us to a place where we ache to go again. It's not called the wheel, it's called the carousel. It lets us travel the way a child travels, round and around, and back home again, to a place where we know we are loved.[63]

The cynicism of this sequence is in its recognition that memory is in some way a product, something that can be manipulated and sold. Nostalgia here is something that might connect consumer with brand, be part of the capitalist movement. Draper recognizes the coming visuality of the past in the present, the way that then–now works as a function of memory – and how his product might underwrite and support this. So, the photograph, the carousel, the slide, all work as bridges to the past: fleeting images of what once was but will never be again, but that is wished for and desired. The series reflects upon its own manipulation of a type of false-consciousness nostalgia, that awakened through engagement with the screened past. The motif of using photographs – literally, still images – in a device that allows them to be moved in sequence at regularly timed intervals, much like a movie camera, allows the script to suggest that the screened past, that which is created visually through the re-presentation of images through a new, technological lens, brings focus to an ache for history that is what makes audiences comfortable and what makes them human. Draper, speaking diegetically in the early 1960s, invokes the space race and science fiction, only to reject it. For him, moving images provoke fantasies, not of newness and travel, but of pastness and prelapsarian harmony. They are a pull backwards to childhood, to the pleasures experienced outside the destructive linearity of chronology.

The 'carousel' scene works as a commentary upon 'American' memory. The images are those from a 'standard' post-war American family (marriage, parties, kids, Christmas) and are clearly intended to work some kind of nostalgic effect on a baby boomer audience. The pitch has an affect diegetically, as one of the executives runs from the room weeping. What is being sold, then, and manipulated by men in suits in New York, is the past, but, moreover, the American past. What the sequence articulates is the fact that the past is product. This is something real and unreal, ghostly and spectral. Diegetically, the images are 'everyman' but also 'no man'; Draper's family is real, but he is an imposter, and so these fundamentally 'American' stories he seems to be selling have a fatal emptiness. The show quite deliberately invokes nostalgia to explode it. On the one hand, it recalls paradisical post-war prosperity and confidence, the sudden expansion of the American economy, rampant, unrepentant capitalism. This is a narrative of American expansion and exceptionalism, of pre-eminence and prosperity. On the other hand, the show gathers much of its historical otherness through its revelation of horrific ideologies in the past – racism, sexism, homophobia, class. The show is revisionist in its approach to the past, disrupting the historical imaginary by undermining the sheen of nostalgia. At first, the viewer is drawn in by the familiarity of some of the cultural caricatures and bemused by historical otherness (most obviously apparent in the constant smoking). *Mad Men*'s obsession with showing the origins of familiar – even nostalgically resonant – marketing (Lucky Strikes' 'They're toasted', Kodak's carousel) creates a sense that the late 1950s/early 1960s were a time on the cusp of corporate, *modern* America. Gradually, however, the beautiful image is revealed to be rotten and fake, the key motif here being the slow way the picturebook household and family that Draper has are undermined and fractured. America was never beautiful and innocent, and any programme that tells you different is selling a lie, is selling a product using nostalgia (this self-referentiality is apparent in the increasing importance of television in the admen's work). As Ellroy argues, it is a narrative of decline only supported by edifices of dreams and lies.

Draper's atypical, out-of-time character has analogues throughout historical 'fiction'. He is able to see through the veneer of the now to the historical verities. He tells his protégés, 'The universe is indifferent', to deflate their bombastic confidence, and:

> The reason you haven't felt it is because it doesn't exist. What you call love was invented by guys like me, to sell nylons. You're born alone and you die alone and this world just drops a bunch of rules on top of you to make you forget those facts.[64]

In contrast, 'I never forget. I'm living like there's no tomorrow, because there isn't one.' He has no sense of himself in history or as part of the normative flow of time. The character who is able to see the skull beneath the skin, to trouble the historicalness of the (fictional) past, is a trope from Walter Scott's *Waverley* onwards. Draper's cynicism enables him to be a brilliant advertising 'creative', because he has a vision unencumbered by the everyday. He intuits the absence in the heart of culture and economy (and the social insanity that this provokes). In this, he assuredly echoes the nightmarish articulation of Joseph Conard's *Heart of Darkness*: 'We live – as we dream – alone'.[65] However, Draper is someone who has stolen his identity, so his assurance and independence are predicated upon an absence and an anxiety, a lack of definition so absolute it can destroy him. He makes his own past, like America itself, denying what happened in order to live in the beautiful, modern moment of possibility. Yet his refusal of idealism leads him to refute 'tomorrow', to reject the idea of future. He lives, therefore, in a state of stasis, and this immobility is something highlighted throughout by the show. He is unable to develop and learn, to evolve and change, and this becomes something quite awful in later series. Others leave (to go to Los Angeles, upstate New York, the Midwest), but Draper abides. His family falls apart, he becomes an alcoholic, and he loses all his meaningful relationships.

Draper is throughout, then, an absence, the centre of a show that articulates the continual state of becoming, of rejection of one's roots, of modernity as a continual denial of pastness, of shiny nowness. Draper thinks he lives his life without history, and the life he leads is 'mad' as a consequence. Similarly, in his work, he helps America to deny and forget the reality for a dream of now, and everything that was solid melts into air. He introduces a nostalgic dream for the 'reality' of the past, a narrative that does not exist. As a character, he articulates Frederic Jameson's point about the schizophrenia of late capitalism, the breakdown between the signifier and signified leading to social psychosis. In his work on postmodernism and historical fictions, Jameson takes up Jacques Lacan's definition of schizophrenia as a language disorder and the insight that psychosis emerges 'from the failure of the infant to accede fully into the realm of speech and language'.[66] He reads Lacanian schizophrenia into postmodern capitalist culture and sees:

> the way in which our entire contemporary social system has little by little begun to lose its capacity to retain its own past, has begun to live in a perpetual present and in a perpetual change that obliterates traditions of the kind that all earlier social formations have had in one way or another to preserve.
>
> (p. 201)

Draper exemplifies this 'perpetual present' and the madness inherent in it. The aesthetics of this particular historical fiction are such that the past is all shiny surface, with no meaning. Post-war American capitalism's inability to connect with the past in any real way, mainly due to the intervention of people like Draper who would turn it into an idealized dream for financial ends, leads to a kind of madness.

Mad Men highlights the unravelling of 'social formations' that Jameson sees in culture more widely. This is linked to a narrative of national decline. The fourth series – as Americans begin to lose assurance during the Vietnam War and after the assassination of John F. Kennedy – shows Draper lose his family, the only person who knows who he really is (the ex-wife of the soldier whose identity he stole), and, increasingly, his hold on the real world, owing to his alcoholism. This is manifested in a self-referential, echoing fashion when Draper gives a drunken approximation of the carousel 'nostalgia' speech at a pitch and steals a jingle from someone he has recently interviewed for a job. This scene demonstrates the recycling, historicist drive of the series and the culture it reflects. It shows how such textual echoes in historical fictions are important historiographically (a fragmented understanding of a past that is only known through aesthetic tropes and representation), economically (the ownership of the words, the importance of repetition and memorability in advertising), and representationally (the series audience has its own memory and comprehension of the 'history' of the show). Draper shows the emptiness at the heart of American life.

In the figure of Draper, *Mad Men* consciously refigures the case of the imposture of Martin Guerre, itself the subject of two related historical films (*Le Retour de Martin Guerre*, Daniel Vigne, 1982; updated to the American civil war in *Sommersby*, Jon Amiel, 1993) and a famous academic book by Natalie Zemon Davis in which she foregrounds the problems of sources in discovering the reality of the past of common people and offers an account that is, 'in part my invention, but held tightly in check by the voices of the past'.[67] Both films highlight the disruption of identity, the way that a society visits order upon the individual through the force of law. One of Robert Rosenstone's key examples for the way that film can 'be' history, *Le Retour de Martin Guerre* explores a celebrated case of identity theft in sixteenth-century France. A peasant farmer, Martin Guerre, leaves his village to go to war. Several years later, a man claiming to be Martin Guerre returns and is welcomed to the village. He farms, takes back his wife, and has a daughter. Then, rumours begin to circle, and a dispute about money leads the villagers to challenge his identity legally. The trial eventually moves to the parliament of Toulouse, where his deception is made evident by the arrival of the 'real' Martin. From the beginning, the film is obsessed with the contrast between the details of 'life' and the material articulations of the law (standing for the nation-state). The film opens with the notary riding to the village to draw up the legal contract of marriage and dwells upon the agreement of the dowry. Subsequent scenes in the first section of the film develop according to the testimony of 'Martin's' wife, Bertrande de Rois. She recounts certain events that are then seen in a kind of narrativized flashback. The judge who interrogates her acts as an avatar for the audience, querying in order to gain narrative development. Thereafter, the film stages several sequences of witnessing, as, repeatedly, participants are asked to recognize, or not, 'Martin'. They must literally bear witness to his authenticity (or not) by comparing him with their memory. The final courtroom scenes again see the testimony of various figures to the authenticity of his claim, with evidence varying from physical scarring to the claims of his wife that their intimacy demonstrated that he was the 'real' Martin. In its reference to these examples of identity theft, *Mad Men* suggests the importance of authenticity in identity and the absence that threatens to disrupt social organization. The nation-state is undermined by the individual who pretends to be other than he is, and the law therefore intervenes to impose order. The nation-state needs coherence, or the semblance of it, to maintain its own particular fiction.

Mad Men, with its empty central signifier (Draper), destroys the sense that history might be anything comprehensible, anything other than a tattered series of lies, rehashed, recycled, and reused to sell an ideal. The key point is about nostalgia. Historical fictions figure a desire for a place where customers feel safe and where the chaos of history – and the inevitability of death within that – is at least obfuscated. Historical product is comforting, as Draper argues. It takes consumers back to a place they recognize, or at least think they do. This nostalgia is illusory, and what fictional historical products might further be argued to do is highlight the fragility of contemporary security. The family life that Draper shows is fictitious, both in the sense that it happens on-screen and in that he, of course, has lied to his wife throughout their life together. The nostalgia that is invoked has, deep within it, a destructive kernel of fiction that obviates its power, rendering it suspect. Draper's comment that advertising might allow audiences to return to a place where 'we know we are loved' suggests that the contemporary world is terrifying and most would desire a return to simplicity and innocence, a regression in order to heal the wounds that capitalism has inflicted upon society. Hence, the crying executive, suddenly conscious of the psychoses haunting him owing to Draper's therapeutic analysis, or, perhaps, repressing them further through his escape. Popular historical texts might work as therapy within the overarching discourse of capitalist

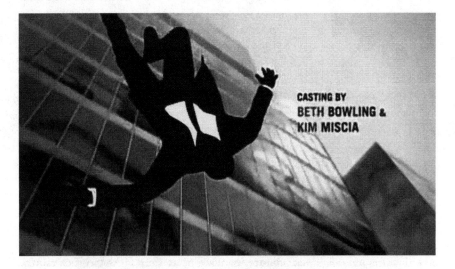

FIGURE 2.4 Falling man from the opening sequence of *Mad Men*

FIGURE 2.5 Final logo of the opening sequence of *Mad Men* (note cigarette, discussed in Chapter 3)

exploitation, commodification, and fetishization. Draper is using nostalgic feelings to force his feeling, but unthinking, audience to consume the product in the present that seems to allow them entry to the past. This past is false, fictional, a lie: photographs of a real event that has its meaning drained owing to its blank central signifier. This traumatic–therapeutic aspect of the show is reflected in its opening sequence, with a figure falling through a cityscape made of tall buildings with advertising slogans on them – clearly referencing the falling figures of 9/11. The traumatic falling man in the opening sequence is clearly an invocation of Saul Bass's famous titles for Alfred Hitchcock's *Vertigo* (1958), a film that itself recounts the gradual psychological unravelling of a protagonist due to a violent event. Yet, the figure is finally seen from behind, seated, watching television (Figures 2.4 and 2.5). America can wake from the nightmare of the present, taking refuge in a fantasy of pastness constructed mainly out of capitalist desire and quite literal renderings of false consciousness.

[*Mad Men* is a popular text that appears to be fundamentally nationalist – it describes the creation and construction of the familiar, modern United States – but also works assiduously to undermine that image. *Mad Men* demonstrates the illusion of the past and the ways in which a nostalgic sense of history feeds into an unbalanced and contorted national identity in the present. Indeed, the series demonstrates how this illusion has been created and constructed simply in order to sell product. This, in a key moment of self-referentiality, includes the heritage and historical industries that produce – among other things – shows such as *Mad Men*. *Mad Men* points out – while outlining a narrative of nationhood – the flaws

[handwritten marginalia: But Don Draper does have those vivid flashbacks to his childhood in the Depression; how do they fit in?]

and cracks in that edifice and, fundamentally, the problems inherent in the whole idea of nation and of a national history. Popular history, in its protean, problematic, challenging dynamism, can contain multitudes. It can undermine mythology and present dissident, challenging readings of events, while seemingly celebrating nationhood. It can allow for difference, while being provocative about similarity. It can be used as a sophisticated critique of the culture it is representing. It is involved in an ongoing historiographical debate about the nature of knowledge, representation, and the aesthetics of understanding. Its complexity, together with the diversity of response to it, gives the lie to the assumption that popular history is somehow passive, unthinking, watered-down and wrongheaded. Much history is nationalistic, and popular historical understanding has often been manipulated in the service of nation; however, it does contain a space of dissonance and challenge that might be manipulated and directed. The past is quite literally a foreign country, somewhere to be colonized or visited as a tourist – but it is also familiar, generically comfortable, innovative, thoughtful, fragmented, unfinished, and challenging. It is other and familiar, strange and capable of giving pleasure, a leisure activity and a call to arms.

Michel de Certeau argues for a fundamental loss inherent in historical writing:

> In this respect writing *is* repetition, the very labor of difference. It is the memory of a forgotten separation. To take up one of Walter Benjamin's remarks concerning Proust, we might say that writing assumes the 'form' of memory and not its 'contents': it is the endless effect of loss and debt, but it neither preserves nor restores an initial content, as this is forever lost (forgotten) and represented only by substitutes which are inverted and transformed according to the law set up by a founding exclusion. Scriptural practice is itself a work of memory. But all 'content' that would claim to assign to it a place or a truth is nothing more than a production of a symptom of that practice – a fiction.[68]

Mad Men's central motif of advertising pushes the face of the audience in this disjunction between real and desired–imagined, showing the dark workings of their imaginations in constructing the 'real'. The emptiness at the centre of *Mad Men* expresses de Certeau's assertions as well as anything (Benjamin's remarks are about memory, rather than history, about Proust rather than 'History', about the ways in which fiction represents the remembrance of things past rather than how it actually happened). The series demonstrates how popular versions of history are often phantasmagoric versions of a pastness viewers must know is not really there, or perhaps was 'invented by guys like me, to sell nylons'. The national history represented by the series is familiar – even within the memory of some of the audience – but fundamentally other and alien. Popular history subverts the idea of nationhood because of its inherent instability, its fictiveness. Indeed, it is the case that popular history – novels, television, film, art, poetry – highlights the gap between knowledge and truth far more explicitly than an admittedly, artfully arch historical discourse might. The 'founding exclusion' of the past is its inherent, inexpressible, alien otherness, and viewers are forever outside, alone, striving to get back in by telling themselves comforting fictions of nation, coherence, identity, and history. *Mad Men* mediates this by demonstrating the pull to, and the shrinking from, the historical enacted by an audience.

The fictions considered in this chapter disclose the work that popular historical texts can do in isolating, comprehending, and critiquing a particular set of cultural discourses (in particular, the establishment and sustaining of nation). In short, such texts engage in a historiographical debate and outline a particular way of thinking about and understanding the present's relationship to the past through the lens of nationhood. Loach showed how film might enable discussion and dissent, and point to ways that utopic thinking can still thrive, despite the imposition of inflexible structures. Subsequently, revisionism became the key to the historiographical positions of the films considered, in particular the Western. This latter genre strives to correct and reconfigure narratives of nationhood, at times seeking an entirely new way of defining the subject. *This Is England* and *Mad Men* demonstrate the emptiness and the horror at the centre of national definitions and nationalism itself, and the way that film and television can represent this. They demonstrate the sophisticated historiographical techniques of historical fictions, but also, further, the ways that they communicate a critique of mainstream, national histories and narratives. Although clearly not comprehensive – there is no account of, for instance, the conservative ideologies of war film or of English versions of India, to take two obvious examples – this chapter has demonstrated the practical implications of popular historiography: that is, the way that film and television might actively engage in historiographical debate, but, further, through their form and their content, might also equip an audience to comprehend and critique the ways in which national histories are narrativized, constructed, and imposed. The next chapter looks in more detail at how historical fictions present the 'dream' of the past, in particular through a consideration of that most ephemeral but material of things, the cigarette.

Notes

1 See, for instance, Amy Sargent, *British Cinema: A Critical History* (London: BFI Publishing, 2005) and Andrew Higson, *Waving the Flag: Constructing a National Cinema in Britain* (Oxford, UK: Oxford University Press, 1995). A demonstration of the wide selection of books on national cinema would include: Marek Haltof, *Polish National Cinema* (New York and Oxford, UK: Berghahn Books, 2002); Jonathan Rayner, *Contemporary Australian Cinema* (Manchester, UK: Manchester University Press, 2000); and the case studies considered in Dimitris Eleftheriotis and Gary Needham, eds, *Asian Cinemas* (Edinburgh, UK: Edinburgh University Press, 2006). Routledge has a series, 'National Cinemas', that currently includes titles on Australia, Brazil, France, Germany, Spain, Ireland, Mexico, South Africa, Greece, Italy, Canada, China, and Britain. See also Stephen Crofts, 'Reconceptualising national cinema/s' in Valentina Vitali and Paul Willeman, eds, *Theorising National Cinema* (London: BFI, 2006), pp. 44–58. On national television, see, for instance, John Caughie, *Television Drama: Realism, Modernism, and British Culture* (Cambridge, UK: Cambridge University Press, 2000); Jonathan Bignell and Andreas Fickers, eds, *European Television History* (Oxford, UK: Wiley-Blackwell, 2008); or

Richard Collins, *Culture, Communication & National Identity: The Case of Canadian Television* (Toronto, Canada: University of Toronto Press, 1990).

2 See, for instance, Vanessa R. Schwartz, *It's So French! Hollywood, Paris, and the Making of Cosmopolitan Film Culture* (Chicago, IL: University of Chicago Press, 2007); Stephan K. Schindler and Lutz Koepnick, eds, *The Cosmopolitan Screen* (Ann Arbor, MI: University of Michigan Press, 2007); and Felicia Chan, 'The International Film Festival and the Making of a National Cinema', *Screen*, 52:2 (2011), 253–60. A more financial viewpoint is provided by Timothy Havens, *Global Television Marketplace* (London: British Film Institute, 2006). On cosmopolitanism, see Kwame Anthony Appiah, *Cosmopolitanism* (New York: W.W. Norton, 2006) and Pippa Norris and Ronald Inglehart, *Cosmopolitan Communications: Cultural Diversity in a Globalized World* (Cambridge, UK: Cambridge University Press, 2009).

3 See Benedict Anderson's hugely influential *Imagined Communities* (London and New York: Verso, 1991) and Tom Nairn, *Faces of Nationalism: Janus Revisited* (London: Verso, 1991).

4 So, for instance, Sir Walter Scott's historical novels outlining Scottish nation identity and freedom fighting were incredibly influential throughout the nineteenth century; see Murray Pittock, *The Reception of Sir Walter Scott in Europe* (London: Bloomsbury, 2014).

5 'Introduction: Narrating the Nation' in Homi K. Bhabha, ed., *Nation and Narration* (London and New York: Routledge, 1990), pp. 1–8 (p. 1). He argues elsewhere:

> The present can no longer be simply envisaged as a break or a bonding with the past and the future, no longer a synchronic presence: our proximate self-presence, our public image, comes to be revealed for its discontinuities, its inequalities, its minorities.
>
> (*The Location of Culture*, London and New York: Routledge, 2000, p. 6)

6 Ato Quayson, *Postcolonialism: Theory, Practice, or Process?* (Oxford, UK: Wiley-Blackwell, 2000), p. 48.

7 In *Too Soon Too Late: History in Popular Culture* (Bloomington, IN: University of Indiana Press, 1998), Meaghan Morris provides a good analysis of the ways that 'history' might provide a space for controversy and dissent.

8 Dipesh Chakrabarty, *Provincializing Europe: Postcolonial Thought and History* (Princeton, NJ: Princeton University Press, 2000), p. 41. On subaltern studies, see Vinayak Chaturvedi, ed., *Mapping Subaltern Studies and the Postcolonial* (London and New York: Verso, 2000).

9 Higson, *Waving the Flag*, p. 6.

10 Quoted in Donal Ó Drisceoil, 'Framing the Irish Revolution: Ken Loach's *The Wind That Shakes the Barley*', *Radical History Review*, 104 (2009), 5–15 (p. 5). Ó Drisceoil provides a strong overview of historians' responses to Loach's film (pp. 11–12).

11 See Jacob Leigh, *The Cinema of Ken Loach* (London: Wallflower Press, 2002), pp. 91–114, and Jerome de Groot, *Consuming History* (London and New York: Routledge, 2008), pp. 214–6.

12 'The Red and the Green', *Dublin Review*, 24 (2006); available online at: http://thedublin review.com/the-red-and-the-green/ (accessed 9 June 2014).

13 A great deal of historical fiction has been interested in the diasporic movement away from Ireland to America in the past years, including Colm Tóibín, *Brooklyn* (London: Penguin, 2009); Roddy Doyle, *Oh, Play That Thing!* (London: Jonathan Cape, 2004); and Sebastian Barry, *On Canaan's Side* (London: Faber and Faber, 2011). This reflection on diasporic and indeed exilic 'national' identity is common in Irish prose; see Liam Harte, *Reading the Contemporary Irish Novel 1987–2007* (Oxford, UK: Wiley-Blackwell, 2014), and Linden Peach, *The Contemporary Irish Novel* (Basingstoke, UK: Palgrave, 2003).

14 *Irish National Cinema* (London and New York: Routledge, 2004), p. 131. She adds that, 'more recent historical films have replaced that almost hysterical sense of the burden of history with a new confidence that the events of the past may be put behind us' (p. 147).

15 See, for instance, Robert B. Pippin's reading of John Ford's 1939 film *Stagecoach* in the Introduction to *Hollywood Westerns and American Myth* (New Haven, CT, and London: Yale University Press, 2010). See also Stanley Corkin, *Cowboys as Cold Warriors: The Western and US History* (Philadelphia, PA: Temple University Press, 2004), who argues, 'the mass of Westerns produced in the period covered by this book had an impact on the terms and tenor of nationalist feeling in the United States' (p. 2). Westerns are regularly read, as are many genre films including science fiction and horror, as reflections of contemporary anxiety; see John H. Lenihan, *Showdown: Confronting Modern America in the Western Film* (Champaign, IL: University of Illinois Press, 1985).

16 André Bazin, 'The Western: American Film Par Excellence', *What is Cinema? Volume II*, trans. Hugh Gray (Berkley, CA: University of California Press, 1971), p. 143.

17 See, for instance, Pippin, *Hollywood Westerns and American Myth*; Richard Slotkin, *Gunfighter Nation: The Myth of the Frontier in Twentieth-Century America* (Norman, OK: University of Oklahoma Press, 1992); and Scott Simmon, *The Invention of the Western Film* (Cambridge, UK: Cambridge University Press, 2003), pp. 99–178.

18 J. Fred MacDonald argues, 'They flattered their audiences by honouring the idealistic and lionizing self-sacrifice in the national past', but points out that such 'nationalistic interpretation of the Western, however, was as selective as it was simple'; *Who Shot the Sheriff? The Rise and Fall of the Television Western* (New York: Praeger, 1986), pp. 110–11.

19 On the problem of revisionism in historiography, see Marnie Hughes-Warrington, *Revisionist Histories* (London and New York: Routledge, 2012), who argues that, 'the neglect of revision in historiography is a neglect of ethics' and 'Histories are what they are *in relation to* other histories' (pp. 3, 120). Furthermore, she argues, it is imperative 'to explore the *meta-ethics* of history: the ways in which historians and historiographers make conclusions about what constitutes a justified, necessary, or "good" revision in history, and, moreover, what *ought* to constitute a history' (p. 2).

20 *No Country for Old Men* (Ethan Coen, 2007).

21 See Pat Tyer and Pat Nickell, '"Of What Is Past, or Passing, or to Come": Characters as Relics in *No Country for Old Men*' in Lynnea Chapman King, Rich Wallach, and Jim Welsh, eds, *No Country for Old Men: From Novel to Film* (Plymouth, UK: Scarecrow Press, 2009), pp. 86–94.

22 See David Cunningham's comments about *Deadwood* and the 'renovelisation' inherent in such long, realist series: 'In this way it becomes possible not only to give a "snapshot" of, but to *narrate*, as Luckás puts it, a time in which "the new opposes itself hostilely to the old"'; see 'Here comes the new: *Deadwood* and the historiography of capitalism', *Radical Philosophy*, 180 (2013), 8–24 (pp. 8, 9).

23 See Matthew Bolton, 'The Ethics of Alterity: Adapting Queerness in *Brokeback Mountain*', *Adaptation*, 5:1 (2011), 35–56.

24 *Brokeback Mountain* (Ang Lee, 2005).

25 *Meek's Cutoff* (Kelly Reichardt, 2010).

26 The 'prehistory of capitalism' argument is forcibly made in Cunningham, 'Here comes the new'.

27 See Claire Monk, 'The Heritage-Film Debate Revisited', in Claire Monk and Amy Sargeant, eds, *British Historical Cinema* (New York and London: Routledge, 2002), pp. 176–98.

28 See, for instance, the discussions in Joseph Brooker, *Literature of the 1980s: After the Watershed* (Edinburgh, UK: Edinburgh University Press, 2010); Kim Duff, 'Let's Dance: *The Line of Beauty* and the Revenant Figure of Thatcher', in Louisa Hadley and Elizabeth Ho, eds, *Thatcher and After: Margaret Thatcher and Her Afterlife in Contemporary Culture* (Basingstoke, UK: Palgrave Macmillan, 2010), pp. 180–98; Kaye Mitchell, 'Alan Hollinghurst and Homosexual Identity' in Phillip Tew and Rod Mengham, eds, *British Fiction Today* (London: Continuum, 2006), pp. 40–51; Katy Shaw, *David Peace: Texts and Contexts* (Eastbourne, UK: Sussex Academic Press, 2010).

29 Montage has been associated with political film-making since the work of Sergei Eisenstein; see, for instance, Gregory T. Taylor, '"The Cognitive Instrument in the

Service of Revolutionary Change": Sergei Eisenstein, Annette Michelson, and the Avant-Garde's Scholarly Aspiration', *Cinema Journal*, 31:4 (1992), 42–59.

30 On nostalgia TV, see de Groot, *Consuming History*, pp. 164–5.

31 *TiE '88*.

32 See Mark Fisher's discussion in *Capitalist Realism* (Ropley, UK: 0 Books, 2009) about the lack of imaginative alternatives.

33 '*This Is England*', *The Guardian*, 27 April 2007; available online at: www.guardian.co.uk/film/2007/apr/27/drama2 (accessed 3 April 2012).

34 Recent popular histories of the 1980s include accounts of the Falklands War and its importance to the collective memory of the decade; see Graham Stewart, *Bang! A History of Britain in the 1980s* (London: Atlantic Books, 2013); Andrew Marr, *A History of Modern Britain* (London: Macmillan, 2007); Andy McSmith, *No Such Thing as Society* (London: Constable, 2010); and Alwyn Turner, *Rejoice! Rejoice! Britain in the 1980s* (London: Aurum Press, 2010).

35 It contrasts, however, with other films that have sought to remember Margaret Thatcher more positively, including *The Iron Lady* (Phylidda Lloyd, 2011).

36 *This Is England*. Maria Hellström Reimer compares the 'polemical use of spatial location' in the film with Paris in *La Haine* [*Hate*] (Mathieu Kassovitz, 1995) and Rio in *Cidade de Deus* [*City of God*] (Fernando Meirelles and Kátia Lund, 2002) in 'Urbanism In-Yer-Face: Spatial Polemic, Filmic Intervention and the Rhetorical Turn in Design Thinking', in Johan Verbeke and Adam Jakimowicz, eds, *Communicating (by) Design* (Brussels: Sint Lucas Hogeschool voor Wetenschap & Kunst), pp. 171–82 (p. 180).

37 *This Is England '88*, Episode 2, Channel 4, 2011.

38 See John Hughson and Emma Poulton, '"This is England": Sanitized Fandom and the National Soccer Team', *Soccer and Society*, 9:4 (2008), 509–19.

39 *This Is England '88*, Episode 2.

40 *This Is England '88*, Episode 2.

41 Cited by Matthew Francis, '"A Crusade to Enfranchise the Many": Thatcherism and the "Property-Owning Democracy"', *Twentieth Century British History*, 23:2 (2012), 275–97.

42 See Francis, '"A Crusade to Enfranchise the Many"'.

43 See Higson, *Waving the Flag*, and de Groot, *Consuming History*, pp. 211–16.

44 See de Groot, *Consuming History*, pp. 214–15.

45 See Iris Kleinecke-Bates, 'Representations of the Victorian Age: Interior Spaces and the Detail of Domestic Life in Two Adaptations of Galsworthy's *The Forsyte Saga*', *Screen*, (2006) 47 (2), 139–62.

46 See Patrick Wright, *On Living in an Old Country* (London: Verso, 1985).

47 See Helen Wheatley, 'Haunted Houses, Hidden Rooms: Women, Domesticity and the Female Gothic Adaptation on Television', in Jonathan Bignell and Stephen Lacey, eds, *Popular Television Drama* (Manchester, UK: Manchester University Press, 2005), pp. 149–65.

48 *Contemporary Costume Film: Space, Place and the Past* (London: British Film Institute, 2004), p. 12.

49 For the affinity between the three, see Samantha Lay, 'Good Intentions, High Hopes and Low Budgets: Contemporary Social Realist Film-making in Britain', *New Cinemas: Journal of Contemporary Film*, 5:3 (2007), 231–44. In terms of the problematic sanctity of the house in working-class historical drama, Leigh's *Vera Drake* (2004) is a useful intertext, as it presents the house as itself a medicalized space.

50 See Emma Hanna, *The Great War on the Small Screen* (Edinburgh, UK: Edinburgh University Press, 2009).

51 See Higson, *Waving the Flag*, and 'Re-presenting the National Past: Nostalgia and Pastiche in the Heritage Film', in Lester Friedman, ed., *Fires Were Started* (London: Wallflower, 2006).

52 This section on *Mad Men* is reprinted from '"Perpetually Dividing and Suturing the Past and Present": *Mad Men* and the illusions of history', *Rethinking History: The Journal of Theory and Practice*, 15:2 (2011), 269–87.

53 'Denial, Anger, Acceptance', *The Sopranos*, Season 1, Episode 3 (1999).

54 'Meadowlands', *The Sopranos*, Season 1, Episode 4 (1999).

55 See Chris Kocela, 'From Columbus to Gary Cooper: Mourning the Lost White Father in The Sopranos', in David Lavery, ed., *Reading the Sopranos: Hit TV From HBO* (London and New York: I.B. Taurus, 2006), pp. 107–21, and Merri Lisa Johnson, 'Gangster Feminism: The Feminist Cultural Work of HBO's *The Sopranos*', *Feminist Studies*, 33:2 (2007), 269–96.

56 Jay Parini, 'The Cultural Work of *The Sopranos*' in Regina Barecca, ed., *A Sit Down With the Sopranos* (New York: Macmillan, 2002), 57–87.

57 *American Tabloid* (London and New York: Knopf, 1995), p. 5.

58 Timotheus Vermeulen and Gry C. Rustad, 'Watching Television With Jacques Rancière: US "Quality Television", *Mad Men* and the "late cut"', *Screen*, 54:3 (2013), 341–54.

59 Sam Wollaston, 'The Weekend's TV: Mad Men', *The Guardian*, 3 March 2008; available online at: www.guardian.co.uk/culture/tvandradioblog/2008/mar/03/theweekendstv madmen (accessed 16 September 2014).

60 See Jeremy G. Butler, '"Smoke Gets in Your Eyes": Historicizing Visual Style in *Mad Men*' in Gary R. Edgerton, ed., *Mad Men* (London and New York: I.B. Tauris, 2011), pp. 55–71.

61 Gary R. Edgerton, 'Introduction: When Our Parents Became Us' in Edgerton, *Mad Men*, pp. xxi–xxxvi (p. xxvii).

62 Rick Fulton, 'Designers Won't Give Me Dresses for Award Shows', *Daily Record*, 27 August 2010; available online at: www.dailyrecord.co.uk/entertainment/celebrity/christina-hendricks-designers-wont-give-1068344 (accessed 16 September 2014).

63 'The Wheel', *Mad Men*, Series 1, episode 13 (2007).

64 'Smoke Gets in Your Eyes', *Mad Men*, Series 1, episode 1 (2007).

65 Joseph Conrad, *Heart of Darkness* (1899), Project Gutenberg E-Book; available online at: www.gutenberg.org/ebooks/526 (accessed 15 April 2015).

66 'Postmodernism and Consumer Society', in J. Belton, ed., *Movies and Mass Culture* (London: Athlone Press, 1996), pp. 185–202 (p. 194).

67 *The Return of Martin Guerre* (Cambridge, MA: Harvard University Press, 1983), p. 5.

68 *The Writing of History*, trans. Tom Conley (New York: Columbia University Press, 1988), p. 3.

PART II

Haunting, ghostliness, and the undead

3
THE MATERIALITY OF
THE PAST

Having discussed ethics, nationalism, paratexts, and self-consciousness in historical fictions, the book now moves on to look at materiality. The following two broadly linked chapters look first at the material object in historical work, and then at the problematic return of the historicized body to the contemporary moment. These two different types of historio-physicality allow for a consideration of the being of the past in the present, and theorizing of the *material* itself. These objects and bodies – distinct and ethereal, absent and present – stand as motifs for the historical experience in fiction of the past. Through them, texts meditate upon memory, haunting, death, and the representation of the past in the present. The body, the thing, is conceptualized as a ghost, a haunting, a revenant, something that transmits the indeterminability of memory and the inability to represent the past fully. The objects and bodies artfully draw attention to the ethical and ontological gap between then and now, and the desire for a wholeness of expression (a firm historiography of actuality) that is impossible. The past cannot be understood or explained; it is other, and any attempts to broker a relationship between then and now should be attempted with some trepidation and read with much suspicion. The object or the body seems to provide a way of moving between the past and the present – it is imagined as having such a quality and represented as being such a palimpsest – but it merely serves to demonstrate the unknowability of the past and its strange presence in the present.

Consequently, these objects and bodies are key to an understanding of the complex aesthetics and historiography of historical fictions. In this present chapter, iterations of two types of object – the cigarette and the ring – are analysed. Both are simultaneously things and motifs, representations and caricatures as well as actual objects that mean diegetically in the fictional world of the past. The chapter uses these somehow indistinct physical objects to pursue Marx's comment in the opening of *Capital* that, 'To discover the various uses of things is the work of history'.[1] Here, the thing is the fulcrum of a kind of historicity and a way of brokering an understanding between the material and the 'imagined' discourse that is a narrative of then to now. Use values are also 'the material depositories of exchange value', that which is outside intrinsic value.[2] The exchange value of an object in the imaginary economy of fiction depends on its use value to an extent, but also on how it might be desired and, therefore, valued as an indicator of historicity. To a certain extent, the chapter takes on Bill Brown's suggestion that, 'They are texts that describe and enact an imaginative possession of things that amounts to the labor of infusing manufactured objects with metaphysical dimension'.[3] Brown continues, discussing Marx's account of how a table supersedes commodification to become an object:

> This is a social relation neither between men nor between things, but something like a social relation between human subject and inanimate object, wherein modernity's ontological distinction between human beings and nonhumans makes no sense. This relation, hardly describable in the context of use or exchange, can be overwhelmingly aesthetic, deeply affective – it involves desire, pleasure, frustration, a kind of pain.
>
> (pp. 29–30)

The object in historical fictions allows for this movement, this time-slip (with ethical implications). The relationships between humans and the non-human objects that are the subject of this and the next chapter sit in the nexus situated by Brown between desire, sensation, pleasure, and frustration. In particular, the chapter is alert to the doubleness of objects in historical fictional renderings and the way that they are made to work in a variety of ways and are freighted with multiple meanings. However, this is always something distinct and politically strange, the thingness of these objects having iteration and purpose in the historiographical universe of the fictions. These fictions consider the materiality of the artefact encountered physically in the 'now' that allows the imaginative journey to the past. The fictionalized object and its manifestation render a relationship to the past and illustrate the problems inherent in commodification and fictionalizing about that unclaimable past. Hence, it dislocates contemporary identity predicated upon *knowing* pastness as other. Consequently, the object allows for the comprehension (and, possibly, ownership) of the past, the jag of misrecognition (what is *that?*), the underlining of contemporariness, the queering of contemporary experience, and the undermining of the self-confidence of modernity. It demonstrates the link to then and the sense of the mediating physical movement within the then/now binary. Through this, it highlights the syncopation of time (that was then, this is now).

The chapter begins by considering the act of smoking, the cigarette, and the importance of smoke in recent historical film and television, to point out the various ways they might mean, or suggest meaning. The chapter is interested in how smoking is an index of pastness. Further, it considers how the cigarette might mean and reflect upon the inability of fiction to communicate anything other than a dream of the past. The (literal) fetishization of smoking in historical television and film allows us to reflect upon the wroughtness, and, hence, the fictiveness, of historical representation (and echoes Marx's comments about the 'mystical character' of fetishized commodities). Cigarettes are used in these fictions to construct an affective bridge between then and now, but also to enable the viewer to gain consciousness of this dynamic. Hence, they are expressive of connection while keeping the viewer at arm's length, and they articulate the fundamental real/unreal paradigm of historical fiction. This very articulation, embodied in an object, is illustrative of a type of historiographical flexibility (a movement between the material and the conceptual). A further section discusses the same issues, but focuses on lack, ghostliness, and rings in Sarah Waters' fiction. The ring is a thing and an absence, an articulation of emptiness, and a physical boundary. It reflects wider ideas in Waters's writing relating to the indeterminacy of knowledge in relation to the past. As the discussions in Chapter 1 showed, detail regarding the physical is paramount in historical fiction and shows an audience historical difference through aestheticizing this disjuncture. Other substances and things might have been considered as indicators of difference. It would be possible, for instance, to discuss alcohol as a connecting and challenging substance, with respect to the same fictions, but, at present, the cigarette has a visual richness in its deployment that allows film and television to reflect upon the construction of their own imaginary and aesthetic. A final shift in the chapter is to consider these material traces in relation to the themes of Jacques Derrida's writing, particularly relating to ethics, Marx, and memory in his later work. The chapter therefore contributes to the book's wider discussions of materiality, memory, sensation, desire, and phantasmagoria in the representation of the past.

Smoking, pastness, and memory in historical film and television

This section and the following two consider smoking, and cigarettes, in historical fictions. This section is interested in the following ideas: how smoking is an index of pastness; how its representation reflects upon the inability of fiction to communicate anything other than a dream of the past; and how it allows us to reflect upon the wroughtness, and, hence, the fictiveness, of historical representation. The argument begins by considering briefly the act of smoking, the cigarette, and the importance of smoke in recent historical film and television, to point out the various ways it might mean, or suggest meaning. It then moves on to thinking more widely about the significance of the cigarette, using some of Marx's ideas, before finishing with a discussion of the series *Mad Men*. The sections, therefore, gesture more widely to the ways in which history works in the public imagination, or at least how it is represented and resourced. They shift terminology – speaking of tobacco, smoke, smoking, and cigarettes as often the same thing but equally individual signifiers – in order to highlight the interchangeability of the conceptually and physically material in historical fictions.[4]

The work here on this topic is in something of a vacuum, in terms of historical studies. There is, however, some work on the ways in which smoking works in culture. Richard Klein's book *Cigarettes Are Sublime* is the most complex, arguing for the multitudinous signification of the cigarette itself in a number of fictional locales, from *Carmen* to Proust. There are many cultural histories of tobacco, smoking, advertising, and popular usage of cigarettes (not to mention accounts of its risks, legal status, and public health consequences).[5] However, as indicated, this discussion instead outlines what smoking means in terms of the now/'then' relationship or binary, how it makes now now and then then. It is interested in how smoking contributes to, and participates in, the rendering of pastness in establishing that binary while undermining it, and in the conceptual creation of an imagined 'history', as opposed to a shiny, modern, healthy, 'now'.

Klein argues that the cigarette is a multilayered and contradictory object: 'a darkly beautiful, inevitably painful pleasure that arises from some intimation of eternity; the taste of infinity in a cigarette resides precisely in the "bad" taste the smoker quickly learns to love'.[6] For Klein, the experience of smoking is affective, complex, strange. Navigating the meaning of smoking in historical fictions can inform, obviously, about contemporary worries and concerns; it can also demonstrate, in a feedback loop, the issues and anxieties that society freights the past with, projects on to 'history' in order to comprehend, control, or other it from contemporary experience. The body is commonly defined as a 'social and discursive object [. . .] bound up in the order of desire, signification, and power' by most cultural theorists after Foucault.[7] The relationship of cigarettes to this socially constructed body involves a multiplicity of discourses: shame, desire, physiology, fear, denial, disavowal, surveillance, ejection, marginalization, eroticism.[8] These concepts sit in the imaginary and cultural field around the body and its relationship to the cigarette.[9] It is inconceivable, then, given this complexity, that the representation of smoking in historical fictions would be merely commonplace. Smoking in historical drama and television resonates because it is something that is contemporarily banned (inside, in most public places in the West), considered a forbidden pleasure or a hidden killer, at the very least fetishized in various ways.

The use of this seemingly simple, contemporaneously prevalent activity signifies multiply throughout culture. So, for instance, *The Shadow Line* (BBC2, 2011) is a contemporarily set, *noir*-ish thriller in which smoking is fetishized. The chief policeman, Patterson (Mark Strong), smokes, but does so in such a studied fashion – even pointing out that he is not allowed to smoke at several points – that the series is clearly making reference to a practice that has somehow been lost, or that is out of time. Previous procedural police shows such as *Prime Suspect* (ITV, 1991–2006) or *Cracker* (ITV, 1993–2006) showed the smoking policeman as out of time, with Helen Mirren's Jane Tennison constantly trying to quit and Robbie Coltrane's Fitz falling foul of bans. Indeed, one of the strange qualities of these relatively recent shows is the prevalence of smoking, together with the ways in which it informs and constructs character. *Sherlock* (BBC 2010–), which plays games with its audience about updating a Victorian hero for a contemporarily set thriller, has the protagonist turn to patches in a bid to break his nasty habit (his cocaine usage is ignored). Sherlock Holmes writes a monograph on the types of tobacco ash (referred to in *The Sign of the Four* (1890)) and ash, cigarette stubs, and cigars in general are often key in his investigations.[10] The textual fetishization of the cigarette is not new, obviously, and yet Holmes's interest in this minor but multipicitous thing demonstrates how objects and things can be clues and carry significance narratively and diegetically. These seemingly minor touches serve merely to demonstrate the peculiarity of cigarettes in contemporary drama and therefore nuance understanding of their use in historical fictions.

Smoking as a narrative indicator of pastness, and a locale of the historical imaginary, can be seen in the conclusion of *This Is England '88*, discussed at the end of Chapter 2. The character of Lol has throughout been a *particular* smoker. Her smoking has been fetishized, particularized, made peculiar, particularly as something that isolates her. Lol returns to hospital, this time as a patient after a failed suicide attempt. Woody, now estranged from her, rushes to the hospital and finds her family and friends sitting in her room around a made bed; he naturally assumes she has died and begins to grieve. It turns out, however, that she has only 'popped downstairs for a smoke', visiting the hospital's smoking room. Smoking is othered here, not allowed in the hygienic space of the hospital room, but something placed outside the mainstream. Yet this is still not 'contemporary', as smoking inside public buildings is still allowed, and so the sequence at once reflects upon the strangeness of smoking while making it historically particular. Smoking makes Lol part of the past. The 'smoking room' is a consciously obvious narrative device, used here to isolate Woody and Lol (and to have him emotionally engaged). It fetishizes her smoking (and her cigarette's smoke still curls around them both as they reconcile), but also points out that it is something not 'right', ejected while being normalized, particularly *located*. Smoking again stands for the difference of pastness, as something that physically intimates the embodied otherness of the experience of those on-screen. Yet the evident 'use' of the smoking room to develop the narrative means that this reflection upon cigarettes as props of the past is also part of the text's self-conscious wroughtness, its pointing towards its own narrative.

The way that the cigarette and smoking are used in historical fictions illustrates Klein's thesis about the attenuated strangeness and importance of the cigarette in culture, its continuous utility as a sign of multiple meaning. It is also clear that the way in which smoking is used and fetishized in 'contemporary' film is different to its iteration in 'historical' texts. The deployment of smoking as a motif means a great deal for the development of the historical imaginary. It is an iteration of authenticity, but there is also something more complex at work. The motif of the cigarette enables an insight into the ways in which fictional historical texts conceptualize and make explicit historicity and allows a meditation upon the ways in which fictional historical texts work in a more conceptual and challenging way than by simply looking at theme, content, and narrative. Such an analysis might be able to say something about the relationship between the props of realism and the imaginative and textual implications they sustain. The cigarette, after all, is a prop that contributes to the reality of the diegesis, the authenticity of the *mis en scène*, and, hence, is part of the performance of the 'costume' drama. It therefore has a double effect, an ethical dimension, and a ghostly materiality all at the same time. It equally contributes to the realist aesthetic while undermining the wholeness of that discourse.

Several examples demonstrate the strange ways cigarettes are used in contemporary historical film. *Tinker, Tailor, Soldier, Spy* (Tomas Alfredson, 2011) is a film that is seemingly infused with smoking and the motifs of smoke and memory. Based on John le Carré's seminal novel, the film recounts George Smiley's search for a mole at the heart of British intelligence in the early 1970s. The film's *mis en scène* is textured throughout with smoke. Smoke suffuses the screen, and the film quality looks as though it has been treated to suggest a quality of unfocused reminiscence at times. In particular, smoke wreathes flashbacks, such as a key party scene, but is equally day-to-day, creating domestic fug in the various offices. This is a quality of the celebrated 1979 TV series, too (Alec Guinness smokes throughout). In the film, the almost obsessive use of cigarette smoke to create a fug contributes to the text's concern with the complex workings of memory, dream, and truth. Smoke is the metaphor for confusion, particularly in the case of Smiley's boss, Control, and stands in for the workings of the mind, obscure and distant. The narrative of the story itself has a cigarette lighter as its fulcrum, something freighted with much meaning in the text. It is both a metaphor for everything and a throwaway object, attaining the metonymic indistinctness and doubleness of the cigarette itself. Smiley recalls an encounter with the Russian spymaster, Karla, and in his story points out the centrality of smoking to the meeting, arguing that Karla's rejection of his cigarettes represented a denial of Western ideology itself.[11] Cigarettes and smoke, then, are both representative of historical difference, part of the texture of the film, and central to the plot and content of the text itself.

In Martin Scorsese's *Shutter Island* (2010), smoking becomes more interrogative of meaning and, particularly, communicates the way that fictionalizing can be used to create a phantasmagoric unreality that smothers an uncomfortable truth. The film is about paranoid delusions. In 1954, a US Marshal, Teddy Daniels (Leonardo DiCaprio), becomes increasingly paranoid and isolated while visiting a psychiatric facility to track down a vanished patient. He begins to see conspiracy and mind-control being used by a shady, and possibly formerly Nazi, doctor. At one point, while talking to a seemingly like-minded escapee, he is warned, 'You tell me at least you've been smoking your own cigarettes!' – the implication being that the patients are controlled by food, water, and inhalation. Cigarettes are carriers, here, of pharmaceutical control and become central to keeping hold of one's identity. The whole film evaporates at the conclusion, as Ben Kingsley's psychiatrist turns to DiCaprio – while lighting his pipe – and says 'What partner?', revealing the fiction created as a part of a cure for the actual patient, Daniels himself. The entire story has been a fantasy, a storyline created by the insane Daniels and supported by the clinical staff in order to bring him to realization of the unreality of the world he inhabits. The film, hence, points out its own wroughtness and suggests that the audience is somehow complicit in Daniels's fantasy. The woodenness and obvious studio-bound quality of the shots, and the film's overly cliché-ridden storyline itself, then, are used to highlight the ways in which an unbalanced mind can seek to construct a narrative and to implement 'realist' tropes to support it. Furthermore, this is part of therapy and treatment.

Flashback is used in *Shutter Island* in a very sophisticated way, both suggesting the horrors that have unhinged Daniels but also providing (for an audience) narrative meaning, which, ultimately, is illusory. Historical film here reflects upon the ways in which role play might be used to deal with the effects of trauma – in this case, the violent horror of the Holocaust, seen in flashback, which provokes the horrific act that Daniels is ultimately incarcerated for. The ways in which filmic techniques are used to construct a kind of visual memory, which is unreliable, reflect upon how all memory is ultimately constructed out of thin air, a fine vapour conjured to explain the absent and unknown past. Smoke, here, is obfuscatory and pharmaceutically problematic. Ultimately, the seeming materiality of cigarette smoke is set against the insubstantiality of memory; the meaning of the text is quite literally effaced, and effected, through smoke and mirrors.

Of course, sometimes a cigarette is just a cigarette, and film-makers have also shown a keen interest in the thing itself. During *Hunger* (Steve McQueen, 2009), Michael Fassbender's Bobby Sands smokes constantly, making roll-ups from the same paper he writes his letters on (Figure 3.1). Smoke is the only thing that Sands imbibes through the film. *Hunger* is an intensely affective film (discussed further in Chapter 6), creating a bodily link with the audience by presenting the abjected body in all its constituent parts. Smoke, though, is somehow both physical and ephemeral, as it is also internal and external. In the context of a film about the denial of bodily appetite, the deployment of smoke and cigarettes as something signifying the inhalation but not digestion of something insubstantial but significant clearly points to the importance of smoking as a complex motif. In comparison, Fassbender's character in McQueen's second film, the contemporarily set *Shame* (2012), smokes at points to connote his lack of control, his descent into personal fragmentation and dejection. It is an act that makes him part of a marginal society, a clear choice to become other. This is literalized when he identifies an after-hours gay sex club by chance, through observing someone smoking outside it; in his desperation, he enters. In modernity, then, smoking is associated with otherness, ejection, and marginalization (literally, as the smoking gay man is divorced from his context and his own community through his habit).

Examples abound in historical film of the particularity of the cigarette in social situations, to signify 'pastness', and as a point of division between now and then. Although, in general, it avoids cigarettes, there is a minor set of communications undertaken in *A Single Man* (Tom Ford, 2010) around lighting a stranger's cigarette (Figure 3.2). Smoking, therefore, attains a great symbolic significance in this film, which seeks throughout to not say various things about hidden sexuality. It enacts the central character's inability to express his desire and loneliness throughout. Smoking is metonymic for a closeted way of life that seems explicitly past, a

FIGURE 3.1 Smoking in *Hunger*

Source: Film4, Blast! Films/The Kobal Collection

marginalized identity that is contemporaneously celebrated. Similarly, *The King's Speech* (Tom Hooper, 2010) does not focus on cigarettes, but they are part of the way in which the film signifies pastness. It is a film in which clarity is central. The overriding motifs of performance and the film's diegetic concern with the construction of a fiction of coherence means that it does not need such overt signals to make its points. The key scene, however, is one in which the King is encouraged to smoke *more* in order to solve his problematic stammer. This foolish, 'historical' medical advice is played for laughs and demonstrates a diegetically 'accurate' state of physiological knowledge that is challenged by his more modern (although, in the world of the film, maverick and odd) speech therapist. Jokes about smoking such as this – echoed in *Mad Men*'s 1950s advertising campaigns emphasizing the health-giving qualities of cigarettes – work to demonstrate the gulf between then and now, a self-righteous, modern sense of health and epidemiology explicitly contrasted with that of the past. They also demonstrate clearly how smoking has been medicalized in the past decades, and how this medicalization affects the way that contemporary audiences view smoking (and think of the cigarettes of the past). Anyone who smokes thoughtlessly (or *unknowingly*), it goes, is foolish, beneath contempt (but somehow innocent, and that innocence is somehow attractive, or the state before knowledge is). The audience is not able to not have an imaginary connection here, nor is presumed to do so.

It is not just historical film. Smoking in anglophone, early-twenty-first-century television culture has become a de facto index of recent pastness. This is particularly pointed after public smoking bans in the UK (2007), Ireland (2004), Australia (state bans enacted 2006–10), and the USA (currently twenty-eight state-wide bans). Smoking in historical television, from *Life on Mars* (BBC1, 2006–7; the sequel, of course, being *Ashes to Ashes*, BBC1, 2008–9) to *The Hour* (BBC2, 2011) to *Eric and Ernie* (BBC2 film, Jonny Campbell, 2011), is deployed very specifically as an aesthetic adjunct and contextual indicator. In the opening sequence of the TV film *Red Riding Trilogy: 1983* (Anand Tucker, 2009; discussed at length in Chapter 6), corrupt policemen gather around to discuss their plot. The men are smoking cigars, and the smoke obfuscates and wreathes their conspiracy. In *Downton Abbey* (ITV, 2010–), only the evil servants smoke cigarettes, their conspiratorial breaks signalling their villainy and excluding them from the harmonious class community of the rest of the house (the members of which, if they smoke at all, smoke cigars). The representation of class, race, and gender suggested in this last example via the use of the cigarette is another key element of its use in historical fictions.[12] It allows a shift through layers of discourse, a very precise and attenuated key to the complexity of past social relations.[13]

Smoking as a sign of historical – bodily – difference is also heavily fetishized in the American series *Mad Men* (HBO, 2007–) and *Boardwalk Empire* (HBO, 2010–15). The logo of *Mad Men* features a cigarette – and no other object. Nucky Thompson, the corrupt politician in *Boardwalk Empire*, smokes throughout the opening sequence of the show. His smoking is affected, particular, precise; the camera lingers on his cigarette and the smoke that he exhales. Smoking in *Boardwalk Empire* is used formally, as striking matches are used as part of an edit. It is also used in terms of content, given that the series is about prohibition (that is, the limiting of appetites, the legal interference with ingesting poisonous substances). 'They might as well outlaw cigarettes', mocks a corrupt politician, early on in the series, pointing out that people will find liquor easily enough.[14] The character of Richard Harrow (Jack Huston) has been so horribly injured during the war that smoking is 'impossible' – a manifestation of the oddness that marginalizes him from

FIGURE 3.2 *A Single Man* (Tom Ford, 2010)

mainstream society. In contrast to these examples, cigarettes were not used in the series about flying in the 1950s, *Pan Am* (ABC, 2011), as the parent company, ABC–Disney, actively discouraged them, despite their diegetic authenticity.[15]

Smoking is made so strange in *Boardwalk Empire* and *Mad Men* that a case might be made that cigarettes' treatment in each text is unique, and should be considered independently. What they mean, and how they mean, are clearly particular. Yet there are also moments of contact, seemingly unconscious, that suggest something more complex. Thompson and Draper both use cigarettes as props. In both series, there are incidents when smoking and sexual health are linked. In the first episode of *Mad Men*, Peggy visits a gynaecologist, who smokes before he examines her; in Episode 3 of *Boardwalk Empire*, Lucky Luciano is treated for gonorrhoea by a smoking doctor. Both scenes are strikingly similar and work by contrasting the intimacy and professionalization of the medical relationship. They also highlight the medicalization of contemporary smoking, by contrasting the unhygienic practices of the past with those of the present. Smoke is unclean and something that should not have a place in an examination room. The past is, hence, dirtier – quite literally – as a consequence of its pastness and its attitudes to smoking. In all other ways, the *Mad Men* scene looks like a standard medical encounter; the key contrast – what makes it *historical* – is the cigarette.

It might be argued that all the instances cited are individual, and the use of cigarettes and smoking is peculiar to each text in which they occur – which is clearly the case – but in itself that peculiarity seems interesting. In the examples given, the common denominator is the use of smoking to make strange, and comment on, historical difference, which is inherently interesting in terms of what it says about the ways in which fictions of the past are made and, hence, how the historical imaginary is resourced. It is instructive too that smoking means so many different things and is deployed so often to such odd, unsettling effect. Smoking is something that reveals different habitual behaviour and bodily pastness (as a prop pointing out historical difference, as something taken into the body). Smoke wreathes the figures in these images, either as smog in offices or individually produced exhalation, and gives an impression of age, unmoving (or unmoved) time, of a certain vagueness of light that might trope nostalgia. It is a point of pressure demonstrating the difference between then and now, but, simultaneously, allowing a relationship and a similarity between the two. Smoke textures these films with something seen and not seen. The indistinct physical presence of the smoke itself is both there and not there, a non-effect with very real iteration. In these films and series, it is diegetically realistic to have cigar or cigarette smoke, but it renders the texture of the film insubstantial and ghostly. This duality – both 'authentic' and having the effect of rendering something seemingly unreal (and formally gesturing towards this, drawing the attention to the real/unreal nature of the realist film text) – allows smoke to be something that inhabits the same doubled representational space as the historical drama itself. The thing/non-thingness of smoke, the organized structure that disappears into bare ash, stands here for the insubstantial ghostliness of historical fiction, real and not real.

Smoke is a revenant of pastness that is barely touchable but that has material effect. It is something unclaimable, a remnant of a physical iteration that is now drifting beyond our grasp and ability to know. It could be considered a motif for the comprehension of the past, or the unravelling of the factuality of the present into the chaos of the future (and, hence, becoming past) – something seemingly solid melting away, drifting out of knowledge and taxonomy. Smoking is practically past, a technology of history; smoke is the signifier or echo of this process (that which marks its occurrence, briefly, before disappearing). Smoke is the diffused impression of something that was once physically organized (a cigarette, a cigar) and packed. Hence, smoke is the historical referent of the cigarette, something that renders in ghostly fashion that which was, before diffusing and disappearing. Smoking allows for the underlining of historical difference, although with the ambiguity of a Derridean *différance* in which its distance from now is bound up with its nearness; smoking is something that is simultaneously past and contemporary, an activity that is at once part of modernity and, at the same time, pushed back into the past.

Pursuing smoke

Tobacco is itself the material legacy of colony, a product desired and fetishized, with an entire modern global industry constructed around it. It has no purpose and no value other then pleasurable; it is highly addictive and party to government legislation, taxation, and surveillance.[16] The packing of tobacco demonstrates capitalism's urge towards the singular, whereas the disapparation of the commodity through its 'use' both undermines this and underlines it. Tobacco might be the most obvious iteration of Marx's articulations of commodity and value: something in which the labour, natural artefact, and use value (from picking tobacco to hand-rolling cigars) are literally destroyed by the consumer, devoured (or rather ingested) and then breathed back out again, ejected. Value accrues from a desire that is based on nothing more than physical craving; it is a constructed, imposed industry that creates nothing real. With cigarettes, there is little actual 'use value' and only 'exchange value'. Cigarettes, then, are elegant metaphors for this aspect of commodity, and their eventual immolation figures the violent processes of industrial capitalism clearly. The way that they are conceptualized and represented, then, relies on this particular oddness and doubleness of identity, which this following section will attempt to elucidate. The material quality of the cigarette in historical renderings depends on its imaginative heft, and this itself is something quite complex.[17] The commodity of tobacco gains only exchange value, and yet this ghostly value is 'absent' and immolated, shown to be purposeless.[18] Smoke figures the uncanny (dis)appearance of exchange value in the commodity. It demonstrates how, in use and exchange value, definitions of a thing or object or commodity always must include the trace of the other. Historical fictions are similarly purposeless retoolings of something 'real' that disappears into the air, something concretized in execution that interferes with the imagination.

The Moon Tiger releases smoke too.
* What about e-cigarettes? Juuls?
Will they come to signify the 2010s?

Given Marx's interest in the spectral quality of money and the ways in which commodity objects can be both distinct and indistinct, material and conceptual, smoke seems a compelling motif.[19] Botting argues that, 'Tobacco articulates monetary and symbolic economies, a differential site at which restricted ciruculation is opened to a more general movement'.[20] Smoke gets in the eyes and suggests phantasms, in the same way that money has a ghostly, unreal–real value that augments itself. Money's spectrality is such that it persuades, creates a dream of itself. In the cigarette might be seen the materialization of exchange value, something constructed purely to create and service an unreal demand. Marx was himself a huge smoker, regularly attempting to find ways of spending less on his ruinously expensive cigar habit.[21] He lived wreathed in the smoke of cheap cigars and pipes.[22] In his writings, though, Marx classed tobacco as a narcotic (similar to coffee), and it was, hence, extremely problematic, being both a commodity and an instrument of control. That said, he considered it a necessity rather than a luxury in *Capital*. Marx uses tobacco when making a key distinction between productive and unproductive labour – 'The producer of tobacco is productive, although the consumption of tobacco is unproductive'.[23] This capital–production disjunct between commodity and user signals the disruption of natural relationships and the creation of singularly economic connections.

Marx reflects upon the various ways that smoke might affect the imagination and stain the memory in an 1856 letter to his wife Jenny, from Manchester:

> I am writing to you again because I am alone and because it is irksome to converse with you all the time in my head without you knowing or hearing or being able to answer me. Bad as your portrait is, it serves its end well enough, and I now understand how it is that even the least flattering portraits of the mother of God, the 'Black Madonnas' could have their inveterate admirers – more admirers, indeed, than the good portraits. At any rate, none of these 'Black Madonna' portraits has ever been so much kissed and ogled and adored as your photograph which, while admittedly not black, has a crabbed expression and in no way reflects your dear, lovely, kissable, dolce countenance. But I put right what the sun's rays have wrongly depicted, discovering that my eyes, spoiled though they are by lamplight and tobacco smoke, can nevertheless paint not only in the dreaming but also in the waking state. There you are before me, large as life, and I lift you up in my arms and I kiss you all over from top to toe, and I fall on my knees before you and cry: 'Madame, I love you', and love you I do, with a love greater than was ever felt by the Moor of Venice. Falsely and foully doth the false and foul world all characters construe. Who of my many calumniators and venomous-tongued enemies has ever reproached me with being called upon to play the romantic lead in a second-rate theatre? And yet it is true. Had the scoundrels possessed the wit, they would have depicted 'the productive and social relations' on one side and, on the other, myself at your feet. Beneath

it they would have written: Look to this picture and to that. But stupid the scoundrels are and stupid they will remain, in seculum seculorum.

Temporary absence is good, for in a person's presence things look too much alike for them to be distinguished. At close quarters even towers appear dwarfed, whereas what is petty and commonplace, seen close at hand, assumes undue proportions. So, too, with the passions. Little habits which, by their very proximity, obtrude upon one, and thus assume the form of passions, vanish as soon as their immediate object is out of sight.[24]

Marx opens a textual dialogue with Jenny because conversing with her imaginatively is not real enough; he seeks a physical connection through writing. Two types of smoke griming occur here – that which turns literal icons black, and that which occludes reality but allows idealization and imagination. The revelation that Marx can recreate the very picture of his wife, despite his eyes being actively blinded by a combination of low light and tobacco smoke, leads him to reflect upon his own performance of theoretical gravitas. He is a player who dissembles; if only his enemies could discern how to create a moral emblem to demonstrate that Marx is committed to only one thing – his wife. She invites him to transgress, and he willingly lies at her feet. She is his religion, his opiate, dulling his senses.

Marx's 'Black Madonnas' similarly are icons covered in soot, women who lose their particular holiness by the action of smoke upon them. They are strangely attractive to followers, more so than the 'normal' icons, their uncanny hybridity mimicking the 'real'. They seem wrong, seen through smoke, but are still attractive. Marx then recounts a photograph that he has 'kissed and ogled and adored', comparing his wife to the Black Madonnas – or, rather, suggesting that the image he has of her is and isn't her: she is veiled in a similar fashion, but this time the dissimilarity (which he has managed to get past in his kissing and ogling) is signalled by an image, a rendering of Jenny Marx in time to which he returns again and again, despite the fact that it actually does not look like her. This image, then, is not sufficient – it is made into an icon (even a fetish) and worshipped, but avowedly is not actually a very good likeness (as the sun makes her squint). He cannot even see the photograph properly, as his eyes are either weakened by, or she is obscured by, 'lamplight and tobacco smoke'; however, this allows him to correct the erroneous image and dream her up in reality (both waking and dreaming, in front of him). In his mind's eye, she appears and allows him to admit his love (although only judged in comparison with a figure from Shakespeare). His eyes 'paint' his lover in front of him. He rejects the 'real' image from the past (from a particular *moment*, when the sun made her squint).

Marx's photograph of Jenny is problematic because it does not look like her, or rather, because the vagaries of the weather have made her react in a particular way. Instead of trusting the image, Marx conjures an icon. The reference to *Othello* is extremely problematic (surely suggesting a skin-colour contrast between the Moor and his Desdemona).[25] This being Marx, who loved Shakespeare, there must be an echo here of the playwright's most famous line about worth – while he may well be alluding to the line 'loved not wisely, but too well', as a reader of the play he would surely know that, two lines later, Othello describes himself as 'one whose hand,/Like the base Indian, threw a pearl away/Richer than all his tribe' (*Othello*, V, ii, 346–8).[26] The imagined sequence also recalls the conclusion of *The Winter's Tale*, when Hermione appears as a statue that then walks and embraces Leontes, her jealous husband. Shakespeare's text is a supreme moment of magicking, and its echo, together with the comparison with Othello's jealous love, suggests Marx's guilt at the spousal demagoguery that he is suggesting here. He then moves to meditate upon the way in which memory works to create a sense (literally) of perspective, a visual means of differentiating between what is important and what is merely irritating. In concluding here, Marx reflects that absence allows one to understand a thing more, to distinguish what is real about it. Smoke-weakened eyes allow the correction of the image of the loved one as they appeared, seemingly erroneously, in the past. He eschews the actual image for an idealized version (which he makes into an icon and falls at its feet).

Marx moves on from the image of Jenny because, despite the almost pornographic, at least physical, succour it offers him, it is not enough either to satisfy him or to persuade him that this photograph is actually 'real'; Jenny is much more 'lovely, kissable, dolce'. Rather than the real woman, he wants something created within his imagination. The frozen moment is incorrect. He turns from the icon, made strange (and black) by a trick of sunlight, to an imagined, constructed idol. He creates for himself an ideal, a spectre of his wife in place of the 'real'. What he prefers is a ghost, constructed from his imagination and rendered by eyes made weak by light and smoke. Yet it is a ghost that he colludes with, that he knows is not 'real', is a fiction created from the raw materials of his imagination, something given value by his desire and his self-acknowledged fetishization. Marx ignores the image, as it is 'wrong', somehow. Although it is real, it does not square with his memory; he invents and supplants the 'real' for something created, iconized, better.

Smoke, and the cigarette that creates it, then, is an index of past otherness, as well as something happily recognized and invoked; audiences want smoke to get into their eyes, in order that they might see more clearly, or, as Marx does, so that they can fantasize something more real. Smoke is both real and imaginary, something that inhabits the hinterland between both then and now, here and absent. In considering the past, it is human to turn from the reality and its reminders of our mortality to easy fictions, wraiths constructed despite the smoke stains on our eyes. Marx creates a dream and rejects the real; this is what audiences do in looking at, and making, historical drama and film; but, similarly, through their concern with smoke, these texts will not allow such an easy, comfortable move, recalling instead historical difference diegetically and formally. Smoke, as in Marx's letter, is mediator of, and reminder of, the unreality of these created things. What the letter allows us to reflect upon is the phantasmagoric quality of memory, the ways in which something material and worldly (tobacco) might destroy the physical (the eyes), leaving the viewer with only imagination to create something sur-real, better than reality (or at least more 'real' than the photographic echoes of the world that are to hand). What they substitute are uncanny presences, things that appear authentic (or more so than the image), but that are insubstantial, conjured by the imagination to console in moments of loneliness. The invocation and use of smoke in contemporary historical drama, then, reflect the tension between then and now. It articulates the physical difference between past and ghost of past and comments upon the insubstantiality of the past in the present, as the following section will elucidate.

Smoking in *Mad Men*

The American series *Mad Men* (2007–) fetishizes period smoking while simultaneously deconstructing our fascination with cigarettes as indices of pastness. *Mad Men* is notoriously full of smoking, to the point that it has been criticized by public health figures.[27] The show's signature trick is to create nostalgia for an imagined, idealized past.[28] *Mad Men* suggests that its audience has a deep desire for something, while at the same time demonstrating to the audience how that need is constructed, serviced, and manipulated, most obviously through the creation of historical TV. The cynicism of the series is in its presentation to its viewers of the ways in which desire, need, enjoyment, and pleasure are all things that are used by the industry to sell the commodity that is the past.[29] This is most obviously enacted during a pitch to Kodak in which Draper successfully articulates a theory of nostalgia-selling, using photographs of his own family's memories to demonstrate how they can be commodified.[30] Draper's genius as an advertising creative is to see that all products can be made into something desirable to fill the empty lives created by post-war American capitalism. Yet he is not real, his identity is stolen, and the things he sells are empty and pointless.

The first episode of the series took this head on. Entitled 'Smoke Gets in Your Eyes', it introduces us to the advertising executive Don Draper and his concerns with selling Lucky Strikes, now that *Reader's Digest* is suggesting that cigarettes might cause cancer. From the beginning, the series is suffused with smoke, at a material, plot, and content level. The first illusion that Don pulls off is to obfuscate: he coins a new catchphrase for his client, a piece of sleight of hand suggesting that, somehow, this product might not be so bad: 'Everybody else's tobacco is poisonous. Lucky Strikes' . . . is toasted'.[31] It is no mistake that the key account at Draper's firm is tobacco. As well as allowing for a discussion of the evolving public health narrative (and the firm's methods of fending this off), it enables the reflection upon one of the very material props of pastness that the series deploys throughout – the cigarette.

In *Mad Men*, the cigarette is an index of the past – liberating, strange, alien, odd, uncanny even (recognizable yet peculiar, that which complicates the relationship between imagination and reality). Yet it is also a product, a commodity, something desired, and something for which desire is constructed. It is an artefact that demonstrates how the show is self-aware – in 'Smoke Gets in Your Eyes', apart from the ironic title, there are references to Freud, smoking and sex, and modern public health discourses – and how the audience is complicit in this self-consciousness. *Mad Men* is a series about consumption and the ways in which materiality is eschewed for product, the way in which things are commodified, fetishized, and made to mean. Its great trick, as a series, is to place history itself, or at least the past, central to this. The trappings of consumption that the show has engendered – fashion, music, other series, social networking, and marketing initiatives – rest on its status as a valued and desired commodity. Yet it is clearly self-conscious about this commodification, and woven into the series itself are both the story of how to fictionalize about something 'real' and the horrific consequences of living according to such dreamt concepts. *Mad Men* is also a critique of consumer capitalism, and the cigarette is its exhibit A, in all its sublimity, familiarity, alienness, and commodity. Once tobacco becomes a cigarette, it takes on the qualities of commodity, that thing with 'mystical character' that emblematizes, crystallizes, and forces the estrangement of man from man for Marx. This estrangement is exactly what *Mad Men* suggests is the central characteristic of post-war American life, and its central emblem is the cigarette – flashy, unreal, physical, and sensual, but freighted with meaning, spectral, sublime, ephemeral.

Cigarettes in *Mad Men* have the double quality that Marx demonstrated was the characteristic of commodity – they are both 'real' and 'imagined', constructed socially through the interrelationship of capital, labour, and production. This is the 'mysterious character' of the commodity, the doubleness that it entails. A cigarette in *Mad Men* is both diegetically 'real' and something that is part of a consensual historical imagination, enabling the viewer to inhabit a space in which there is an awareness of both, and hence – surely – the ability to critique, or at least to recognize, the workings of capital. They are a thing/not-thing, and in this they allow an audience to reflect upon the commodity of historical television itself. The self-reflexive quality of *Mad Men* almost demands that an audience sees how it is being sold a product, marketed a dream of something. Marx argued that, 'the mystical character of the commodity does not therefore arise from its use value', and *Mad Men* elevates the cigarette both diegetically – through the various advertising campaigns recounted in the show – and textually – through the use of the object itself.[32] This doubleness of the motif – an ability to be both metonym of 'past' and simply a prop, albeit one loaded with meaning – demonstrates the flexibility and the significance of the cigarette in historical fictions about the recent past.

By focusing on cigarettes to such an extent, by effectively fetishizing them, the series hides in plain sight its central emblem. The cigarette is both diegetic – authentic, a prop of pastness – and something that can reach outside, resituating the viewer in a dynamic relationship with the show. Cigarettes are historical but also something that might be experienced now; viewers can share the smoke of the past while understanding that it is not-now. Popular historical texts work by reinserting the body back into history, creating an affective bond between 'now' and 'then'; smoking seems to construct that bond, to remind an audience of the fragility of the body in the past. Like tobacco, historical film and television reflect

And then Betty gets lung cancer . . .

the way that the past has been made commodity – tightly wrapped together to create something with no iteration in the modern world other than a nearly empty echo of something that might have been. The solidity of the past goes up into the air, coiling around in an insubstantial, ghostly fashion. At a material level, smoke allows the visual text to reflect upon its historicity, to put in plain sight for the viewer a veil that demonstrates a physical otherness, and a representational aporia (literally, a gap) is opened/filled. Smoke is insubstantial but physical, concrete but transparent. It is a complex and sprung-loaded motif for pastness and, as a consequence, is used regularly in historical drama (fetishized visually from pipe-smoking to cigars, from candle smoke to steam-engines).

Smoke leaves the body that it was once, temporarily, part of (a kind of horrific grey physiological other of generally unseen breath). Exhaled cigarette or cigar smoke itself is a remnant of a past action, a ghostly recollection of something that has already happened, an invasion into the *now* of something that had significance and physical meaning *then*. The fetishizing of this evacuation of something that was inside the body might be conceptualized as concern with abject materials, the waste of immediate pastness. It is a momentary manifestation of something that was once within, a way of literally modelling the inside of the physical human form (or the spaces within it; see the discussion of the abject in Chapter 6). Smoke is a ghost of what once had structure, something that revisits briefly, insubstantially, the present moment, only to disappear. It provides a brief moment of mourning and an insight into the ways in which that which is past haunts the present, albeit momentarily and insubstantially. In contemporary historical TV and film, the smoke of the past is shorthand for the difference between then and now, a ghostly index of the progress that has been made from the uncivilized to the modern. In the bourgeois rush to now, away from then, all that is left of the past are these smoky traces, these echoes of former relationships and reminders of what was once but is no longer. The deployment of smoke as a trope in historical drama enables a reflection upon the ways in which coherent 'history' drives towards wholeness, coherence, singularity. The use of smoke in the frame, and the content, of historical drama, then, signifies a historiographical intervention at both a visual and a material level; it places the bodies of the past in history, while articulating the fact that those smoking on-screen are merely using the cigars to perform pastness, as props to signify their alterity. It is something that articulates the difference between then and now, both through demonstrating the chaotic fragility and ephemerality of a past moment, and by suggesting a particularity of experience that is atomized and never attainable. Cigarettes are never just cigarettes: they are time machines that burn themselves up, measures of moments, period-specific indicators of a past that is never reachable.

[handwritten margin note: sometimes a cigar is just a cigar!]

Rings as things and non-things[33]

Sarah Waters's novel *The Night Watch* reflects on the ability of things – ruins, rings, cigarettes – to provide presence in absence or emptiness. As such, it provides a counterpoint to this chapter's discussion of the ephemeral/material cigarette by demonstrating how historical fictions are obsessively concerned with material objects that are loci of historiographic meaning. The novel concerns a set of relationships during the Second World War, with a narrative that runs backwards. Thus it formally challenges heteronormative linearity to provide an alternative set of narrations and to reflect upon the ethics of historical representation (in ways that were also discussed at length in Chapter 1).[34] By its simple inversion of linearity, *The Night Watch* demonstrates to the reader how the act of engaging with a historical product is inherently insightful and, hence, powerful. As Lucie Armitt and Sarah Gamble argue about her earlier book, *Affinity* (1999), 'history is not just revisited but revised'.[35] The position of the reader is that they *know*, and therefore have an ethical conflict when engaging with the text. The strength, and awful power, of that knowledge – that the character will die, will be in pain, will suffer loss – is often hidden by linear, positivist, realist fictions that invite the suspension of this historical othering in the service of comfort. Time-slip fictions have long allowed a meditation such as this, as the protagonists (those who fall through time) are left to reflect upon their ethical relation to those in the past and the value and status of their knowledge (this is discussed further in the following chapter).

The temporal dislocation that fiction demands on the part of the reader, an imaginative movement between here and wherever, is brought into focus by the historical novel.[36] These specific iterations of the novel show in relief key concerns of all writing: death, knowledge, identity. The reader is empowered in relation to the text through this 'foreknowledge', but also forced to think about their ethical relation to both text and historical event. *The Night Watch* undertakes this kind of work, but, furthermore, demonstrates to the reader how all historical fiction is time-slip of a type, with the reader themselves in the problematic ethical position in relation to the text. 'We might all be dead tomorrow', says Viv, and, of course, they are.[37] They never lived, but people like them did, their manifestation in the past is over, and they are 'dead' to the contemporary. Waters' formal innovation in *The Night Watch* is to render elegantly the novel's deconstruction of linearity as part of the fragmentation of identity and selfhood that are its themes. The unravelling of self that is undertaken in the plot, and in the workings of the narrative, reflects the concomitant fragmentation of meaning and infects the historiography of the text, ensuring that the novel's version of the past itself is contingent and insubstantial.

The text demonstrates this through its concern with an object, a ring. Kay gives Viv a ring when she is in her most extreme pain, a moment of comfort and anonymous connection. The ring allows Viv to pass as married, and so it works to concretize her heteronormative identity (performatively, rather than in actuality, given that she is not *actually* married). This is ironized by the fact that the ring has been given to her by a queer character. It is a metonym and a material actuality, and this doubleness – both presence and absence, freighted with imaginary meaning and composed of something simple and elegant – informs the entire text retrospectively. The physical itself is invoked as a way of linking together disparate people through time. As Viv thinks to herself when, 'She caught the dusty, nasty smell of the hotel carpet', it might be something to take a kind of pleasure in:

she pictured all the men and women who might have embraced on it before, or who might be lying like this, now, in other rooms, in other houses – strangers to her, just as she and Reggie were strangers to them [. . .] The idea was lovely to her, suddenly.

(p. 188)

This affective connection figures the material bodies in the novel as imaginatively conjoined with others. Such sympathy and synchronicity are illusory, of course, but they create an imagined connection that works through the conceptualization of the physical. The ring has a similar ability at once to connect and articulate difference, its invocation of physicality (the finger) seeming to link both Viv and Kay. Viv's restoration of the ring is one of the first things to occur in the novel, and it works to return Kay to the evening she gave it away and her life fell apart. It is, therefore, an object that allows for conceptual, imaginative, memorial work to be done both by the character and, later, by the reader. It renders Viv's happiness and Kay's tragic loneliness simultaneously. It stands for a physical link between the two women – and their personal histories – while demonstrating quite how far apart they are. As an object that suggests connection, it also signifies fragmentation and disconnection. The ring has an actuality – its 'use value' – and 'exchange value' within the imaginative economy of the novel. Both are wrapped in one another, again highlighting the spectral duality of the object in historical renderings.

A ring describes an absence (both geometrically and conceptually). It is both specific and common, gathering meaning from its physicality and its imaginative iteration. It needs the body of an individual to give it significance, but that meaning itself is prey to change or misinterpretation (malicious or otherwise, given Viv's use of it). *The Night Watch* is a novel that is interested in the banality of some objects and their sudden transformation into, for instance, things that might kill (razors) or allow time-travel (Kay's ring). Material objects and things in texts allow a reflection of 'not just the physical determinants of our imaginative life but also the congealed facts and fantasies of a culture, the surface phenomena that disclose the logic and illogic of industrial society'.[38] Kay's ring is diegetic and authentic, something with physical heft that clearly is only imaginatively/fictively constructed by the text (it does not *actually* exist). The concern with the physical object renders the text in thrall to materiality while it points out its unreality; like the ring, it is substantial and empty. Kay's ring is an echo, a spectre, a trace of the past diegetically in the present. It is an object fetishized and given value and meaning. It is also a clue, something the reader looks for throughout the subsequent narrative owing to the inverted chronology of the novel. It provokes a range of interpretations but at the same time is simply a ring, a band of metal, without inherent 'value' or meaning.

The absences/presences inherent in the ring, the physical emptiness it enacts as an object, serve as a motif for *The Night Watch*'s intense interest in ghostliness and memory and, more, how these issues interact with 'history'. The novel is obsessed with the gaps between solid objects, particularly in its concern with ruins and the way that the destruction of the urban landscape fosters new, innovative relationships: 'She supposed that houses, after all – like the lives that were lived in them – were mostly made of space. It was the spaces, in fact, which counted, rather than the bricks' (p. 195). That which is physical *means* only in relation (and not outwith relation) to the spaces in between, the echoing, dusty, lonely places. Objects – bricks – only have significance in social/spatial relation, only describe meaning (rather than geometrical shape) in dynamic interaction.[39] The ring, again, stands for a motif that inflects the whole book's conceptualization of the space between people (diegetically and in terms of the audience's response to these other lives, these 'dead' characters). It is real and it is false, empty and full, and this ability to broker an interrelationship between such states demonstrates inherently the power of the historical novel, not simply to dislocate history, but also to provoke new ways of thinking about the past, to construct new relationships and possibilities.

Julia says at one point of her work surveying the bombed buildings of the city, 'We're recording ghosts, you see, really' (p. 269) This quite physical sense of the lost, the way that 'ghosts' can be recorded and archived and taxonomized, but still never really understood or comprehended, is key to Waters's practice as a historiographer. The insubstantiality of the historical revenant, or the ghostliness of the referent, and its near-rational (but not quite) link with the reality of modernity are her subjects through the spiritualism of *Affinity*, the performativity illusions of *Tipping the Velvet* (1998), and the 'actuality' of haunting explored in *The Little Stranger* (2009). Things, ghosts, and the spaces between, then, are central concerns for Waters's fiction and elements that enable the works to reflect upon their own fictiveness. This self-consciousness, an interrogation of historicity imbibed via gender theory and the last vestiges of the aesthetics of postmodernism, enables the articulation of a dissident sensibility at the same time that her work cleaves to authenticity, realist tropes, and the modes of a form long thought conservative. The ring motif – empty and material, object/fiction, real and ghostly, remembered and textualized – stands for the ways in which Waters is concerned with brokering the relationship between the real and the fictive.

Remnants and mourning

To conclude this discussion of the material and the ghostly and to shift towards the discussion of the physical return of what should be dead, which is the concern of the next chapter, the argument turns to the work of Jacques Derrida and, particularly, his late work on ethics and haunting. Derrida's work on spectres is concerned with seeing that which reminds those in the present of the fragility of the concretizing discourse that is history. The revenant is valuable, as it suggests the interruption of a kind of history that seeks singularity and linear temporality. The return of the unknown dead 'thing' disrupts this singularity and demonstrates its speciousness. In articulating his ideas about spirit and spectre in relation to Marx, Derrida seeks to show how usefulness and uselessness are things that are always inherent in the definition of a thing, and how having both qualities simultaneously undermines the distinction between use and exchange:

> Just as there is no pure use, there is no *use-value* which the possibility of exchange and commerce (by whatever name one calls it, meaning itself, value, culture, spirit[!], signification, the world, the relation to the other, and first of all the simple form and trace of the other) has not in advance inscribed in an *out of use* – an excessive signification that cannot be reduced to the useless [. . .] only beyond value itself, use-value and exchange-value, the value of technics and of the market, is grace promised, if not given.[40]

Smoking seemingly undertakes this address to useful–uselessness, in its excesses deconstructing the binaries imposed upon commodity and definition, splitting apart the imaginative unity underwritten in the capitalist imaginary.[41] Similarly, the ring winks in and out of value-meaning, refusing definition and, hence, demonstrating the spectral quality of commodity and the mad dance of capital. These objects allow a critique of representation and suggest the disintegration of modes of comprehension and representation, including realism and authenticity among others.

In his working through of the incursion of the trace of what is not known into the present, Derrida discusses the revenant that is the ghost of Hamlet's father. Key for him is the undecidable, which disrupts any attempt at systems and the organization of knowledge:

> *It is* something that one does not know, precisely, and one does not know if precisely it *is*, if it exists, if it responds to a name and corresponds to an essence. One does not know: not out of ignorance, but because this non-object, this non-present present, this being-there of an absent or departed one no longer belongs to knowledge. One does not know if it is living or if it is dead. Here is – or rather there is, over there, an unnameable or almost unnameable thing: something, between something and someone, anyone or anything.[42]

[handwritten margin note: Ghosts represent a kind of liminality?]

That which 'returns' is outside knowledge, a challenge in its non-ness. It is an anachronism, a dislocation, something undecidable. The ghost of Hamlet's father represents, for Derrida, 'that which is neither present nor absent, neither dead nor alive'.[43] The past is evidently part of the present, but unfamiliar although (simultaneously) familiar. When Derrida discusses Hamlet's father in *Hamlet*, he is talking about a spectre that, in the diegesis of the play, is part of the 'past'. Hamlet's father is diegetically realistic, part of a former chronological moment. Here, the past is uncanny in its appearance in the present, its uncategorized, problematic return to haunt the now. If the past is uncanny and unsettling during its incursions into the present, History is a way of attempting to organize, narrativize, and control this fracturing, problematic echo, to make it speak or silence it in the archive. Frederic Jameson interprets Derrida's invocation of the unknown ghost as an ethical intervention:

Spectrality does not involve the conviction that ghosts exist or that the past (and maybe even the future they offer to prophesy) is still very much alive and at work, within the living present: all it says, if it can be thought to speak, is that the living present is scarcely as self-sufficient as it claims to be; that we would do well not to count on its density and solidity, which might under exceptional circumstances betray us. Derrida's ghosts are these moments in which the present – and above all our current present, the wealthy, sunny, gleaming world of the postmodern and the end of history, of the new world system of late capitalism – unexpectedly betrays us.[44]

The doubleness of things in the fictive past gives them unpredictable life in the present and undermines our presumed understanding of the 'now'. The incursion of the revenant into the now, the thing that is no-thing or a 'non-object', the thing that is in and outside knowledge, forces an awareness of the fragility of identity in the now and its shaky foundations. Looking at the past, something that should be comprehensible and understandable, something that is the foundation of now, historical fictions present an audience with a set of insubstantial elements.[45] These transitory 'things' are there and not there, just as the historical fiction is physical and imagined. The material objects of the past that historical fictions dwell upon undermine the 'density and solidity' of a present that is predicated upon an understanding and an ownership (and a dominance) of the past through a discourse that is history. The material object in historical fictions corresponds to this insubstantial non-thingness, the kind of unnameable horror that Derrida recounts here. It fragments understanding of the world, challenging an audience with an echo of reality to confront something unknown.

Historical fictions problematize the material of the past in the present, as what is brought into the present is 'past' but not past, something that has similar uncanny qualities through what it is not (real) and what it is (fiction). The mimicking of the otherness of the past might seek, therefore, to make it flat, inert, controllable. Yet, in historical fictions, the past mimics the present, appearing familiar (even featuring famous faces, places, or events) but clearly other in a strange way. Historical fictions present, hidden in plain sight, something profoundly unsettling. In their mimicking of the past, their playing and performance of 'history' (and often of a history that cannot, could not, did not happen), they render a ghostliness within popular culture, something outside 'knowledge'. The representation of the material in these fictions, then, allows an insight into the way in which memorialization is conceptualized. Smoking, for instance, is an echo, a reminder of something that once was, something that reminds us of mortality (work through the permutations of the word 'ash', for instance, or think about cremation), a way that 'reality' is undermined and challenged. It is that which returns and is unknown. It might be used to hide the face of the past and to conceal. Smoke created by smoking is an echo–other, an imprint of pastness. It briefly intimates the past before diffusing and disappearing, creating an uncanny non-shape. It is something indistinct and fleeting, suggesting recognition, but denying it. Smoking in historical film and TV refers to this indistinct quality, suggesting that the brief, diffuse echo of tightly wrapped pastness that is the smoke of a cigarette sits as a motif for the way in which the film acts as a revenant of the past – indistinct, unreal, ghostly, translucent. Similarly, the ring is something material and insubstantial, an interzone between known and absent, actual and empty. As motifs for a way of connecting with the past, then, these two material elements provide a doubleness, an uncanniness, and something that might provoke anxiety. They are real and unreal, present and absent. They represent the incursion of the past into the present, but, simultaneously, the inertness of the things of the past until made to live in the now.

What of that which is left by the fire, the remnant that is not blown away, the physical remains? In Derrida's late impressionistic text on ethics, *Cinders*, he ponders the resonance of a particular phrase, '*il y a là cendre*' ('cinders are there'), that returns throughout his work, often being used as a citation or epigraph:

> The phrase came from very far away to meet its supposed signatory, who did not even read it, who scarcely received it, dreamed it rather, like a legend or a saying, a whiff of tobacco smoke: these words leave your mouth only to be lost in unrecognizability.[46]

Derrida likens words from the text/dream/myth/legend/commonplace of the past to tobacco smoke, an echo of something immediately lost. The cinders are a way of thinking through both spectrality (in terms of presence, absence, and physicality) and the trace that erases itself while presenting itself.[47] The point of using the word '*cendre*/cinder', furthermore, is to invoke domestic fires and the space of the hearth, a place of both hospitality, archives, and law, as much as the fire of the Holocaust.[48] The work done in comprehending the insubstantiality of the cinder but its centrality is the moment of remembrance and the aware- ness of mourning: '– But why would you have given it to the fire? To preserve the hiddenness of mourning's ashen grayness, or to undo it by letting it be seen, the half-mourning that persists only as long as the time of a cinder?' (p. 37). The ashen remnant enacts within it the unknowability of a past and, hence, a movement to mourning; it also allows the sense of the past, a half-seen trace of some other moment.[49] In Derrida's text, the remnants of something burnt become that which eschews representation or iteration, the trace itself, the thing–not thing, 'embody- ing' within its lack of entity the spectrality of the past in the present:

> But that is just what he calls the trace, this effacement. I have the impression now that the best paradigm for the trace, for him, is not, as some have believed, and he as well, perhaps, the trail of the hunt, the fraying, the furrow in the sand, the wake in the sea, the love of the step for its imprint, but the cinder (what remains without remaining from the holocaust, from the all- burning, from the incineration the incense) [sic].[50]

Ash is the best way of expressing the trace because of its 'effacement', its being–not–being, its resonance from the past (and as something that survives the fire to force us to remember the other and mourn).[51]

That which is left by burning is precise: 'The cinder is exact: because without a trace it precisely traces more than an other, and as the other trace(s)'.[52] The cinder seems to have iteration and physical presence while it simultaneously effaces itself; in this, it is the perfect motif for the material insubstantiality of the trace, as what it signifies is not part of (although is clearly constituent of) what it now is. For Derrida, that which remains, the ash, the remnants of the destruction of history, is significantly different from that which is ephemerally lost:

> What a difference between cinder and smoke: the latter apparently gets lost, and better still, without perceptible remainder, for it rises, it takes to the air, it is spirited away, sublimated. The cinder – falls, tires, lets go, more material since it fritters away its word; it is very divisible.
>
> (p. 73)

Smoke disappears, can be forgotten; cinders are the representational work of the past in the present, the spectre of substance in their insubstantiality. Smoke pretends to suggest meaning, disarticulates the object into being ash.

The material thing in historical fiction is representative of an absence. There is *nothing* that it stands in for. It is insubstantial and incoherent. Both the objects considered here – the cigarette and the ring – are holes in the diegetic, only physical when considered in one dimension and prey to being interpreted or interpolated or immolated in differing ways. They stand as motifs for the way in which historical fictions conceptualize a relationship to pastness, as something inherently physical but immaterial, somehow ghostly and solid at the same time. These revenants of the past, then, are solid and airlike, ghostly and physical, just as the ghost of Hamlet's father, for Derrida, is both real and unreal, flickering on the edges of consciousness in a way that disrupts contemporary identity and an ability to become complete. It is and is not and, in this duality, renders real and not real the concept of the trace. The returning spectre is something that provokes questions that must remain unanswered and, in this uncertainty, is the challenge to our modern rationality: 'One does not know if it is living or if it is dead. Here is – or rather there is, over there, an unnameable or almost unnameable thing: something, between something and someone, anyone or anything'.[53] The revenant challenges 'normality' through its refusal to be defined; it fragments and fractures. The past is something indistinct, smoky, something that recalibrates the now in undefined ways and provokes anxiety and distress; it is the evidence of the traumatic event that demands witness while avoiding definition. It is strange, queer, uncanny. The duality of the object in historical fiction is a motif for the historical fiction itself, something real and insubstantial, with heft and weight, but empty and ephemeral. In this it haunts the present, introducing into knowledge an insubstantial but significant other that cannot, but must, be acknowledged. It shows the fragmentation of the past and its unknowability. Ultimately, these ghosts may be nothing at all, but they point to the emptiness in understanding. The present cannot become complete, because of the absence of certainty about the past. Such ghosts render 'knowledge' complete by pointing to its insubstantiality. These hauntings from the past suggest a desire for a completeness that is never there, a mourning for a complete past that can never be attained. All that remains is the ash of something that might once have been, uncategorizable, unknowable, to be mourned and recollected through our investigations, to be borne testament to perhaps, and to be memorialized through a reading practice that recognizes this emptiness.

The drive of Derrida's work on spectrality and Marx is towards an understanding of the melancholia of the trace. Using a particular type of reading practice to understand the things of the past is part of a process of sympathy, empathy, and tribute:

> First of all, mourning. We will be speaking of nothing else. It consists always in attempting to ontologize remains, to make them present, in the first place by *identifying* the bodily remains and by *localizing* the dead [. . .] Nothing could be worse, for the work of mourning, than confusion or doubt: one *has to know* who is buried where – and it is *necessary* (to know – to make certain) that, in what remains of him, *he remain there*. Let him stay there and move no more!
>
> (p. 9)

Disruptions to knowledge, or texts that demonstrate the insubstantiality of epistemology, suggest a way of understanding the mournfulness of the present. The haunting of the present by the past, by bodies or things that should be dead but refuse to sleep quietly, and therefore disrupt normality, will be discussed in depth in the following chapter. The argument moves to consider the return of the dead, literally – zombies, vampires – and how this figures anxieties about the unknown, what is and is not, and the disruption of normalizing historicity by the alterity of the past.

Notes

1 *Capital*, opening section; available online at: www.marxists.org/archive/marx/works/ 1867-c1/ch01.htm (accessed 16 April 2015). Marx makes the distinction between the thing and its exchange and use value in his definition of commodity here. See David Harvey, *A Companion to Marx's Capital* (London: Verso, 2010).
2 *Capital*, opening section.
3 Bill Brown, *A Sense of Things* (Chicago, IL: University of Chicago Press, 2003), p. 4. Thing theory has been criticized for moving away from the commodity definitions of Marxist theory, but this chapter attempts to situate the two ideas in the same space.
4 There is a great deal of terrific work on material culture itself, but the cultural representation of fetishized objects within a fictive historical discourse has not been investigated greatly; see, for instance, the essays in Gillian Partington and Adam Smyth, eds, *Book Destruction From the Medieval to the Contemporary* (Basingstoke, UK: Palgrave Macmillan, 2014).

5 Iain Gately, *Tobacco: A Cultural History of How an Exotic Plant Seduced Civilization* (London: Simon & Schuster, 2001); Eric Burns, *The Smoke of the Gods: A Social History of Tobacco* (Philadelphia, PA: Temple University Press, 2006); Matthew Romaniello and Tricia Starks, eds, *Tobacco in Russian History and Culture* (London and New York: Routledge, 2009); Jordan Goodman, *Tobacco in History: The Cultures of Dependence* (London and New York: Routledge, 1994); Judy Vaknin, *Smoke Signals: 100 Years of Tobacco Advertising* (London: Middlesex University Press, 2007); Xun Zhou and Sander L. Gilman, eds, *Smoke: A Global History of Smoking* (London: Reaktion Books, 2004); Matthew Hilton, *Smoking in British Popular Culture 1800–2000: Perfect Pleasures* (Manchester, UK: Manchester University Press, 2000).

6 Richard Klein, *Cigarettes Are Sublime* (London: Picador, 1995), p. 2.

7 Elizabeth Grosz, *Volatile Bodies: Toward a Corporeal Feminism* (Bloomington, IN: Indiana University Press, 1994), p. 19. See also Elizabeth Freeman, *Time Binds: Queer Temporalities, Queer Histories* (Ralegh, NC: Duke University Press, 2010), pp. 8–12, 95–6, on the relationship between history, historiography, and the socially constructed body.

8 See Fred Botting:

> Within modernity's rational, useful, and moral codes of production and social organization, the art of smoking introduces an excessive and heterogeneous element associated with the sacred and the profane, luxury and poverty, sovereignty and abjection, habit and freedom, *jouissance* and death.
>
> ('The Act of Smoking in an Age of Techno-Moral Consumption',
> *new formations*, 39 (2000), 80–100 (pp. 81–2))

9 On these imaginative interrelationships and history, see, for instance, Alison Landsberg, *Prosthetic Memory: The Transformation of American Remembrance in the Age of Mass Culture* (New York: Colombia University Press, 2004).

10 Not least in relation to opium, something that introduces a set of discourses around trade, legality, globalization, intoxication, and empire that this chapter does not have space to cover; see, for instance, Susan Cannon Harris, 'Pathological Possibilities: Contagion and Empire in Doyle's Sherlock Holmes Stories', *Victorian Literature and Culture*, 31:2 (2003), 447–66.

11 In the 1982 TV sequel, *Smiley's People*, it is revealed that Karla, despite being an ideologue, smokes American cigarettes; at the conclusion, he returns Smiley's cigarette lighter, which falls uncollected into the Berlin gutter.

12 See Penny Tinkler, *Smoke Signals: Women, Smoking and Visual Culture in Britain* (Oxford, UK: Berg, 2006).

13 See Scott McCracken on the 'use' of smoking in Dorothy Richardson's fiction: 'In this context, smoking, far from being useless, is a material practice that enables the public performance of a new gendered subjectivity'; *Masculinities, Modernist Fiction and the Urban Public Sphere* (Manchester, UK: Manchester University Press, 2007), p. 64.

14 'Boardwalk Empire', *Boardwalk Empire*, Season 1, Episode 1 (2010).

15 Lynette Rice, 'Why you won't see stewardesses smoke on *Pan Am*'; available online at: http://insidetv.ew.com/2011/08/07/pan-am-smoking/ (accessed 16 January 2012).

16 Allan M. Brandt, *Cigarette Century: The Rise, Fall, and Deadly Persistence of the Product That Defined America: A Cultural History of Smoking in the United States* (London: Basic Books, 2009).

17 I owe much of this discussion and the later discussions regarding Derrida (and his book *Cinders*) to Sue Chaplin.

18 'The phantasmagoria, like capital, would begin with exchange-value and the commodity-form. It is only then that the ghost "comes on stage"', Jacques Derrida, *Specters of Marx*, trans. Peggy Kamuf (New York and London: Routledge, 1994), p. 200.

19 See Derrida, who quotes 'The body of money is but a shadow' (*Specters of Marx*, p. 45) in his general discussion of spectrality and value. Derrida argues that Marx is obsessed with ghosts, spirits, and the indistinct revenants of the past throughout his work.

20 'The Act of Smoking', p. 83.

21 Francis Wheen, *Karl Marx* (London: 4th Estate, 1999), p. 294.

22 Another great smoker was Freud, who would eventually die from related cancer. Those who were involved in his sessions remember the smoke and smell of his cigars, and clearly this association of cigar smoke with the memorial practice of psychoanalysis chimes with the ideas being worked through here (and on the ghostliness of the uncanny). See Peter Gay, *Freud: A Life for our Time* (London and Melbourne: J.M. Dent, 1988), p. 170.

23 *Grundrisse* footnotes; available online at: www.marxists.org/archive/marx/works/1857/grundrisse/f293-330.htm (accessed 23 May 2011).

24 From Marx in Manchester to Jenny Marx in Trier, 21 June 1856; previously available online at: www.marxists.org/archive/marx/works/1856/letters/56_06_21.htm (accessed 23 May 2011).

25 'Her name, that was as fresh/As Dian's visage, is now begrimed and black/As mine own face', *Othello*, III, iii, 386-8.

26 Marx's use of Shakespeare is examined in Jerry Phillips, 'Cannlibalism Qua Capitalism: The Metaphorics of Accumulation in Marx, Conrad, Shakespeare, and Marlowe' in Francis Barker, Peter Hulme, and Margaret Iversen, eds, *Cannibalism and the Colonial World* (Cambridge, UK: Cambridge University Press, 1998), pp. 183-202. See also Wheen, *Karl Marx*, pp. 19, 387, 394, n. 19.

27 Gerard Gilbert, 'Smoking in Films: Light up, Camera, Action', *The Independent*, 14 January 2014; available online at: www.independent.co.uk/arts-entertainment/films/features/smoking-in-films-light-up-camera-action-9059744.html (accessed 5 September 2014).

28 Jeremy G. Butler, '"Smoke Gets In Your Eyes": Historicizing Visual Style in *Mad Men*' in Edgerton, *Mad Men*, pp. 55-72.

29 See an expanded discussion of this in Jerome de Groot, '"Perpetually Dividing and Suturing the Past and Present: *Mad Men* and the Illusions of History', *Rethinking History: the Journal of Theory and Practice*, 15:2 (2011), 269-87.

30 'The Wheel', *Mad Men*, Series 1, Episode 13 (2007).

31 'Smoke gets in your eyes', *Mad Men*, Series 1, Episode 1 (2007). The obsession with smoking persists until the final episodes of the show, as Betty Draper contracts lung cancer and is given months to live. Her reaction is to not fight it, recognising that it is 'the end'.

32 'The Fetishism of the Commodity and its Secret' in Martyn J. Lee, ed., *The Consumer Society Reader* (Oxford, UK: Blackwell, 2003), pp. 10-18 (p. 10).

33 This section on Sarah Waters is reprinted, by permission, from '"Something New and a Bit Startling": Sarah Waters and the Historical Novel' in Kaye Mitchell, ed., *Sarah Waters* (London: Continuum, 2013), pp. 56-70.

34 See Kaye Mitchell, 'What Does it Feel Like to Be an Anachronism? Time in the *Night Watch*' in Mitchell, *Sarah Waters*, pp. 84-99.

35 'The Haunted Geometries of Sarah Waters's *Affinity*', *Textual Practice*, 20:1 (2006), 141-59 (p. 141). Armitt and Gamble explore the way that Waters uses the haunted form of the Victorian novel 'as a vehicle for the exploration of alternative versions of history' and to create 'deliberately subversive revisitings' (p. 142). See also Kate Mitchell, *History and Cultural Memory in Neo-Victorian Fiction* (Basingstoke, UK: Palgrave, 2010).

36 See the discussion of Genette, narrative time, and the impossibility of realist narrative in Jeremy Tambling, *On Anachronism* (Manchester, UK: Manchester University Press, 2010): 'the nature of narrative is to be falsified by its necessity to be set within time', p. 38.

37 *The Night Watch* (London: Virago, 2006), p. 298.

38 Brown, *A Sense of Things*, p. 4.

39 See Svetlama Boym, *The Future of Nostalgia* (London: Basic Books, 2001), for a key discussion of ruins and nostalgia.

40 Derrida, *Specters of Marx*, p. 201.

41 'Tobacco [. . .] for Derrida symbolises the symbolic and, when burnt, turns from commodity to value', Botting, 'The Act of Smoking', p. 83.

42 Derrida, *Specters of Marx*, p. 6. On Derrida and hauntology, see Gayatri Chakravorty Spivak, 'Ghostwriting', *Diacritics*, 21 (1995), 65-84.

43 Colin Davis, '*État Présent*: Hauntology, Spectres and Phantoms', *French Studies*, 109:3 (2005), 373–9 (p. 373). See also Mark Fisher, *Ghosts of My Life* (London: Zero Books, 2014).

44 'Marx's Purloined Letter' in Michael Sprinkler, ed., *Ghostly Demarcations: A Symposium on Jacques Derrida's 'Spectres de Marx'* (London and New York: Verso, 1999), pp. 26–67 (p. 39).

45 'The annihilation of the remainder, as ashes can sometimes testify, recalls a pact and performs the role of memory', Jacques Derrida, *Given Time: I. Counterfeit Money*, trans. Peggy Kamuf (Chicago, IL, and London: University of Chicago Press), pp. 111–2. I owe this citation to Botting, 'The Act of Smoking'.

46 Jacques Derrida, *Cinders*, trans. Ned Lukacher (Lincoln, NE, and London: University of Nebraska Press, 1991), p. 33.

47 Simon Choat, *Marx Through Post-Structuralism: Lyotard, Derrida, Foucault, Deleuze* (London and New York: Continuum, 2010), pp. 81–2.

48 Derrida, *Cinders*, p. 37. The cinder is the 'the remainder of the destruction of memory [. . .] is itself a performative: the incineration of the cinders', Herman Rapaport, *Later Derrida: Reading the Recent Work* (London and New York: Routledge, 2013), p. 91.

49 Robert Eaglestone discusses the way that the cinder is itself a 'haunting' through Derrida's work and argues that deconstruction has always been concerned with the Holocaust, at least obliquely; 'Philosophy of Cinders and Cinders of Philosophy' in Martin McQuillan and Ika Willis, eds, *The Origins of Deconstruction* (Basingstoke, UK: Palgrave, 2010), pp. 226–43 (p. 234).

50 Derrida, *Cinders*, p. 43.

51 See the discussion of *Cinders* and the Holocaust in Peter Baker, *Deconstruction and the Ethical Turn* (Gainesvile, FL: University Press of Florida, 1995), pp. 128–30.

52 Derrida, *Cinders*, p. 57.

53 Derrida, *Specters of Marx*, p. 6.

4

THE PROBLEM OF TIME AND
THE RETURN OF THE DEAD

The analysis here develops the ideas of haunting and ghostliness that were considered at the end of the previous chapter. This present chapter argues that the prevalence in culture of certain types of horror trope – possession, the undead, the walking dead – articulates an anxiety about the way that the past might affect the present. These hauntings give aesthetic voice to a concern about how history – as something that provides typology, order, and structure in the contemporary world – might be challenged and disrupted. The threats to normal, mainstream, ordered, harmonious existence, to a sense of identity defined through accepted norms relating to time, historicized experience, authenticity, memory, and bodily sanctity that are discussed in this chapter articulate a deep unease about contemporary social relations and orderings. The return of something thought safely inert and dead is deeply problematic to the rational everyday. The horror creature troubles humanness through different temporality and a challenging agency. Discussion of zombie, possession, and vampire films allows a consideration of the past as a moment of horror that erupts into a present that continually attempts to discipline and control it. A contrasting strand in mainstream film demonstrates a desire to cheat death and to bring the dead back to life, often through a concern with new technology, time travel, or scientific innovation. Throughout the chapter, the centrality of time, and ways of contorting and confronting linearity are uppermost. The discussions here circle around questions of the body and/in history and discussions of affect that will be picked up in the final two chapters.

Horror films are often concerned with the revelation of something from the past dislocating the present. They articulate a fear of the revenant, the unquiet ghost, the voice calling from the past. The disruption of the rational and the eruption of the uncanny form the basis of much work in the field of Gothic studies and horror over the past decade. Fred Botting comments on twentieth-century Gothic:

In the continuing popularity of ghost stories, in the development of fantastic, horror and occult fiction [. . .] Gothic shadows flicker among representations of cultural, familial and individual fragmentation, in uncanny disruptions of the boundaries between inner being, social values and concrete reality and in modern forms of barbarism and monstrosity.[1]

Indeed, the turn to Gothic in popular culture has been so prevalent, particularly post-millennium, that Catherine Spooner can confidently argue, 'Gothic has arguably reached saturation point in contemporary popular culture', and talk of the 'bewildering range of contemporary manifestations of the Gothic'.[2] Gothic is a prevalent discourse of contemporary popular culture, and this suggests that a concern with ghosting, haunting, uncanniness, and the eruption of the unseen is increasingly part of the imaginative economy of Western nations. Linnie Blake suggests that horror films express quite explicitly the traumas of the past, in a way that other cultural texts struggle to:

Critical engagement with a nation's horror cinema offers a significant means of not only grappling with the traumatic past and in so doing measuring the effects of social, political, and cultural transformation of the nation on its citizens, but of exposing the layers of obfuscation, denial or revisionism with which those wounds are dressed in service of dominant ideologies of national identity.[3]

For Blake, horror texts are a way of understanding how a nation finds memory problematic and challenging. They open up understanding of how national stories have been constructed purposefully to ignore or obfuscate traumatic events. Similarly, Adam Lowenstein argues for something he calls the 'allegorical moment [. . .] a shocking collision of film, spectator and history where registers of bodily space and historical time are disrupted, confronted, and intertwined'.[4] This is 'a complex process of embodiment, where film, spectator, and history compete and collaborate to produce forms of knowing not easily described by conventional delineations of bodily space and historical time' (pp. 2–3). So, for Lowenstein, moments of rupture, openness, and particularly elements from horror films of bodily revenants such as the living dead of all kinds lead to a challenge to binary oppositions and ordering narratives such as temporality and 'history'. In particular, Lowenstein argues that horror films can work to challenge entirely the ways in which historical events are represented, particularly the 'naïve verisimilitude of realism' (p. 4). Blake and Lowenstein are both particularly working with discourses of trauma and pointing out the horror film's concern with return, the body, and showing the unpresentable. Furthermore, they argue for the importance of non-traditional representational techniques in film's comprehension of national and social historical traumas. As will be seen, horror films' engagement with history is complex and often at the level of the allegorical, rather than the straightforwardly representational.[5]

Furthermore, the various texts considered here demonstrate a flexibility with – and an anxiety regarding – concepts of time and linearity. It might be argued that such an anxiety has been the case since at least the writing of H.G. Wells, and obviously these texts are in a heritage of cultural product that, since the late nineteenth century, has been concerned with reconceptualizing time and, therefore, history. This malleability of intellectual engagement, a willingness to consider different 'times', situates the texts within a set of philosophical challenges to straightforward 'historicity', as defined by Paul Ricoeur. Contemporary engagement with historicity and models of temporality has affinity with the discourses of 'new time' that Peter Fritzsche suggests occur in the early nineteenth century.[6] Certainly, a sense of differing 'ways of being in time' are prevalent, and the texts investigate the social, cultural, ethical, and moral aspects of different modes of time and, ultimately, seek to test the limits of mainstream ideologies of time and, hence, history and the past.[7] The texts considered here attempt to account for what Ricoeur calls the 'aporia' of time, that is, the thing that exists but does not, and, in a post-Einsteinian world, has been disconnected from linearity and causality.[8] Ricoeur works through the close relationship between narrative form and time, seeking to use the one as a way of comprehending and critiquing historians' use of the other.[9] As Bevernage and Lorenz argue:

> Hartog has rightly argued that terms such as 'past', 'present' and 'future' are invariably invested with different values in different regimes of historicity. When taken to its logical conclusions, this observation suggests that historians must ask whether historical time is a neutral medium or whether it is in fact inherently ethical and political.[10]

The texts considered here demonstrate that types of time are always ethical and political. Understanding these different times, from 'dominant' modes of proto-colonization to melancholic understanding of the fragility of modern consciousness, might allow an investigation of the discourses of temporality that bind the contemporary mind. Peter Burke discusses 'systems of time reckoning and time perception (*Zeitbewusstein*) as social or cultural constructions'.[11] These texts demonstrate the construction of 'time perception' to pressure the limits of ontological primacy and rationality in thinking about time: that is, to remind an audience that it does not know what time is, although it might think it does.

As Bevernage and Lorenz suggest, via Hartog, the ideology of time, its reckoning, and its ontological comprehension (experiencing) are things that have direct consequence for the ethical and political dimensions of history. Those texts that most cleave to mainstream narrative time are exactly the costume dramas that contribute to discourses of progress, heritage, modernism, and civilization: texts that demonstrate Lowenstein's 'naïve verisimilitude' in many ways. So, the different temporalities considered here and the new temporal agencies considered in the texts present a challenge to these ordering discourses of time. The zombie, the vampire, the possessing spirit, and the body brought back from the dead demonstrate a clear anxiety about temporality. The time experience of the vampire and the zombie is different to that of the human. They have a different temporal agency. Similarly, time travellers and those who can beat death also have something of this different temporal agency. These cultural productions, then, demonstrate a concern with different time experience. In some, the different linearities represented are to be feared; in others, they are to be desired. They demonstrate the fragile foundations upon which 'time' is founded in contemporary civilization, and how 'othered' experience can point this out. Time is an ideology, and the undead creatures upset it, demonstrating to the viewer and reader how they might be interpellated into temporality. The creatures also suggest the seduction of stepping outside history, becoming something other than human as a consequence. Fundamentally, then, they demonstrate how a particular understanding of chrononormativity is constructed.[12] Maria Mulvany argues that Emma Donoghue's *Slammerkin*, a novel relating to prostitution in the eighteenth century, is 'a haunted text that offers a subtle queering of both temporal normativity and the sequential temporal logic that heteronormative culture is contingent upon'.[13] This 'sequential temporal logic' is challenged and queered by particular types of writing and, particularly, accounts of the past in fiction. Analysis of the various horror and fantastic film tropes demonstrates an abiding concern with stabilizing temporality. The chapter finishes with a consideration of how the cinema itself allows for the dream of different temporal experiences, and, further, how historical representation and time might be bound up in this illusion.

Horrible history

It is initially important to gain a sense of how horror tropes and history combine in film. Period-costume horror film and television invite an exploration of many of the issues associated throughout this book with historical fictions generally. The ghosts that have been seen as prevalent in relation to historical fictions are here made physical – ethereal – flesh. The tension of the 'realist' mode with the supernatural or fantastical can be problematic and often leads to self-conscious historiographical and metatextual work, such as *A Field in England* and *Berberian Sound Studio*, discussed below. Perhaps owing to its relative rarity, historical horror is an underconsidered genre. It encompasses Gothic horror, literary adaptation, and some complex meditations on representing the past. Period horror also includes regular or revisionist versions of familiar monster stories (*Dracula* (Sky TV, 2014), *I, Frankenstein* (Stuart Beattie, 2013), and *Dracula: Untold* (Gary Shore, 2014) all attempt the latter). Period horror films and television series often use their quasi-fantastical setting to invoke folklore or tradition (*Sleepy Hollow* (Tim Burton, 1999), *Van Helsing* (Stephen Sommers, 2004)). They regularly echo a cinematic concern with European or English Gothic (*The Others* (Alejandro Amanábar, 2001), *The Woman in Black* (James Watkins, 2012)). Similarly to the texts discussed in Chapter 2, they demonstrate an anxiety and a concern about the house, in contrast with other period drama. Period horror films often revolve around the revelation of a

[handwritten marginal note: Not horror, but Against the Day also highlights a different experience of time.]

past horror, the discovery of something disquieting that erupts into the present. So, films as diverse as *Sleepy Hollow*, *From Hell* (The Hughes Brothers, 2001), *The Others*, or *Shutter Island* rely upon the thrilling psychological effects of revelation and fear of the unknown. These films use their period setting purposefully to investigate the horrors of history and, more generally, seek to suggest that the past is itself a scary, uncanny place. The historical setting of the film engages with the story beyond aesthetics, contributing a pervading sense of chaos and ominous worldly events. The paranoia of *Shutter Island*, for instance, invokes the cinematic world of Hitchcock's movies, as well as the geopolitical anxieties of the 1950s. *From Hell* suggests that Victorian society was fatally diseased.

Demonic and ghostly possession films are key demonstrations of a kind of ghostly haunting that is problematic in the present. They are concerned with that which still resonates, lives, echoes in the present, offers harm to those living, and attempts to do violence to the now. Possession films take their lead generally from *The Exorcist* (William Friedkin, 1973) or *The Amityville Horror* (Stuart Rosenberg, 1979). Both films suggest the malevolent influence of the dead in the now. Modern possession narratives are concerned with the eruption in the rational 'present' of the supernatural past. *The Conjuring* (James Wan, 2013), for instance, is both a historical possession film set in 1971 and a film that dramatizes the vengeance of an unquiet ghost from the mid 1800s. A witch called Bathsheba possesses the central character, Carolyn, and it is only when she is reminded of special family memories that she is partially recalled to the 'real' present. Possession suggests the actual disruption of identity that zombies or vampires do not achieve. The simultaneity of the possessed figure, both themselves and their demon, figures a truly disquieting kind of haunting. The presence of the past in the present fragments contemporary identity and traumatizes the now. That which should not be 'alive' is recalled to the present; time is disrupted and made nonlinear. The thing from the past challenges the order of the present.

Period horror often depends on the uncanny strangeness of the past to disrupt a sense of linearity and temporality. *A Field in England* (Ben Wheatley, 2013) is deeply concerned with rendering the otherness of the past through the presentation of horrific events. Although not strictly a possession film per se, it involves a kind of embodied haunting. Set during the English Civil War, the film articulates a nightmarish experience as a rag-tag group of deserters come under the spell of a man named O'Neill. He forces them to dig for treasure, and various alchemical and unpleasant events happen. Nothing is overtly or explicitly said about what is going on, and the narrative is constantly disrupted by editing, strange interludes, hallucinogenic moments, and seemingly meaningless exchanges. It is a disturbing film that is intended to confuse and disquiet the audience, suggesting that the experience of communing with the past might be strange and terrifying. The film consciously echoes the immediate, hand-held visual style of Peter Watkins, the director whose *Culloden* (1964) had challenged the documentary frame by interleaving modern techniques of war reporting with the representation of the battle.[14] *A Field in England* is self-consciously strange and inconclusive, refusing narrative form and order. Shot in black and white, it is in many ways extremely realistic in its deployment of tropes of authenticity. Wheatley was inspired in part by his experience shooting a film about the Sealed Knot Civil War re-enactment society. However, the diegesis of the film contends with this realism, and the odd events – repetitions, resurrections, drug-fuelled religious awakenings, the probable presence of the devil – render the very 'realism' of the film itself uncanny, full of uncomfortable second meanings only half seen. Wheatley makes the 'real' – the tropes of authenticity found in all costume drama – suspicious, and his veracity is in communicating the unsayable difference between then and now. This film's historiographical approach is to undermine what Lowenstein called 'naïve verisimilitude' by infiltrating it and impregnating it with shadow. Realist time and the illusions of representation are challenged here.

A similarly self-conscious and metatextual British horror film is *Berberian Sound Studio* (Peter Strickland, 2012). Similarly to Wheatley, Strickland undermines the tropes of realism and attempts to render them strange and disturbing. The actual form of film itself becomes something uncanny. In the 1970s, a mousey sound engineer named Gilderoy travels to a famous Italian studio to help make a pulpy *giallo* film about the torture of women thought to be witches. The film deconstructs the making of 'horror' by showing that the sound of particularly gory moments is made by hammering fruit. As Gilderoy becomes more concerned about the psychological effects on him of making the movie, the director attempts to calm him by pointing this out: 'This is just a film. You're part of it. You can see how all this is put together, what's your problem with this?'.[15] The audience is shown how the narrative is made to have an affect, but is still scared by it. Somehow, the sound effects are grimmer for being made by such innocent means. The director claims that his exploitation horror is in fact important: 'This is history. And a filmmaker must be true. I hate what they did to these beautiful women. But the world must see the truth . . . brutal, and honest'. His 'truth' is the representation of torture and a true rendering of the violence of the past. It becomes indivisible from reality for Gilderoy, who succumbs to insanity and loses his sense of identity. In both these films, a self-consciousness regarding representation is important. Both stage the past as uncanny and terrifying, possibly outside rationality, and the location of horror. The past is materially part of the uncanniness of the *mis en scène*, as the texts echo others very carefully. They are self-consciously haunted by the traces of other texts. This is also the case for the tranche of horror remakes that have been made through the past two decades, an echoing of past terrors in new settings. As Catherine Spooner argues, horror and Gothic texts are very much predisposed to remakes, revivals, and reinvention and, through this, enact within their diegesis a kind of cultural echoing.[16]

Engagement with historiography through challenging the frame of representation, then, is key in how many historical horror films function. They attempt to undermine epistemologies and challenge normative temporality. By stepping outside realist representational paradigms, the films can reflect upon the way in which stories of the past are constructed and, particularly, how authority is imposed. Fantastical, uncanny moments are used to undermine the focused rationality of repressive systems such as 'history'. The fantasy–horror film *Pan's Labyrinth* (*El labertino del fauno*, Guillermo del Toro, 2006), set during the Second World War, demonstrates how the elements of horror and terror can also reflect, aesthetically and imaginatively, the disruptive and destructive events of the contemporary moment. The film communicates clearly the nature of internecine war, while similarly reflecting upon the way that such an event is remembered. The child protagonist, Ofelia, discovers a secret world, the labyrinth, which holds many treasures and strange beasts; outside this space, the war becomes increasingly bloody and horrific. Ofelia withdraws into the labyrinth to escape the vicissitudes and violence of the 'real' world, seeking an aestheticized ideal (something that echoes fairy and folk tales) rather than face what is happening around her. The film articulates the desire to escape into a world that – although scary at times – is other to the real world and somehow more attractive (and holds the possibility of redemption and happiness).[17] This forgetting – this avoiding of the realities of the war – is what history has done in Spain, seeking oblivion rather than face how the events of the 1930s still shape and warp contemporary Spanish society.[18] The labyrinth is emblematic of how the past might be aestheticized and made into something imaginatively beautiful but unreal.

Pan's Labyrinth reflects the experience of the past moment, but also enacts the desire of society to eschew and avoid this reality, to seek meaning elsewhere. Similarly, del Toro's earlier film, *The Devil's Backbone* (*El espinazo del Diablo*, 2001), set during the Spanish Civil War, uses Gothic traditions – apparitions, visions, shadows – to explore once more concerns relating to the war, memory, and to being without a legitimate or defining past (the film is set in an orphanage). *Pan's Labyrinth* is an example of a fantasy–horror historical film that communicates something about the historical moment through its aesthetics, but also reflects upon the impossibility of remembering. The film meditates upon the way that innocence might be corrupted, or how a moment of origin in childhood innocence might be something that looks more to fantasy than to grim reality. This incredibly stylized film performs historical work. Its aesthetic leads to an affective and diegetic communication of a sense of the past. Additionally, it works historiographically through its concern with articulating a version of the war period (and how it is or is not remembered) and reflecting upon how popular media such as film might communicate key elements, issues, and ideas more effectively than other modes. It plays with differing time signatures and modes of understanding the past in the present. The film works by demonstrating that innovative formal techniques can challenge the centrality of narrative realism in conceptualizing pastness.

Similarly, the 'vampire' story *Let the Right One in* (*Låt den rätte komma in*, Tomas Alfredson, 2008; remade as *Let Me In*, Matt Reeves, 2010) uses its setting to reflect upon the bleakness of the 1980s in Sweden as much as to think about the traumas of childhood.[19] Oskar, the child protagonist, befriends a new arrival, who helps him with his bullying problem but also turns out to be undead. Oskar accepts this in return for some form of companionship and even love. The horror here is the other people, the society full of drunks and liars and broken homes that Oskar rejects. These films' concern with the child as avatar of the contemporary audience, traumatized by the events of the past (and, hence, attempting to escape somehow), chimes with a general concern over the past 20 years with childhood and innocence, as Erica Burman argues:

> The child as signifier of either the 'true' self, or even the (biographically prior, or never experienced but longed for) 'lost' self, has coincided with a historical sensibility of even greater personal alienation and dislocation. [. . .] Hence childhood becomes a site for multiple emotional as well as political investments: a repository of hope yet a site of instrumentalisation for the future, but with an equal and opposite nostalgia for the past.[20]

Contemporary historical film often uses the child, or childhood scenes, to signify innocence, a simpler time, this sense of nostalgic pastness (before the grimness of experience sets in). A contemporary voice-over often distinguishes between the sadness of now and the openness of then. Yet both Alfredson and del Toro seek to meditate upon the traumas of childhood and strategies that children might deploy to deal with them. The horror of these films lies in the 'alienation and dislocation' both characters feel in their contemporary moment, and their attempts to escape. Burman's words also point out the obvious sense of futurity (or a bleak ending of this) inherent in the contemporary deployment of a child's point of view in a historical film. These films articulate a fear that is somehow associated with the pastness that they invoke; part of the process of making a historical horror movie scary is about communicating a horror that belongs inherently to the time period. Period horror seeks to understand a set of fears set in a very particular historical moment, but suggests that the horrific might be precisely associated with that time itself.

Shuffling into history: Zombies

The next two sections focus on how key motifs of the past decade demonstrate palpable cultural anxieties regarding haunting, time, and the return of the dead. In particular, the sections meditate upon the phenomenon of the undead in contemporary popular culture, notably the zombie and the vampire. Given what Erik Butler calls the 'cultural teratology' inherent in establishing which monsters a society fears, it is evident that, in the late twentieth and early twenty-first century, anxieties accrue around bodies that are undead, outside history, othered by their physical and temporal stasis.[21] This present section considers the way that the zombie reflects anxieties about the return of what should be dead and the disruption of anthropocentric linearity. Zombies are an inescapable trope, a flexible and instantly recognizable way of communicating contemporary fears about violence, apocalypse, and the end of the way that life was. They introduce a new, monstrous temporality in their eternal, hungry, undead shuffling and provoke an uncanny terror in the recognition of that which was once human, now twisted and horrific.

The prevalence of zombies as a central trope within popular culture over the past decade or so is clear.[22] Successful films such as the remake *Dawn of the Dead* (Zack Snyder, 2004), *Resident Evil* (Paul W.S. Anderson, 2002; there are five sequels), *Shaun of the Dead* (Edgar Wright, 2004), *Zombieland* (Ruben Fleischer, 2009), and *World War Z* (Marc Foster, 2013) show the mainstream popularity of the genre. Numerous pulpy horror texts have been produced, as well as the films about those infected with 'rage', *28 Days Later* (Danny Boyle, 2002) and *28 Weeks Later* (Juan Carlos Fresnadillo, 2007). *Shaun of the Dead* and *Zombieland* are comedies, but still cleave to the same principles of apocalypse. *Zombieland* delights in explaining the 'rules' for avoiding and defeating zombies, referencing a set of well-known clichés and characteristics as an in-joke with the audience. Massive-selling games such as *Call of Duty: Black Ops* (Activision, 2010, 2012) have zombie survival mode (not to mention the hugely popular *Plants vs. Zombies* (PopCap, 2009) smartphone game). Marvel Comics has produced *Marvel Zombies* (2005–6). There are television series including *Dead Set* (Channel 4, 2008), *The Returned/Les revenants* (Canal+, 2013), *iZombie* (The CW, 2014), and *In the Flesh* (BBC3, 2013). This last series and the novel/film *Warm Bodies* (Jonathan Levine, 2013; novel by Isaac Marion, 2011) demonstrate how the zombie as a trope is evolving. *In the Flesh* is set after an outbreak has been quelled, and there are numerous survivors suffering from 'partially deceased syndrome'. *Warm Bodies* gives human characteristics to zombies in a rom-com revolving around an inter-mortality relationship. The trope is immensely flexible as much as it is prevalent.

Many commentators argue that the apocalyptic nature of most zombie movies responds to an American sense of bleakness engendered, in part, by the attacks of 9/11. The trope became more resonant after the 2008 global financial crisis prompted (particularly in the USA) the economic destruction of communities and the fragmentation of cities and towns. Similarly, the USA has been at war in Iraq and Afghanistan since 2002 (and more widely engaged in a 'war on terror'), and the zombie might be a cultural echo of discomfort and anxiety provoked by this fact.[23] The multiple and various uses of the zombie – as articulation of fears, from miscegenation to contagion to annihilation – demonstrate its protean quality in representation, springing from its fundamentally uncanny nature – that which has returned, that which was repressed. The zombie represents the past in the present, and this makes the present fearful. How that fear is focused and what it might mean to an audience are predicated upon the fundamental disjunction of then in now. The zombie, after all, is a reminder of things an audience would like to forget (death) and a harbinger of the end of normality. They trouble identity by being dissonant physical embodiments of living death. They challenge normative identity literally, as being bitten – invaded – will turn someone into one. In Gothic terms, they are familiar but horrific, something emphasizing the abjection of the physical body (they are bloody, rotting, interested in brains and blood). Their inhumanity is inextricably linked to rationality and temporality: 'Beyond sense, meaning, reason, its passion for destruction goes nowhere, does nothing but consume [. . .] Living after the end, zombies are neither human nor monstrous but remain revolting all the same'.[24] They are uncanny, the recognizable (often loved ones or friends) turned into relentless killers. This is one of the reasons why the child zombie is particularly unsettling, and such a figure is used regularly in order to shock a numbed audience.

The zombie defies normative existence and brings the past into the present, embodying that revenant that should be excised and (as much as possible) forgotten. Their flesh revolts, and they seek to feed upon the living – particularly the brain – as a means of challenging a rational, humanist typology of the universe. The catastrophic event that has created them is in the past, but rendered in the now, as these monsters come alive. Zombies are the physical enactment of death, a constant reminder of a violent end that awaits all. They are an embodiment of the fear of the past, and of that fear stalking the present. Society seeks to control the fears of its populace by rationalizing, explaining, and organizing, but the past trudges remorselessly onward, intent on the quotidian. Zombies are the thing that reminds the contemporary to live in the now rather than the past, to live in the moment. As entities they are constantly now, ageless, with no timeline or sense of future, and their 'victims' (those who have to make lives around them) are not able to create a community or recall the past without pain. Zombies are inherently postmodern, it might be argued, in their historicity, blank and directionless, shuffling around to no purpose, past without narrative. Botting argues that this directionlessness is key to their contemporary resonance:

> Neither angels nor cyborg-vampires but basely material, they embody not joyous states to come, but states, beliefs and habits that recur with possibility of supercession, shadowy figures of a permanent and inescapable contemporaneity unable to achieve distance from itself and incapable of moving on.
>
> (p. 508)

Zombies rarely appear in anything other than the contemporary world (apart from the novel *Pride and Prejudice and Zombies*). The zombie is a fear in the *now* of the then (or the should-be-then). They are anachronistic, out of their time, something that should be dead. They are not consciously undead in the same way as vampires, and do not attain death-in-life. Rather, they are reanimated, living on out of their time and, hence, disturbing linearity and chronology. Like the time traveller or the hero who cheats death, discussed below, they express a primal desire to develop and surmount the logic of rationalist chronology, challenging models of linearity. Their material pastness (they are rotting artefacts of a human that was) ensures that there is no future (or not a recognizable one). They generally do not learn or develop or become anything, instead simply shuffling around without intent or purpose.[25] Zombies also represent an unthinking mass, driven by appetite and rage, dehumanized echoes of people in a way that ghosts are not. The zombie is the spectre of the cosy world that was, which has been destroyed, a constant reminder of what might have been.

Zombies have also regularly been used as motifs to meditate upon capitalism and time.[26] The zombie interrupts capitalist time. Part of the horror of chaos that the zombie represents is their untemporal or intemporal existence, outside contemporary modes of comprehension. This is consistently linked to a fear of the collapse of society and capitalist ordering. George A. Romero's film *Dawn of the Dead* (1978) famously took place in a shopping mall and made a series of points about the mindlessness of consumer capitalism.[27] One of the central arguments was the mindless *boredom* of consumption. Once trapped in the mall, the survivors, with every commodity they would ever need, lose any sense of the 'value' of the objects. Yet they fight tooth and nail to keep their consumer existence. Similarly, Robert Kirkman's *The Walking Dead* (2003–) series of comics explicitly undertakes a critique of capitalism. The series sets itself up to argue for a kind of purity of life after the apocalypse, a new conception of the now:

> How many hours are in a day when you don't spend half of them watching television? When is the last time any of us really worked to get something we wanted?
>
> The world we knew is gone.
>
> The world of commerce and frivolous necessity has been replaced by a world of survival and responsibility.
>
> An epidemic of apocalyptic proportions has swept the globe causing the dead to rise and feed on the living.
>
> In a matter of months society has crumbled. No government, no grocery stores, no mail delivery, no cable TV.
>
> In a world ruled by the dead, we are forced to finally start living.[28]

This sense of hopeless bleakness – but a kind of vital new life emerging from the encounter with a vengeful, cleansing monster – pervades the series. Life in the new world eschews consumer capitalism for something that is more 'real'. The encounter with the zombie horde makes the now more important, and, as the protagonist, Rick, says, 'Thinking about the good times makes all this seem so much worse' (p. 32). The past is embodied now by shuffling corpses, and memories are to be ignored for the sweet, nostalgic innocence that they represent (and the pain in the now that they provoke). The world no longer has history, just a set of ravenous things that should be dead. The opening of the TV adaptation of *The Walking Dead* features a pocket watch spinning out, signalling the disruption of capitalist and modern time by the zombie invasion. Such catastrophes render the survivors outside history, living in a moment without pastness, a very now time. The zombies particularly represent the attempted invasion of time, as they are intent on dragging the living into a non-time, a temporal neutrality of unlife. They disrupt normal, capitalist, modern time and linearity. They are interventions of the past in the present and, as such, they challenge the comfortable, historicized identity in the now. They have a different temporal agency to the human, much as the ghost does. As a central cultural trope, therefore, they suggest an anxiety surrounding the temporal logic of the contemporary. They literally disrupt the imaginative economy of the now with an invasion of that which should be then. The definitions of self in the now are intricately related to a firm understanding of how the past is in strict relation to the present. Zombies interrupt this and, hence, destabilize this contemporary historicized identity.[29]

In zombie films, though, the zombie is never really the most terrifying thing. Other people are what make living in a post-apocalyptic world so problematic, as Cormac McCarthy's novel *The Road* (2006) or the game *The Last of Us* (Naughty Dog, 2013) demonstrates. The zombie apocalypse leads to a refiguring of social relations, particularly as figured in the USA. It is a violent rending of post-Enlightenment accord, with a society founded on the principles of reason reduced to aggressive frontierism and hunter–gathering. The zombie film often leads to a refiguring of social relations and the establishing of a frontier-town society that is *now* but echoes a representational *then*. The set of tropes invoked is from the Western, a primitive society of sorts, held together by force of will and whoever has the most guns. In this, again, there is an echo of critique of nationalist myths, as discussed in Chapter 2. In *The Walking Dead*, Carl's stetson (his father's police hat) and Rick's position as the last cop alive and self-appointed sheriff of the post-apocalyptic badlands explicitly reference the Western mode to suggest the new lawlessness is simply a recurring of events from the national past. Rick often rides a horse, owing to the lack of petrol. The zombie text here is about the organization and establishment of the nation, a desire for an order that has been lost. *The Walking Dead*'s concern with the law is demonstrated when a group of survivors take refuge for some time in a prison, making themselves inmates to escape the horrors outside. The survivors remake their society and sacrifice those who do not share their aims. Ejecting difference, the series demonstrates the ways in which communities organize themselves and the dirty secrets that they keep in order to maintain sanity. The series, therefore, inscribes the formation of modern society through attention particularly to the ejection of that which is different – other people, and zombies. In *The Walking Dead*, this refiguring happens in recognizably modern architectural spaces, the war for now fought in the echoing places of then. The spaces of combat are Marc Augé's postmodern non-spaces – motorways, malls – made horrifically meaningful through the invasion of the undead.[30] For the zombie film, the contemporary is past, something to be lovingly remembered but that can never be attained. To have the luxury of history would be nice; simply staying alive is a struggle.

Glibly, it might be possible to figure the historical film as, not just ghostly, the present haunting itself with these spectres of the past, but also – given the materiality and physical temporality of the film medium – as zombie or vampire films. In them, the dead return to walk, upsetting the rational world. They become liminal figures, between death and life, challenging the rational smoothness of the now with the intrusion of then. They are not echoes, revenants, ghosts, but physical entities reanimated, uncanny and recognizable, disturbing and dislocating. They perform horrific past–presentness, caricaturing that which is known and seeking to reorder the rational comprehension of the world (brains). This way of using 'zombie' as a metaphor is not new – everything from urban emptiness ('zombie estates' in post-recession Ireland) to economics (John Quiggins' book *Zombie Economics* was published in 2010) has been characterized as 'zombie' – the empty shells of once-living ideas or structures remaining to hurt and haunt the contemporary world with their echoes of something past that should not exist now. The historical fiction as zombie would figure it as something analeptically shuffling around, undermining the rational and the order of the everyday. It would challenge contemporary identity through its rendering of the past as empty echoes with a troubling violence.

The zombie is also an expression of that which is unfeeling and undead, without thought or reason. It might represent the past that society would hope buried, or a death it would rather avoid, but it also embodies an atavistic physicality without present, or future, something *now* and, hence, non-human. Like the vampire, the zombie demonstrates that to be human is to be in history, to appreciate the change and shift of things, to have a temporal sense that leads towards death. The zombie has a past, but that has stopped – it is no longer the person it once was. Like the vampire, the zombie represents the arresting of time. So, the zombie text generally represents an anti-utopic strain in contemporary culture, a way of thinking about the thing from the past as something parasitic and violent, to be shut out rather than invited into the home. It figures a clear anxiety about that which should be dead and should remain in the past.

Humanness and temporality: The vampire

In recent years, the vampire has been the biggest of popular cultural tropes – possibly even more so than the zombie – mainly owing to the worldwide success of the *Twilight* franchise of books and films (2005–8, 2008–12).[31] As Erik Butler argues, the vampire outdoes 'most other forms of monstrosity in the twentieth [century]'.[32] Similar to the zombie, although with rational sense, the vampire is undead, a physical and material revenant of that which should not be in the present. This physical and temporal dislocation works to disrupt linearity. The vampire's desire to stay alive outside the strictures of human life challenges the taxonomizing effect of history by undermining its totalizing ability. Vampires, hence, represent a fear of continual life (and infection by this), invasion, the disrupting of boundaries, and of being cast out of human existence by being forced to live without history. The vampire challenges capitalist, normative, mainstream temporality and seeks to make others do this too. Their enemies are the rational, the scientists, the religious – those who wish to sustain the power of certain ordering structures.[33] Yet, at the same time, the vampire is often the ultimate capitalist, representing the abiding establishment: 'Because of its inimical relationship to stability, tradition, and order, the vampire embodies the transformative march of history'.[34] As creatures, vampires challenge selfhood and knowledge, undermining the wholeness of the body, invading it, feeding on it. In this, they are the key element of a tranche of Gothic writing that expresses the fear of a challenge to rationality and to self-definition.

As Markman Ellis argues, 'the vampire has a perverse modernity: a terror of recent invention manifested as a monster from time out of mind, from deep history'.[35] This 'perverse modernity' bespeaks a simultaneity allied to a sense of historicized identity. Vampires dislocate the present because they appear from the past, disavowing the ordering of history. They query modernity and the comforting temporal linearity of the contemporary.

In *Abraham Lincoln: Vampire Hunter*, the racists in the South are the vampires, feeding on the slaves. Lincoln's desire for truth and nobility and equality becomes a rallying cry to rid the world of evil: 'Vampires aren't the only things that live forever', he says, suggesting that morality is also timeless. For Lincoln, in this film, social and moral actions are what make one human – freedom and liberty are the things that define the living. Lincoln ensures that the United States will be a nation of 'living men' rather than undead creatures, a nation, moreover, defined in its 'living' status through its historicized conception of itself. The film situates itself as a 'secret' history, presenting something unseen and unknown – recounting a marginalized but incredibly important set of events. Other historical films, such as *The Mummy* series (1999–2008), articulate a clear sense of historical relativism and quasi-orientalism (the chaotic and othered past attacking modernity; the threats to the taxonomizing Europeans – scientists and archaeologists – represented by the horrors of the East). In both these examples, the horror in the past represents a possible challenge and disruption to modern time and linearity, the return of something that will fragment linear temporality.

The vampire disrupts because it brings the past into the present and challenges human temporal, normative experience. As Newitz argues, 'Slavery and genocide may be part of the past, but they wreak havoc in the present. Zombies, vampires, and mummies bear in their half-alive bodies the signs of great social injustice whose effects cannot ever be entirely extinguished.'[36]

These revenants have a political agency, a nightmare of the violence of the past intruding into the present to remind those living there that their existences are built on horror. Set in Bon Temps in rural Louisiana, *True Blood* (HBO, 2008–) imagines a contemporary world in which vampires have been legalized, freed from their desire for human blood by synthetic blood substitute.[37] Vampires have been recognized and are beginning to demand rights as citizens (the series echoes, very deliberately, the civil rights movement). In Series 1, Episode 5, Bill, the central vampire figure, has been persuaded by his human lover Sookie's grandmother to address the meeting of the Descendents of the Glorious Dead. The interest in Confederate history (the Confederate flag is raised in the church) is seen to be both innocent (the joy that the grandmother has in the past) and distasteful (the black character Tara stares at the flag in disbelief; she has already asked Bill if he owned slaves). The past is still very much alive and problematic in this Southern community.[38] The 'descendants' idea, of course, suggests a direct link to those who took part in the Civil War or the Revolution, a sense of historic racial purity that has affinity with, but is much more heightened than, general genealogical interest. It suggests a link that echoes through the ages, like the vampires themselves. The meeting is itself popular history, the local community coming together to remember in certain amateur ways (and to celebrate their link with the past). Bill's involvement makes the past more real to them (and us, through flashback) – his body and his story (not a textual narrativizing) make the past live, because it is still alive in him. He demonstrates the way that popular history returns the viewer/audience/ genealogist to the body of and in the past.

The use of a vampire to transcend time and disrupt linearity in this way is not unusual. Anne Rice's *Interview With the Vampire* begins in Louisiana in the eighteenth century (*True Blood* has many connections with this classic novel), and the central figure is doomed to walk alone through time. Similarly, there are various jokes in the *Twilight* series about how the vampire family has gone to college multiple times. The use of Bill's experiences in *True Blood*, though, contributes to a queering element that the series undertakes more generally. It is interested in blurring boundaries of sexuality, anthropology, and identity throughout, using its status as Southern Gothic to do this (and to add in layers of ghostliness, haunting, and revenants throughout). Its use of history is no less complex. The vampire is literally a relic, something that lived then and lives now; anti-historical longevity combined with true, authentic historicalness. Bill tells a story about the death of one of the congregation's ancestors during the war. He was fighting for the Confederates and attempting to save another (whose ancestors are also in the hall). It is a moving story, and the shifting of viewpoint from Bill, to his memory, to the dying boy, and then into the head of his drugged ancestor both contributes to this account (Bill's voice in the voice-over renders the sequence diegetically recalled into the present) and makes it clearly resonant and effectual in the present. Bill is the conduit for the past, a witness and participant who, despite his claims to be human, is very much not so – and the thing that defines him as such is his ability to stand outside history, or, perhaps, to stand in historicity and not care. The show thus argues that death is what makes people human, and the point of death is to recall them to memory and history. Without this and the ineffable sense of poignancy and fleetingness that it evokes, they are above – or outside – humanity.

What happens next, however, shifts the tone. In the same way that the vampire in Rice's novels is lonely (a trope that harks back to Byron and echoes through vampiric writing), Bill's isolated state historically is recalled. The mayor of the town gives him a picture of his family taken just before he went to war. The pain in his face demonstrates how it affects him, and he sees and comprehends his loss – the loss of his humanity and his history. He weeps. Being outside history is possible, but you can still, even if you are undead, be brought back in (and the conduit for that is the memory of death, the recollection of the death and loss of his family, friends, and comrades). Later, he has visions of his family (children, wife) in his house. The vampire who made him appears outside his family home in a flashback sequence, telling him, 'You can never enter . . . do you wish to see them grow old and feeble, year after year? [. . .] They are as good as dead'.[39] Being human means being in history, which means being mortal; popular historical texts have this at their heart. Popular history, or the manifestation of the past in the cultural text, reconciles the audience at the same time as repelling them from death. They recognize the otherness of the past and its complete difference from now – that otherness allows them to control their reactions to it. However, the vampire stands outside this, queering the linearity and smoothness of history and disrupting our understanding and comprehension, in the same way that it complicates our notion of humanness, sexuality, and science. The vampire queers the linearity of history by disavowing the otherness of the past (and, hence, demonstrating the falsehood of the narrativizing of that past into history), by not allowing death to make a binary of then and now. Its body – refreshed by the lifeblood of others – stands materially for what should not be alive. The manifestation of the past in the present in *True Blood* demonstrates a malleability of trope, an ease with the ways in which a kind of history might be iterated in the now (and, hence, a new way of comprehending ourselves as contemporary figures). Georg Lukács argued that Walter Scott's historical fiction allowed, for the first time, a popular sense of historicity, of the individual in history of some description (and of history as process): 'Hence the concrete possibilities for men to comprehend their own existence as something historically conditioned, for them to see in history something which deeply affects their daily lives and immediately concerns them'.[40] The versions of the past that are presented in vampire texts allow a new conceptualization of the contemporary self through a renewed/reanimated/renovated modelling of engagement with the ways in which history might be seen to work (or how it might be undermined). The different time of the vampire's experience undermines the normative quality of human time, exposing how anthropo-temporality is simply a constructed discourse.

Modern times

Time is, of course, an abiding concern of texts that are not strictly defined as 'horror', although the anxieties described by them might suggest concern about the horrific quality of different temporalities. Common in science fiction, children's novels, and graphic fiction, time-travel and time-slip texts eschew rationality and historiographic positivism, instead concentrating on the strangeness of the encounter with the past and the ethical trauma associated with any experience of history. Such motifs invoke an ethical dimension to lived experience of, or engagement with, the past.[41] A good example is the whimsical *Midnight in Paris* (Woody Allen, 2011), in which Owen Wilson moves between 1920s Paris and the contemporary moment. The film introduces a number of ethical issues, not least regarding relationships and lives that Wilson's character knows too much about (those of Scott and Zelda Fitzgerald, for instance). He writes a novel that involves someone working in a heritage shop, selling memorabilia, and the film makes much of its self-conscious meditation upon timeliness, history, and memory. The film concludes that the dream of the past might be able to help life in the present, but to live constantly in the past is a nostalgic illusion. Such films challenge the realistic, positivist, authenticist epistemology often found in contemporary historical culture, suggesting a potentiality and imaginative innovation that are lacking elsewhere.[42] These texts provide a skewed, strange reflection of various key ideas in contemporary physics and neuroscience, particularly relating to quantum mechanics, string and chaos theory, parallel world theory, and mental time travel.[43] Furthermore, they offer a useful way of conceptualizing memory, historicity, and the spectre of the past in the present. As with the zombie and vampire examples, these texts demonstrate an anxiety in popular culture in relation to time, and revenant narratives of the past. What is dead, or out of time, might somehow return; indeed, the entire rational model of temporality that structures the Western imaginative universe, the ideology of absolute time, might be troubled and undermined. Modern culture's concern with time travel, or the literal return of the 'dead', illustrates an obsession with the way in which temporal comprehension works. Conceptualizing on a multi-temporal basis is something that is fundamentally human, according to modern neuroscience, and these texts allow for a diversity of approaches to something that wrongly seems comprehensible, transhistorical, and transcultural: that is, *time*.[44] Time apprehension – and its mind-bending complexity – is often the subject of jokes in such texts: 'I don't want to talk about time travel because if we start talking about it then we're going to be here all day talking about it, making diagrams with straws'.[45] What is key to note is the malleability of time in contemporary renderings, with the consequences of this flexibility for cultural understanding of contemporary agency in relation to discourses of temporality, chronology, memory, and narrative.[46] Additionally, it might be argued that European time is the last key ideology to remain relatively untroubled in the mainstream. As discussed below, models of historical time have been primarily challenged within the academy for their contribution to discourses of progress, not least in relation to Western and colonial time.[47] However, the robust centrality of ideologies of time in mainstream culture has proven hard to shift. These current texts provide a forum of discussion for the ways that time works and, importantly, how it is constructed as an interpellating and interpretative discourse. They go someway, therefore, to providing a space of critique of totalizing, oppressive models of temporality and, hence, of identity.

Emblematic of this cultural concern with time travel is the BBC TV series *Doctor Who*. Since the 1960s, the show has played with notions of 'time' and enjoyed bending its own logic, while also challenging cultural conceptions of linearity and progression.[48] In the final episode of the 2013 series, for instance, an enemy enters the Doctor's timeline – which he has hidden – and destroys the present by changing the past. The Doctor is saved by his companion, Clara, who enters his timeline and continually saves him from death – and thereafter is the 'impossible girl', who herself has to be saved from such fragmentation by the intervention of the Doctor into his own timeline ('The Name of the Doctor'). Earlier in that series, the Doctor had argued against events being in any way fixed or concrete ('Cold War'), suggesting a temporal flexibility (although the series has also, on occasion, argued for 'fixed points' in time that are impossible to change). Certainly, the show disavows a temporal harmony, asking that viewers be comfortable with shifts in time, particularly those that wipe memory (one whole episode in this series, 'Journey to the Centre of the Tardis', simply does not happen, as it is written 'out' of time). There is logic, but it is not an ordering symmetry. The Doctor reflects the fragility of 'History', something that might be both physically changed and edited into something textually new. History is not a fixed point, something ineffable, a set of coordinates. Time travel in popular culture enables this rewriting – in fact, the ability to change the past (and, hence, the future) is a fundamental trope in much film and television. It is at once a pop cultural version of psychoanalysis (bad things happen in the past; changing them can heal the psychotic present) and demonstrative of an overarching linear sense of temporality and causality.

This is taken to a logical extreme in the film *Source Code* (Duncan Jones, 2011), in which an agent is repeatedly sent back to the same moment (just before a train explodes) to discover who did the crime. In *Source Code*, Jake Gyllenhaal revisits the last 8 minutes of a man's life in order to try to discover who bombed the train he was on. Through a combination of high-tech mastery and the hokey revelation that the mind contains an afterimage or memory of the last 8 minutes, the film suggests that the final moments of a life might be crucial. Similarly, in *Déjà Vu* (Tony Scott, 2006), Denzel Washington's ATF agent uses space-bending technology to avoid the bombing of a boat in New Orleans. Both films demonstrate a tendency in recent Hollywood film to use 'science' to provide an alternative account of how the past and the present might relate to one another, seeking to provide an escape from death through the potentiality of time travel. This allows a conservative, closed-down sense of pastness, despite the seeming radicalism of the disruptions to linearity. Consequently, both films ultimately allow their protagonists to subvert and change the past in order to usher a new, hopeful future (breaking the film's own logic in *Source Code*), complete with a certain romantic resolution. There is a tragedy to this – a clear sense that, had people known in advance of a terrorist attack (something that Paul Greengrass's 2006 dramadoc *United 93* deals with thoughtfully), then it could have been averted somehow. There is a desire to be able to return and make amends – but these amends are to be the elimination of (internal) threat, rather than restitution of any other kind. The counterpoint with *United 93* is instructive – these films suggest an anxiety about bombing and a desire to be able to return to the moment of attack and undo it, a post-9/11 haunting of the possibility of traumatic events simply not happening if anticipated correctly. *Source Code* is gruelling in the constant replaying of the moment of explosion, constantly reviewing the horror of the past in the hope that it might not occur. Both *Déjà Vu* and *Source Code* allow for resolution – the bombers are found – and, hence, suggest that a constant return to the past might allow for a happier resolution in the present and future. Yet the logic of *Source Code* is that the events are repeatedly happening in a variety of timelines, and that the only one that includes a happy ending is that of the film. Therefore, 'escape' is clearly a narrative and formal convention, a resolution that is constructed.

The mournfulness of time travel, together with its dehumanizing nature, is continually represented in *Doctor Who*. The alien character of the Doctor is numbed owing to his being outside history and without linearity. This alienation is similarly addressed in the conclusion to *Captain America: The First Avenger* (Joe Johnson, 2011). While saving the world during the Second World War, the superhero crashes in the polar ice cap, where he is frozen, and subsequently wakes into the modern world. His last conversation before he crashes is with a woman he loves, who is brutally consigned to the 'past' by the film (there is a clear echo here of the dying pilot who cheats death through love in Michael Powell's and Emeric Pressburger's *A Matter of Life and Death* from 1946).[49] A further Marvel/ Disney film, *The Wolverine* (James Mangold, 2013) features a titular character who does not age between 1945 and the present owing to a healing ability. Wolverine, hence, lives physically outside time, does not have material time in his existence, and this is seen to be his tragedy. He is figured as someone without family or definition, a loner wandering in search of purpose. Both *The Wolverine* and *Thor: The Dark World* (Alan Taylor, 2013) have moments when seemingly dead characters return to life, showing again the Hollywood–Disney obsession with surmounting mortal linearity. *Tangled* (Nathan Greno and Byron Howard, 2010), for instance, similarly features a magical resurrection. Much like the vampire, the undying hero in these instances is suggested to lose (or never have) something manifestly human, that is, a clear sense of their specific historicity and place within the *linear* movement of time. The texts suggest that shifting through time is problematic, something to be feared, something that challenges the boundaries of humanness and historicized identity. To be 'human' in the strictest sense of the term is to be within linear temporality. However, the characters in these examples are super- and supra-human, heroes to be celebrated, as much as their uncanny inhumanity might be problematic (see also *The League of Extraordinary Gentlemen*, Stephen Norrington, 2003).

In the second Captain America film, *The Winter Soldier* (Anthony and Joe Russo, 2014), the palpable sense of being out of time is part of the film's critique of the military–industrial complex governing modernity. The Captain, now living in the contemporary world, despite being 95 years old, finds solace in visiting dying elderly friends and the exhibit of his wartime exploits in the Smithsonian Museum. He feels melancholic, unable to connect, unhappy, and anxious. The modern world cannot understand him, and the incomprehension is mutual. He is literally strange, but, more than this, he is stateless, off the grid, without identity, and therefore written out of modernity. He is a refugee from the past, without family, nation, or friends, an orphan. The film communicates the undesirability of this kind of communication between the past and present: what is then should never be now, without the correct linear time in between making then into now. The intrusion of something past into the present is traumatic and troubling. Yet it is also something that reminds the present of what it has lost. Peggy Carter, the now-dying woman who was his lover in the first film, says to him that the world was made worse by those in charge after the seemingly morally clean victory of 1945, suggesting a clear critique of post-war American policy. The modern S.H.I.E.L.D. organization, a thinly veiled Homeland Security, seeks increasing surveillance of the entire world and the ability to address threats before they happen. This 'modern' warfare is contrasted with the Captain's 'greatest generation', who would only respond to violence. This idealized and nostalgic sense of the fairness of the past, in comparison with the overly complex and terrifying present, feeds the film's tone of paranoia and anxiety. Although the appearance of the Captain in the present is troubling, it also exposes modernity to an ethical challenge. Together, the Captain and his maverick associates destroy the 'future', literally, by blowing up the helicarriers that would undertake global surveillance.

Although it is important to recall the constraints (and possibilities) of genre, it is clear that films that have a more flexible sense of time are actively challenging those that are more fixed. So, in this case, for instance, both *X-Men: Days of Future Past* (Bryan Singer, 2014) and *Captain America: The First Avenger* shift between past and present in order to illustrate a contrast between timelines. This is illustrated culturally (through behaviour) and aesthetically (the shiny modernism of 'now' and the future, as opposed to the somewhat tattered realistic versions of the 1960s and the 1940s). They lay bare, therefore, the different aesthetic and representational (and narrative) strategies of 'fantasy' or science-fiction films and 'costume drama'. In this, they open up a space of critique of the realist authenticity of costume drama, demonstrating how it cleaves to a particular type of nationalist, absolute time (that of the house, truth, order, the family, dominant ideologies, heteronormative relations, stability, modern capital, class, and conservatism). By incorporating elements of period drama – moments of 'authentic' representation of past moments – these two films interrogate the reified version of the past, and of time, that the genre articulates. They are suggestive of the ways that costume drama plays with anachronism (and is itself fundamentally anachronistic). Their proleptic qualities mimic the time-travelling aspect common to all historical fictions.

Challenges to history and temporality might be virtuous rather than worrying. *Source Code* seeks to solve 'crimes' by locating the evil and neutralizing it, hence rendering the present a more peaceful place. *Déjà Vu* similarly looks to make the change in the past to correct the future, to literally challenge one timeline by silently replacing it with another. *Looper* (2012) involves a man attempting to kill a future version of himself. The film is self-conscious about the vagaries and paradoxes of time travel, but seeks a way out, some means of avoiding the logic:

> Then I saw it. A mom that would die for her son. A man that would kill for his wife. A boy angry and alone. Laid out in front of him, the bad path, I saw it. That path was a circle. So I changed it.

This demonstrates the way in which Hollywood uses time travel to escape and change history to become anew, to render the world innocent again. In order to create something 'good' and a happier world, time might be challenged and transformed. These texts demonstrate a fascination with the implications for time of quantum mechanics (and parallel universe theory). The films strive to use an interpretation of contemporary pop 'science' to provide an alternative account of how the past and the present might relate to one another, seeking always to provide an escape from death through the potentiality of time travel. This allows a conservative, closed-down sense of pastness, despite the seeming radicalism of the disruptions to linearity. They are also the most recent manifestations of cinema's interest in staging encounters with or in the past as something that impacts upon the contemporary moment (and that might be changed or reconstructed somehow). This is most obvious in *Back to the Future* (Robert Zemeckis, 1985) and other time-travel films such as *Bill and Ted's Excellent Adventure* (Stephen Herek, 1989), but it might be argued to be clear in non-generic films. Such films present a particular relationship to pastness, a dynamic engagement with events that shape the now. The relationship to what has happened is flexible and might be changed. The point is that pastness in contemporary Hollywood cinema is somewhat malleable. This is a subversion of 'history', insofar as it argues a malleability of linearity and a way of challenging what has happened, but it also suggests a dynamic sense of pastness rather than the construction of a narrative of past (i.e. a 'history'). Furthermore, the very fact that these films are working through a model of the contemporary's relationship to the past implies a clear historiographic sense that arguably pervades (in multiple manifestations) contemporary popular culture. Finally, these films seek to valorize a future through their tinkering with the past. They address an idealized point some time from now, suggesting that a shift in pastness can lead to the development of something in time to come.

A key element of these films is the chance to conquer, or delay, death. Death is continually mastered in science-fiction films, ranging from *Star Wars* (George Lucas, 1977) to *The Matrix* (The Wachowski Brothers, 1999). The overtly Christian notion of sacrifice and rebirth is a narrative arc that is reworked repeatedly, contrasting in some ways with the materialist, secular inhumanness of the horror tropes discussed elsewhere in this chapter. Films as diverse as *Edge of Tomorrow* (Doug Liman, 2014) and *Groundhog Day* (Harold Ramis, 1993) demonstrate a concern with temporality and particularly with repetition – in the former, a soldier fighting aliens 'loops' or resets events and can replay them more successfully; in the latter, the same day is played out repeatedly until the 'correct' outcome ensues. *Edge of Tomorrow* mimics gaming structures where storylines can be replayed repeatedly with more success (and avatars never really 'die'), but also suggests, along with many of the military-led science fictions discussed here, a Western concern with combat loss and a desire for a type of invulnerability. The possibility of surmounting death through tinkering with time or changing a timeline is fundamental. These texts illustrate a desire for futurity to be saved as much as the present or the past. Certainly implicit in the re-rendering of the past is a reordering of the future, as *Doctor Who*, *Looper*, and *X-Men: Days of Future Past* overwhelmingly demonstrate. Therefore, new configurations of time might lead to new possibilities of futurity; maintaining Western, anglophone, mainstream, 'authentic', truthful versions of time not only constrains the past but limits the future.

A more generically mainstream text that interrogates contemporary temporality in order to critique it both diegetically and formally is *True Detective* (HBO, 2014). Consideration of this series will also lead us towards ideas of the archive and models of trauma that will be discussed in Chapter 6. This series also sees the collapse of 'authentic' models for rendering past events in the face of the horror of inflexible temporality. Formally, the series works as a kind of time-shift narrative, as it presents versions of a story from several different temporal viewpoints. It begins with the retelling of the discovery and investigation of a crime in 1995. This retelling is in the 'present', which is not actually a diegetic 'now' but 2012; other action happens in 2002. The original crime investigation is itself being investigated, which means each participant is giving a witness statement regarding events (and it is clear that they are not telling all of the truth). The show, therefore, participates in the discourse of authenticity in rendering the past, while playing self-conscious narrative games with the audience. It dramatizes shifts in time and anxieties about memory; it also renders clear the relationship between occurrence and textual trace (i.e. narrative 'event' and archival recording).

This is common enough in contemporary drama, particularly in relation to crime. Numerous series deploy multiple viewpoints or temporal locations to complicate narrative. What makes *True Detective* key to a discussion of temporality is its diegetic contemplation of a set of philosophies, from Nietzsche to Heidegger. Cohle (Matthew McConaughey), one of the two partners investigating the original crime, is incredibly cerebral and pessimistic–nihilistic. His bleak worldview is communicated through a set of conversations during drives with his partner, Hart (Woody Harrelson). He claims that, 'human consciousness is a tragic misstep in human evolution'.[50] This becomes a bombastic critique of the modern self:

> We became too self aware; nature created an aspect of nature separate from itself [. . .] We are things that labour under the illusion of having a self, a secretion of sensory experience and feeling, programmed with total assurance that we are each somebody, when in fact everybody's nobody.

The only solution, Cohle claims, is as follows: 'I think the honourable thing for our species to do is deny our programming, stop reproducing, walk hand in hand into extinction, one last midnight, brothers and sisters opting out of a raw deal'.

Cohle's verbose and articulate philosophical musings foreground a series of questions about genre, ethics, and representation of the past.[51] He sees humanity as its own 'other', an aberration in natural law, and something, tellingly, that depends on a misguided sense of self that depends on teleology and development. The only way to answer this is simply to *stop*. His dread of the world is used to force the audience to consider the ethics of representation and what it is to be human and in time. He argues, echoing Nietzsche (and the 'circle' of *Looper*):

> Why should I live in history, huh? I don't want to know anything any more. This is a world where nothing is solved. Someone once told me, 'time is a flat circle', everything we've ever done or will do we'll do again.[52]

The horror of the repetition of a type of temporality, the bleakness of this philosophy, reflects a certainty that humanity is lost and without purpose. It also suggests something about genre (someone will always have to be murdered for the form to exist) and simultaneity (all moments happen at once, returning us to the earlier discussions of Einsteinian physics). The climactic scene of *True Detective* has Cohle, near death, hallucinating a vision of a vortex. He − and the audience − looks into the void, the abyss, the bleak inhumanity of space. This vision is shared with the audience, placing them directly in line with Cohle's nihilistic understanding of the utter futility of things (and the echoing darkness). That a television text should be engaging with these issues is not at all extraordinary − crime TV has been engaged with a discussion of pessimism and nihilism through its protagonists for decades. Yet this particular example is overridingly concerned with the way in which time works and how that relates to testimony, memory, and identity.

Yet the series is forced into narrative resolution, unable to simply leave things unresolved, messy, chaotic. The demands of genre (itself a kind of temporality) and narrative form (similarly concerned with telling only the important bits of the story within a temporal framework) undermine its address to something more ineffable. This awkward conjunction adds to the self-consciousness of the text. The audience is encouraged to see the problems inherent in narrativizing events, turning the chaos and violence of the world into a 'story'. Hence, *True Detective* is a popular cultural text engaging with complex historiographical and philo-sophical issues and expecting its audience to use these concepts, not only to understand the show, but also to critique it. It introduces multiple temporalities to dislocate an understanding and to challenge the idea of an affirming whole-ness of time. Consequently, it challenges underlying assumptions about time and history, particularly relating to linearity, chronology, teleology, and positivism.

Time and magic and narrative: *Hugo*

To conclude this chapter's consideration of time, rebirth, the possible revenant, and the haunting of history, it is necessary to consider a key text regarding the representation of the past *on film*. The rendering of the past in the present is the work of the illusionist, as the 1930s-set *Hugo* (Martin Scorsese, 2011) articulates clearly. The relationship between time, narrative, illusion, pleasure, and identity are explored in the light of the desire, through dreaming film, for the return of the dead, or the re-rendering of what once was. *Hugo* both articulates and decon-structs the idea of pleasure in the text. On the one hand, the film is a celebration of dreaming and the joy of cinema. On the other, its obsession with the mechanics of film-making and time-making demonstrates the way in which things are created through technology and the manipulation of machinery. The film obsessively pairs the ephemeral with the mechanical, showing how dreams are made, as shown early on by this line from the film historian René Tabard: 'My brother worked as a carpenter making sets for [George] Méliès. He took me once to see a set − it was like a dream'. The great director encounters the child Tabard and asks if he dreams, because 'this is where they're made'.[53] This conjunction of making and dreaming demonstrates the film's interest in the material construction of something seemingly indistinct. [On the one hand, then, *Hugo* meditates on the pleasure of the text – books, films, clocks, and magic are all celebrated for the sense of wonder that they might engender – where, on the other hand, there is a strong awareness that illusions are made, simple constructions that people believe in because they lack something – a father, a family, wholeness, the heart-shaped key that is lost throughout the film.]

From the outset, with the camera zooming in on Hugo looking at Montparnasse station through the action of its clock (see the cover of this book), the film demonstrates an obsession with time and the mechanics of temporality. Hugo's father is a watchmaker, but he also works at a museum – he combines the task of keeping the now *now* with those of preserving and remembering the past. After his death, Hugo is brought by his rough uncle to keep the clocks in the station going. The film relishes the clockwork complexity of the station's margins, swooping around and following the running boy as he adjusts, oils, tinkers, and makes precise the various clocks that ensure social accuracy. Hugo's unseen work is crucial to the functioning of the station and, hence, to urban capitalism and its associated modernity – as demonstrated by the faceless masses of business people who stampede through the station at times (nearly killing the child Isabelle), by the unstoppable careering of the train that nearly kills Hugo (and does, in a dream, destroy the station), or by the constant checking of the time by characters through-out (particularly the lawmaker (the station constable), keen on disciplining the society of the station through his imposition of models of governance). The workings of modernity's linear time are represented here by power and violence, then, and a challenge to the innocence of childhood. Both children in the film are threatened by the overpowering, trampling progression of capitalist modernity – the mass, the train – in ways that suggest the onward rush of time is implacable and inhuman. Yet this rush of time is constructed, made, the product of social networks that impinges upon the body and the relationships between people.

Time in this film becomes a character. That is, the ways that time might be made – recorded, marked, audited – play a supporting role. This is literalized at one point, with Hugo hanging from the hands of the station clock, an image that both demonstrates the material reality of 'time' and is, of course, a reference to something from *another* time, that is, the Harold Lloyd film *Safety Last* (Fred C. Newmeyer and Sam Taylor, 1923) that Isabelle and Hugo watch a little earlier in the film. Hugo himself *makes* the time, ensuring that the thing that forces people into this implacable action is maintained. The film lovingly dwells on the clockwork elements that he tends to. The automaton he discovers, the machine that 'lives', also works in the same way – is powered by clockwork, by time – as are the toys that Papa George sells on the station platform. The cinema itself is also driven by time, both in terms of chronology – film works in a linear fashion, technically, being wound through a camera in front of light – and in terms of freezing time, holding action on celluloid. Scorsese himself notes, in an essay discussing the film history important to *Hugo*, 'that's the third aspect of cinema that makes it so uniquely powerful – it's the element of time'.[54]

At one point during a sequence about film-making, a cameraman is shown with a metronome, reminding the audience that film works according to a precise sense of time (although, obviously, one that is mechanically produced). The mechanics of early film production were dependent on certain technical aspects – lighting, the winding of film – being as precise as possible in order to create the requisite 'reality' and, hence, illusion required. So, the creation of time and the creation of film are aligned, both being material activities – using clockwork, light, machinery, and human interaction – that both ensure illusion and collaborate in the sense that this illusion is somehow *not* made. Industrial-capitalist time similarly requires that the subject renounce their agency by accepting chrononormativity; that is, by allowing their body to be governed by a time that is itself in thrall to the wider system, but also collaborating in making this time, or at least observing it and making it worthy of worship. The clocks are raised high in the station (itself a monument to new industrial capital), reified rulers and surveyors of those below them.[55] Hugo himself expresses a very modernist sense of the city, suggesting, when overlooking Paris, that the metropolis is one big industrial machine with no spare parts (so that everyone has a function).[56] The imperial capitalist city is a watch, imposing structural time upon the bodies of its inhabitants and ensuring compliance in a particular way of acting and living.

The children encounter film historian René Tabard, who outlines the story of film from the early 'realism' of the Lumière brothers' *Arrival of a Train at La Ciotat* (1895). He argues that film moved from a 'sideshow' once people realized that they could 'use the new medium to tell stories'. The contrast is between the 'documentary' realism of the Lumière film – shown twice in *Hugo*, with a fearful audience fleeing the train on both occasions – and the imaginative excursions of the true geniuses such as Charlie Chaplin, Buster Keaton, Louise Brooks, and the like. This is the progression of early cinema, from the 'real' to the imagined, via the imposition of an illusory temporality. George Méliès tells the story of film similarly in a later scene, but claims that the war in 1914 ended 'hope' and the magic of cinema. The onset of a particular type of European modernity (and a kind of horrified sense of chronology and time) renders his work marginal and forgettable, rejected by a newly cynical and traumatized public. The men who came back from the war, he claims, did not want escapist fantasy but something harder and more 'real'. Méliès and Tabard, in their accounts, both point out the key role of *editing* in creating film, dramatizing the way that reality can be bent, warped, distressed. They reflect upon the ways that narrative is created through the manipulation of screen time and the construction of an illusory temporality.

The film highlights, through the character of Tabard, the taxonomization of film (and culture) through the actions of the archive and the academy. Seeking to understand the automaton's drawing, the children seek out the Film Academy Library, as 'you'll find all you need to know about movies there'. Film has become something that has an archive, a history, and, hence, authority and order. As a medium now, it participates in the disciplining of the past through this collecting of information. Scorsese is himself a historian of film, archivist, reconstructor, and director of the Film Foundation archive that is dedicated to film preservation. When

Méliès cannot pay his creditors, his film is melted down into its constituent chemical parts and sold. This demonstrates the physical materiality of film – celluloid is simply a confection of chemicals that somehow produces something engaging and beautiful. Yet, at base, it is nothing more than stuff that would be worth more if sold for industrial purposes. *Hugo*'s concluding sequence shows a festival of forgotten film, celebrating those fragments, offcuts, and edits that have been saved from the fire and now live as reified objects of wonder. *Hugo* is here a loving reconstruction of films that have been lost, a re-enactment of the early stages of cinema. It includes footage of Louise Brooks, Charlie Chaplin, and Buster Keaton. It creates a clear sense of cinema history and, therefore, acts as something of an educator about the teleology and development of film.

At the same time, the movie argues that film is a dream, a revenant of the past that can provide pleasure and make us happy in the present. It is something captured and frozen, but edited and manipulated, a way of communicating a story of the past that viewers know to be untrue. Méliès says this when discussing the form's move from 'sideshow' and early documentary: 'they could use the new medium to tell stories'. This tension between entertainment, fact, and storytelling is inherent in all film, but becomes more epistemologically important when one considers historical representation. *Hugo* is interested in the work of George Méliès in the main because his films are fantasias, rather than realist – they express a phantasmagorical strangeness and wonder at the opportunity afforded by cinema, rather than attempting to record reality.[57] The film comments upon the enjoyment of cinema by itself being enjoyable cinema, pointing out the falseness of such a construction. It is in a realist mode but highly wrought, both in terms of the storyline, which involves flashback and some fantasy sequences, but also formally, given that it was shot in stereoscopic 3D. This new technology itself invites the audience to be excited about innovation as well as challenging the traditional space–time relationship of audience to film.[58] It prompts audience members to think about their own pleasure and the ways that it is being constructed and manipulated. Stereoscopic film allows an audience to rethink its relationship to the 'real', immersive authenticity of the cinema.

Roland Barthes famously considered historical photographs to chronicle death foretold:

> I read at the same time: This will be and this has been; I observe with horror an anterior future of which death is the stake. By giving me the absolute past of the pose (aorist), the photograph tells me death in the future. What pricks me is the discovery of this equivalence.
>
> In front of the photograph of my mother as a child, I tell myself: she is going to die: I shudder, like Winnicott's psychotic patient, over a catastrophe which has already occurred.[59]

Barthes sees death in still photography and argues that the tropes of the picture work so powerfully on him that the human need not appear; the photograph (whatever it is of) reeks of the death that defeats linearity.[60] He continues:

Whether or not the subject is already dead, every photograph is this catastrophe. This *punctum*, more or less blurred beneath the abundance and the disparity of contemporary photographs, is vividly legible in historical photographs: there is always a defeat of Time in them: that is dead and that is going to die. These two little girls looking at a primitive airplane above their village (they are dressed like my mother as a child, they are playing with hoops) – how alive they are! They have their whole lives before them; but also they are dead (today), they are then already dead (yesterday). At the limit, there is no need to represent a body in order for me to experience this vertigo of time defeated.[61]

The picture stands outside History insofar as it records the 'defeat of Time'; images are powerful because of their ability to draw the viewer back into a past they know is no longer, to act as a mediating point between then and now (but a then that is no longer). They force the beholder to recognize their own historicity through conceptualizing their relationship to that-which-was (and is no more), and, presumably, to recognize the inevitability of their own death. This 'catastrophe which has already occurred' forces a visceral reaction ('I shudder'), despite an intellectual comprehension. The text from the past forces Barthes to see rationally his relationship to this unrecognized but uncannily familiar 'past', to interrogate the idea of a 'history' with any kind of ordering principle, and, importantly, to physically respond (unconsciously) to the violent otherness depicted.

Every image contains this end – 'Whether or not the subject is already dead, every photograph is this catastrophe'. This is 'Barthes's insistence that photography is haunted by the morbid promise of death'.[62] The picture communicates something that has already died; for Barthes, this reveals the 'equivalence' between future and past. The past is horribly other, but the real shock of understanding is that the future is similarly other, as is the present. The still photograph reminds us of mortality – it is a moment frozen in time. He describes the '*punctum*', the moment of then–nowness that the image creates. The queer simultaneity of the image in this instance also suggests the 'syncopated time' articulated by Rebecca Schneider (using the ideas of Gertrude Stein) when discussing re-enactment and performance, 'where *then* and *now* punctuate each other'.[63] What this syncopation creates is an awareness of the strangeness of time in performance, the ways in which then is part of now, and vice versa. Historical fictions achieve a type of syncopation, insofar as they gesture towards the strangeness of the then in the now, striving for such an affective *punctum* while presenting a fictional representation. What, then, of film of a past the audience knows did not occur? Does it matter? Do moving images still have this jolt of recognition for an alterity (but one of equidistance)? Does the fictional representation of the past in images have this effect? Similarly, how might Benjamin's idea of 'aura' work in relation to the representation of a non-time and idealized memory, a narrative of a past?

The moving image is a revenant of that which was past, a representation of something recognizable but other, a ghost of something that an audience might somehow comprehend. It also looks at them, refiguring identity in the now. Historical images might make the shock of recognition happen, but images that are 'historical' – that is, wrought to look like the past – figure a self-conscious ghosting, a death foretold but not real. Such images are consolations, ways of mediating the imminent/immanent death of the image. Barthes sees the 'vertigo' induced by the images as something that heralds the defeat of death, or the end of Time. Yet what is seen is – self-evidently – a fiction, something dreamt up by us to supersede the real. This is because the real will decay and die, or it has already done so. The performance of the past in historical fictional texts, then, provides some kind of recognition of this then–now–death nexus. It is a victory over time (this is unreal and, therefore, undead), but it also ensures the desire for the dream, the imagined version of the past, rather than the reality. Viewers would rather look at the fiction than consider the actual, horrific obscenity of the 'real'. Barthes reflects upon the images that are echoes of an otherness, and they allow him to contemplate the end of time; he uses them to force himself into an ethical position with relation to the ways in which the past is communicated to us. He articulates a position that is surely historiographical, but, with the idea of *punctum*, something that is unavoidably affective at the same time.[64]

Hugo can never bridge the gap between his father and his current position in 'time' and space. Film both suggests a connection and denies it. When Hugo discovers the automaton, he believes he has found a way to bring the dead to life. The automaton can 'speak' for the dead father, bringing his memory from the past somehow and articulating, through machinery and clockwork, something that will heal the trauma of his death in the present. It provides a bridge between times. In his disappointment (leavened with enchantment) at the automaton's performance – his father does not return – can be seen the distinction between the material and the memory. Literally, what separates the living from the dead here is time. The automaton is given a kind of life through clockwork technology, but is not actually 'alive'; it is as dead as Hugo's father. Rebirth here is not possible, but some kind of interaction with a past – albeit through a 'dead' medium – is possible through various technological interventions, notably, the dream of the cinema. This is counterpoised with the industrial, colonial time of the station.[65] *Hugo* suggests that film might be a repository for memory and some kind of way of surmounting, in a fragile although pleasurable way, the end. This, in itself, is a comment on temporality, arguing for the connectivity of the text, an immediacy of engagement between then and now, unmediated by the actuality of intervening time. However, following Barthes, this connection is never real. It must take place, therefore, within an imagined idealized space – that is, within the dream of the historical fiction. The fiction here becomes utopic, a desired space of reordering and restoration. The *punctum* of the historical fiction is its affective element in the now and the way that this creates syncopation between 'now' and 'narrated then'. The comforting element of the fiction, then (in the case of *Hugo*, the film), is that the loop is not 'then–now' (hence including death in the now) but 'now–then'. There is no death here. The audience is located in a carefully syncopated relationship with the 'past', and this comforting fiction enables the restitution of a contemporary identity. Mourning has no place in this relationship, as *Hugo* argues, because the simultaneity and 'nowness' of film can somehow surmount the temporal and spatial gaps between bodies.

The various texts considered in this chapter – horror, children's fantasy, time travel – demonstrate a concern with the way that time works and is experienced. They undermine phenomenologically normative models of temporality, presenting instead a range of different ways of experiencing and comprehending time. As Bevernage and Lorenz argue, challenges to temporal ordering are themselves articulating a radical, new historiographical position:

> Although many historians have noticed these developments, only few have developed new conceptualisations of historical time. Even though the traditional notion of (linear) time has been heavily criticised in the decades since Einstein's relativity theories, the time-concepts of historians, as well as philosophers of history, are still generally based on an absolute, homogeneous and empty time. Not accidentally, this is a notion of time presupposed by the 'imagined community' of 'the nation' as Benedict Anderson famously suggested.[66]

Manuel de landa's "1000 years of Non-Linear History" is one example of a rethinking of linear time.

Models of time are used to impose structures upon social groupings through the intervention of linear and solid models of history. Ordering structures such as nationhood, empire, capitalism, modernity, and history itself are dependent on particular, linear, monolithic modes of temporality. If time is understood to be complex and in flux, then the articulation of an ordering history is similarly troubled. Rather than accept the ideological implications of particular definitions of time, the texts considered here experiment and interrogate them. They provide an insight into contemporary thinking about the relationship of the past and the present. Apart from anything else, they reflect upon different temporal states and experiences. In particular, *Hugo* reflects upon the way that the representation of time through celluloid and image exemplifies an abiding need for a connection that is impossible. Contemporary monster films demonstrate an anxiety regarding the disruption of time and, hence, the interruption of a kind of historiographic normality. They challenge the uninflected representation of time in 'mainstream' costume and period fictions, substituting instead a clear understanding of the fragile nature of temporal experience and, hence, contemporary identity. The past, here, is terrifying in many ways, but a renewed conceptualization of how it relates to the now and how it is represented and narrated in the contemporary moment might provide some comfort.

Notes

1 *Gothic* (London and New York: 2005), p. 102.
2 'Introduction: Gothic in Contemporary Popular Culture', *Gothic Studies*, 9:1 (2007), 1–4, p. 1; *Contemporary Gothic* (London: Reaktion, 2007), p. 9. See also Glennis Byron, 'Global

Gothic' in David Punter, ed., *A New Companion to the Gothic* (Oxford, UK: Wiley-Blackwell, 2012), pp. 369–79.

3 *The Wounds of Nations: Horror Cinema, Historical Trauma and National Identity* (Manchester, UK: Manchester University Press, 2008), p. 23.

4 *Shocking Representation: Historical Trauma, National Cinema, and the Modern Horror Film* (New York: Columbia University Press, 2005), p. 2.

5 Jerrold E. Hogle, 'History, Trauma and the Gothic in Contemporary Western Fictions' in Glennis Byron and Dale Townshend, eds, *The Gothic World* (London and New York: Routledge, 2014), pp. 72–83.

6 *Stranded in the Present: Modern Time and the Melancholy of History* (Harvard, MA: Harvard University Press, 2010), p. 8.

7 François Hartog, 'Time and Heritage', *Museum International*, 57:3 (2005), 7–18 (p. 8).

8 Paul Ricoeur, *Time and Narrative*, trans. Kathleen McLaughlin (Chicago, IL: University of Chicago Press, 1990), p. 7.

9 Ricoeur (*Time and Narrative*, p. 86):

> At times it will be the hermeneutic phenomenology of time that provides the key to the hierarchizing of narrative, other times it will be the disciplines concerned with historical and fictional narrative that allow us to resolve poetically – to use an expression already employed – the most speculatively intractable aporias of the phenomenology of time.

10 Berber Bevernage and Chris Lorenz, 'Introduction' in Chris Lorenz and Berber Bevernage, eds, *Breaking Up Time* (Gottingen and Bristol, CT: Vandenhoeck & Ruprecht, 2013), pp. 7–39 (p. 11).

11 Peter Burke, 'Reflections on the Cultural History of Time', *Viator*, 35 (2004), 617–26 (p. 617).

12 There is much work in this area in queer and performance studies; see particularly Elizabeth Freeman, *Time Binds: Queer Temporalities, Queer Histories* (Raleigh, NC: Duke University Press, 2010); Carla Freccero, *Queer/Early/Modern* (Durham, NC: Duke University Press, 2006); and Rebecca Schneider, *Performing Remains* (London and New York: Routledge, 2011). This scholarship builds on the large body of philosophical work on time, from Benjamin, Stein, and Heidegger through to Paul Ricoeur.

13 Maria Mulvany, 'Spectral Histories: The Queer Temporalities of Emma Donoghue's *Slammerkin*', *Irish University Review*, 43:1 (2013), 157–68 (p. 158).

14 J. Cull Nicholas, 'Peter Watkins' *Culloden* and the alternative form in historical filmmaking', *Film International*, 1:1 (2003), 48–53.

15 *Berberian Sound Studio* (Peter Strickland, 2012).

16 Spooner, *Contemporary Gothic*, p. 11.

17 Roger Clark and Keith McDonald, '"A Constant Transit of Finding": Fantasy as Realisation in *Pan's Labyrinth*', *Children's Literature in Education*, 41:1 (2010), 52–63.

18 See David Archibald, 'Re-framing the Past: Representations of the Spanish Civil War in Popular Spanish Cinema' in Antonio Lázaro Reboll and Andrew Willis, eds, *Spanish Popular Cinema* (Manchester, UK: Manchester University Press, 2004), pp. 76–92.

19 J.M. Tyree, 'Warm-Blooded: *True Blood* and *Let the Right One In*', *Film Quarterly*, 63:2 (2009), 31–7.

20 Erica Burman, *Developments: Child, Image, Nation* (London and New York: Routledge, 2008), p. 13. I owe this quote to Christopher Vardy.

21 Erik Butler, *Metamorphoses of the Vampire in Literature and Film* (Rochester, NY: Camden House, 2010), p. vi. See also the still influential arguments made by Jeffrey Jerome Cohen: 'Monster Theory: 7 Theses' in Jeffrey Jerome Cohen, ed., *Monster Theory* (Minneapolis, MN: University of Minnesota Press, 1996), pp. 3–20.

22 Kyle Bishop, 'Dead Man Still Walking: Explaining the Zombie Renaissance', *Journal of Popular Film & Television*, 37:1 (2006), 16–25.

23 See, for instance, discussions in Robert A. Saunders, 'Undead Spaces: Fear, Globalisation, and the Popular Geopolitics of Zombiism', *Geopolitics*, 17:1, 80–104, and Kyle Bishop, 'Raising the Dead', *Journal of Popular Film and Television*, 33:4, 196–205.

24 Fred Botting, 'Post-Millenial Monsters' in Glennis Byron and Dale Townshend, eds, *The Gothic World* (London and New York: Routledge, 2014), pp. 498–510 (p. 509). See also his 'Love Your Zombie: Horror, Ethics, Excess' in Justin D. Edwards and Agnieszka S. Monnet, eds, *The Gothic in Contemporary Literature and Popular Culture* (London and New York: Routledge, 2012), pp. 19–36.

25 Although one of the key develements in the anthropomorphizing of zombies has been their ability to develop and evolve, as is the case in *Land of the Dead* (George A. Romero, 2005). See also Sarah Juliet Lauro and Karen Embry, 'A Zombie Manifesto: The Nonhuman Condition in the Era of Advanced Capitalism', *boundary 2*, 35:1 (2008), 85 108.

26 David McNally, *Monsters of the Market: Zombies, Vampires and Global Capitalism* (Leiden, Netherlands: Brill, 2009).

27 Annalee Newitz, *Pretend We're Dead: Capitalist Monsters in American Pop Culture* (Durham, NC: Duke University Press, 2006).

28 Robert Kirkman and Tony Moore, *The Walking Dead: Days Gone Bye* (Berkley, CA: Image Comics Inc, 2010), back cover.

29 A good account of this latter idea is in Martin L. Davies, *Historics* (London and New York: Routledge, 2006).

30 Marc Augé, *Non-places: An Introduction to Supermodernity*, trans. John Howe (London: Verso, 2009).

31 Angela Tenga and Elizabeth Zimmerman, 'Vampire Gentlemen and Zombie Beasts: A Rendering of True Monstrosity', *Gothic Studies*, 15:1 (2013), 76–87.

32 Butler, *Metamorphoses of the Vampire*, p. vii.

33 Ken Gelder, *Reading the Vampire* (London and New York: Routledge, 1994).

34 Butler, *Metamorphoses of the Vampire*, p. 1.

35 *The History of Gothic Fiction* (Edinburgh, UK: Edinburgh Univeristy Press, 2000), p. 161.

36 Newitz, *Pretend We're Dead*, p. 91.

37 This section on *True Blood* is reprinted from 'Afterword' in Barbara Korte and Sylvia Paletschek, eds, *Popular History Now and Then* (Bielefeld, Germany: transcript, 2012), pp. 281–95.

38 See, for instance, Tony Horwitz, *Confederates in the Attic* (New York: Vintage, 1999), in particular pp. 275–80.

39 'Sparks Fly Out', *True Blood*, Series 1, Episode 5 (2008).

40 Georg Lukács, *The Historical Novel*, trans. Hannah Mitchell (Lincoln, NE: University of Nebraska Press, 1983), p. 24.

41 See Adam Roberts, *Science Fiction* (London and New York: Routledge, 2005). On time-slip, see Tess Cosslett, '"History from Below": Time-Slip Narratives and National Identity', *The Lion and the Unicorn*, 26 (2002), 243–53, and Linda Hall, 'Aristocratic Houses and Radical Politics: Historical Fiction and the Time-Slip Story in E. Nesbit's *The House of Arden*', *Children's Literature in Education*, 29:1 (1998), 51–8.

42 See the discussions of Martin Davies in *Historics* and *Imprisoned by History: Aspects of Historicized Life* (London and New York: Routledge, 2010).

43 On, for instance, Einstein in popular culture, see Katy Price, 'On the Back of the Light Waves: Novel Possibilities in the "Fourth Dimension"', *Essays and Studies*, (2008), pp. 91–110, and Peter Galison, *Einstein's Clocks* (London: Sceptre, 2003).

44 Mental time travel as something specifically human is a controversial topic in neuroscience; see the Special Issue 'Predictions in the Brain: Using Our Past to Prepare for the Future', *Philosophical Transactions of the Royal Society*, 364:1521 (2009).

45 *Looper* (Rian Johnson, 2012). The best-digested version of pop culture's time-travel horrors, possibilities, and dangers is 'Treehouse of Horror V: Time and Punishment', *The Simpsons*, Season 6, Episode 109 (1994).

46 For overviews of time-travel narratives, see Paul J. Nahin, *Time Machines: Time Travel in Physics, Metaphysics, and Science Fiction* (New York: Springer-Verlag, 1999).

47 Key here is the work of Dipesh Chakrabarty, discussed in Chapter 2; see *Provincializing Europe: Postcolonial Thought and History* (Princeton, NJ: Princeton University Press, 2000).

48 There is not space here to consider *Doctor Who* in sufficient depth, and so only the most recent series are concentrated upon. There is a surprising lack of critical work on the series, but see, for instance, John Kenneth Muir, *A Critical History of Doctor Who on Television* (Jefferson, NC: McFarland, 1999), and Courtland Lewis and Paula Smithka, eds, *Doctor Who and Philosophy: Bigger on the Inside* (Chicago, IL: Open Court, 2011).

49 See Andrew Moor, *Powell and Pressburger: A Cinema of Magic Spaces* (London: I.B. Tauris, 2005), pp. 126–68.

50 'The Long Bright Dark', *True Detective*, Series 1, Episode 1 (2014).

51 This was first explored by Michael Calia in a blog and then in an interview with the series writer, Nic Pizzolatto, in the *Wall Street Journal*; available online at: http://blogs.wsj.com/speakeasy/2014/01/30/the-most-shocking-thing-about-hbos-true-detective/ (accessed 24 July 2014); http://blogs.wsj.com/speakeasy/2014/02/02/writer-nic-pizzolatto-on-thomas-ligotti-and-the-weird-secrets-of-true-detective/ (accessed 24 July 2014).

52 'The Secret Fate of All Life', *True Detective*, Series 1, Episode 5 (2014).

53 *Hugo* (Martin Scorsese, 2011).

54 Martin Scorsese, 'The Persisting Vision: Reading the Language of Cinema', *New York Review of Books*, 15 August (2013); available online at: www.nybooks.com/articles/archives/2013/aug/15/persisting-vision-reading-language-cinema/ (accessed 25 July 2014).

55 W.G. Sebald writes at length on the way that the clock in Antwerp station organizes and controls both the building and, by extension, the imperial city; see *Austerlitz*, trans. Anthea Bell (London: Penguin, 2011), pp. 1–3.

56 This is a version of Walter Benjamin's understanding of modernity through considering the arcades of Paris; see Rolf Tiedemann, ed., *The Arcades Project*, trans. Howard Eiland and Kevin McLaughlin (Harvard, MA: Harvard University Press, 2002).

57 See Thomas Elaesser, ed., *Early Cinema: Space, Frame, Narrative* (London: BFI Press, 1990).

58 On concerns regarding stereoscopic film, see Peter A. Howarth, 'Potential Hazards of Viewing 3-D Stereoscopic Television, Cinema and Computer Games: A Review', *Ophthalmic and Physiological Optics*, 31:2 (2011), 111–22. On the mechanics of shooting in 3D, see Bernard Mendiburu, *3D Movie Making: Stereoscopic Digital Cinema From Script to Screen* (Oxford, UK: Focal Press, 2009).

59 Roland Barthes, *Camera Lucida*, trans. Richard Howard (New York: Hill & Wang, 1981), p. 96.

60 See George Kouvaros, 'Images That Remember Us: Photography and Memory in *Austerlitz*', *Textual Practice*, 19 (2005), 173–93.

61 Barthes, *Camera Lucida*, p. 96.

62 Geoffrey Batchen, 'Palinode' in Geoffrey Batchen, ed., *Photography Degree Zero: Reflections on Roland Barthes's Camera Lucida* (Cambridge, MA: MIT Press, 2011), pp. 3–31 (p. 14).

63 Schneider, *Performing Remains*, p. 2.

64 See Michael Fried, 'Barthes's *Punctum*' in Batchen, *Photography Degree Zero*, pp. 141–70.

65 See Sebald's *Austerlitz* on station clocks and time and empire, and, further, J.J. Long, *Austerlitz: Image, Archive, Modernity* (New York: Columbia University Press, 2007).

66 'Introduction' in Lorenz and Berber, *Breaking Up Time*, p. 13.

PART III

Pleasure, affect, and performance

5

PLEASURE AND DESIRE

Enjoying popular history

The magic of cinema and the pleasure of the text are critical commonplaces and cultural clichés, and yet there is value in unpicking their meaning within a historiographical context. The concept of being 'entertained' in various ways is clearly ideologically and culturally coded. Simple *entertainment* is something that does not exist and never has. Historical fictions that engage with models of popular entertainment in their communicative strategies – that is, all of them – run the gamut of ideo-historiographical articulation, from being actively conservative (shutting off types of interpretation) to being actively radical (seeking to undermine, through popular culture, more hegemonic or monolithic interpretative structures).[1] Little theoretical work has been undertaken on why popular audiences enjoy historical fictions on-screen and consume them in such huge quantities (and, thence, engage with them, as Hughes-Warrington puts it: 'We have yet to chart the effort involved when a viewer first encounters a construction of history on film').[2] Consequently, one of the key things to have been ignored in many accounts of popular historical fictions is the fact that they provide pleasure to their readers and audiences. The texts themselves are, instead, often accused of simplicity and encouraging passivity, which in many ways is part of a lazy critique of the kinds of pleasure in which the texts are considered to deal. Rather than simply repeat this, the next two chapters argue that pleasure and affect might be considered fundamental to the historiography of the texts. Or, rather, that enjoyment might somehow have to be figured into an understanding of how these texts create an effect, both in terms of their fictive work but also in terms of their historiographical impact. Audiences are complicit in their rendering of another, unreal world, and their collusion argues an understanding of what they should be doing, of what is at stake ethically and ideologically in ignoring 'reality' for escapism. These texts often stage within them discussions of pleasure and enjoyment, or of horror and disgust, particularly in relation to costume, gender, and sexuality. So, while they reflect upon these issues, they articulate a way of knowing the past through these various lenses.

These two chapters, therefore, build on the work of the previous discussion of the body in order to outline a potential historiography of desire for the past, brokered through a kind of demagoguery or 'heritagolatry'. In particular, this present chapter suggests, tentatively, that the pleasurable encounter with the historical text might in itself be thought of as a historiographical, and certainly epistemological, experience. Instead of dismissing escapism and fantasy, such concepts might be modelled as articulating a historical comprehension of some kind. This is so even when the intention of the fiction is for some kind of passive viewing experience. The chapter argues that the 'escapist' moment might create a space for a historical comprehension different from that of more 'active' reading. Costume dramas and historical fictions do not reflect academic historiography but create anew moments, encounters, and positions that involve elements that mainstream professional history might find troubling – desire, conservatism, humour. They create, stage, and enable different historic encounters, new modes of pastness, a new historicity. In particular, the contemporary costume drama articulates a way of 'looking' at the past, of visualizing and controlling it, of, therefore, desiring it, which is in many ways akin to the ways that romance fiction works. This desire for the past suggests a way of conceptualizing the then and the now, and of traversing that distinction.

The pleasure of the text – economically, formally, or affectively – is something that has exercised literary and cultural scholars for decades.[3] How might this enjoyment be articulated, and does it in some way enact an epistemological interface with models of the past? Might delight in costume drama be in itself historical work? Does gratification – within the commodified nexus – become part of a very complex transaction, of which a historiographical understanding might be considered a part? This notwithstanding, it is key to comprehend this enjoyment as a way in which audiences engage with the past. As the case of *Downton Abbey*, discussed below, eloquently demonstrates, it is immaterial whether critics or historians are comfortable with such TV series, as their influence, impact, and reach are profound. In order to understand these texts, then, and what they mean for the historical imagination and the popular historiographical sensibility, it is necessary to analyse and think about them in creative and challenging ways. Given much recent work looking at the affective relationship with the archive and relating the scholar's enjoyment, political or sexual identity, or their physical position to their understanding of pastness (and their narrativization as a consequence of a version of that past), it should not be too much to suggest that general audiences might have a similar experience.[4]

In an episode of *Boardwalk Empire*, Haneen, the magician brother of Houdini, cynically describes the pleasing effect of his work: 'Deception requires complicity – we want to be deceived'.[5] His words are suggestive as a model for the ways in which audiences engage with historical fictions generally. The combination of pleasure with knowing self-deception – a critical awareness, even a distance, inherent, if consciously disavowed – describes well the contention involved in viewing texts that undermine their own authority. The keyword 'complicity' articulates an active engagement, a conscious choice to view the deceiving action as 'magic' or illusion, rather than simply a lie. Similarly, the desire for the fictive – 'we *want* to be deceived' – figures the encounter with the deceptive as something that satisfies some kind of need. Somehow reconciling complicity and deception, the audience of the costume drama enjoys the text that enables both.

All historical texts are clearly works of deception, inherently fictive in their attempts at fixing some kind of meaning and describing a past that cannot be grasped. Encountering a fictional history demands a level of self-conscious forgetting, an active disavowal of the deception that is going on. However, too little attention has been paid to whether audiences might wish the illusion and derive pleasure from this actualizing aspect. Historical fictions only work, like magic, if people believe in them while knowing their falsehood. This is well worked through in historical films about illusion itself. *The Prestige* (Christopher Nolan, 2006), for instance, spends a great deal of time undermining its own narratives about magic and showmanship in order to demonstrate, with exactitude, the ways that illusions are made, constructed, and formed for the enjoyment of the audience. What is important is the performance of 'reality', the convincing display. The virtuoso illusionist makes an audience believe, but only if they have convinced themselves first, and inherent in this conviction is a wish to be entertained.

This present chapter, then, is broadly interested in the various pleasures of the historical text. It suggests that various critical models that have been applied to reading historical fiction can be softened by considering issues of passivity, affect, emotion, desire, and enjoyment as fundamental to the workings of the series *and* as part of their contribution to a historical and historiographical imaginary. Claire Monk argues that women 'looking' and women's pleasure are key diegetic components of the heritage film. She argues that *A Room With a View* 'is particularly astonishing for its repeated representation of active female looking *on-screen*, and its central diegetic thematisation of female looking and female pleasure'.[6] Certainly, period drama's diegetic analyses of desire, surveillance, and the gaze might suggest that the genre is self-conscious about the ways it might practicably work. Affect, emotion, pleasure, desire – these are all things that are bound up in the 'enjoyment' and, hence, consumption of popular historical fictions. If scholars are to understand how these texts work on a historiographic level, then the matrix of these seemingly corporeal elements will have to be recognized. The costume drama is a genre that allows for an investigation of this amorphous and seemingly irrational (as the antithesis to rational) historiographical engagement. This chapter is interested in these texts as renderings of history within the present, representations of a past that, in their formal and aesthetic workings, show the diverse ways in which the historical and historiographical imaginaries are resourced by fictions.

Downton Abbey, escapism, and passivity

The chapter begins, however, with a consideration of how costume drama might be criticized for ensuring a passivity of response. Although this is often seen as a problem, this section seeks to understand this model of passive escapism as a more complex phenomenon than has hitherto been considered. Critique of the costume drama in many of its guises – period drama, lit flick, frock flick, historical film, heritage film, adaptation, costume series – has often emphasized its conservatism and the lack of dynamism in its audience.[7] Andrew Higson's work in the field began this way, with his seminal article on the innate conservatism of films from the early 1980s, but then opened out to consider the diversity and challenging quality of much of the work produced over the past 30 years.[8] In Higson's later account, the films contain diversity and possibly contradictory meanings. This division in interpretation is at the heart of scholarship on costume drama, with the debate demonstrating both the vibrancy of the genre and its range. In some ways, this chapter is not concerned with whether the texts are conservative or radical, but is concerned with how, in their representation of pastness, they might be engaged with and what kind of historiographical experience they are offering. In particular, it is key to consider the texts as products that work fundamentally to entertain and, therefore, occur within an economy of heritage consumption and use a generic vocabulary of familiarity.

They are also generally concerned with relationships, and, as Alison Light argued, 'It is as romances that [they] might be best understood, criticized, and (I dare say it?) enjoyed'.[9] Light was suggesting that certain criticism of the form was inherently critical owing to a misunderstanding of the mechanics of genre and audience expectation (and, in Higson's words, suggesting that the films offer 'a vision of a more inclusive, democratic, even multicultural England').[10] However, she also offers the texts as romances, fantasy texts enabling an audience to project their desires upon the past.[11] This sense of the doubleness of enjoyment, as something that is passive but also part of a historical engagement, is key to the chapter's argument. The key word here is 'enjoyed', as Light reminds critics that it is key to understand how exactly this pleasure might work, and how it relates to, and is different from, more 'rational' engagement. The yoking of the three investigative terms – understood, criticized, enjoyed – suggests that, in Light's thinking, they are cognate or related. This parity of response is important when one is considering the historical effect of the texts.

Certainly, the conservative, passive reading of such texts has been uppermost in criticism of the globally successful *Downton Abbey* (ITV, 2010–). Set in the fictional titular house, this show considers the Grantham family and its servants and is particularly interested in the relationship between the two sets of characters. The series has had huge international success, but, after a first series that was praised for raising some unusual questions in the context of costume drama (inheritance by a commoner, miscarriage, colonialism in Ireland), it has been increasingly criticized for demonstrating an innately conservative and patrician view of class politics and English national history.[12] This historiographic trend away from social history towards soap history has not prevented the series from being hugely successful, and indeed it can be argued that the lack of complexity is what makes it excellent historical entertainment.

In fact, the need for the show to be comfortable and 'unchallenging' is demonstrated clearly in reviewers' responses. It is expected from the series. Previewing the 2011 Series 2 of *Downton Abbey* in *The Daily Telegraph*, Ceri Radford discussed what viewers had in store. Her account of the strengths of the show argued that it had won 'over audiences and critics with its combination of human drama, period detail, romance, skulduggery and beautiful evening dresses'.[13] This conjunction of elements demonstrates a central appeal of the series, both domestically and abroad. Indeed, Radford's outline serves to illustrate the key elements of all Sunday-evening costume drama. The historical element, 'period detail', is only part of the workings of the series, and a relatively minor one at that. Finery, excess, sensationalism, and visual pleasure are as much a part of the show's appeal as anything else, and so need to be read together. The 'experience' of the historical is buttressed by these several elements.

Radford discusses the various relationship developments, the impact of new historical events (the First World War), and how Julian Fellowes's writing communicates 'a sense of smaller human dramas playing out against the backdrop of seismic events'. She concludes: 'The new series looks set to become another Sunday evening national fixation, and a significant source of cheer once the nights start drawing in'.[14] This suggestion that the show provokes a national conversation – something seemingly lost (and mourned) in critiques of a multichannel, on-demand television culture – suggests that the costume drama both contributes to the development of an identity and also harks back to a time when television was an event. The show brings 'cheer' to a populace, and this sense of escapist enervation, that period drama allows the population to forget the cold realities of the contemporary, is crucial to understand in the context of this type of period drama. Its functions are comforting and they return, as Higson argued, to contemplating an idealized past through a nostalgic template. Sam Wollaston, describing the series in *The Guardian* in 2012, argued that it was shifting from drama to soap opera: '*Downton* is her ladyship's soap, *Emmerdale* with a posh frock on'. This series has reached new heights of melodrama, absurdity of storyline and clichéd writing'.[15] Again, he emphasizes the sensationalism of the series and highlights its dramatic excesses. The shift in generic definition, he suggests, renders the show even less engaged with historical process and more something that should be considered as entertainment. This hybrid, then, of 'historical' and entertainment is what needs to be understood more deeply.

The response to a key event in the fourth series demonstrated this status of *Downton* as entertainment rather than drama. The controversy around the episode and the fact that ITV ran a warning relating to the events before the beginning of the show highlight how the formal conventions of costume drama rarely allow for the invasion of violence or grimly unpleasant events. In Episode 3 of the series, a popular character, Anna (Joanne Froggatt), resisted the advances of a valet, who then raped her. This scene was intercut with Kiri Te Kanawa singing opera as Dame Nellie Melba, a conscious contrasting of high culture with the brutal quotidian. Ian Hyland, writing in the *Daily Mirror*, argued that such 'challenges' to the audience were unnecessary and ended up 'punishing the audience':

It just needs the routine quota of births, deaths and marriages, some nice frocks, the odd nostalgic shot of a steam train, a liberal sprinkling of class war, the occasional nod to historical events, and a weekly stock of neat put-downs from Maggie Smith.[16]

Again, Hyland emphasizes the need for costume, emotional sensationalism, caricatured period detail, and some reference to class entanglements. For many critics, the rape scene disrupted the smooth functioning of the drama as palliative, something that provided an undemanding version of pastness. Responding to criticisms of implausibility and irrelevance, the fourth series had introduced homosexuality, jazz, and feminism. However, the reactionary element is central to the appeal of the show. The series' most celebrated character, Maggie Smith's arrogant dowager duchess, regularly expresses sentiments that articulate contempt for normality and modernity ('what is a *weekend* exactly?', she asks in the first series). As these critics argue, this kind of conservatism is key to the working of the drama that demands a passivity of viewing. Similarly, most 'costume drama' is obsessed with surface, class, desire, and relationships.

Attempts at constructing a passive viewer – either on the part of the series or by the reviewer – suggest a great deal about the perceived value of the costume drama and its effect as a translator of the past. A conservative version of the past is still an attempt at writing that past in the present and contributing to a sense of how history might work. Sunday night TV of the kind that is being described here, from *Poirot* (ITV, 1989–2013) to *Heartbeat* (ITV, 1992–2010), attempts to obviate the trauma of the past through the forgetting, or erasure, or marginalization of anything challenging. This demonstrates a cultural need for a nostalgic engagement with the past, a sense that a show that brokers a relationship with history needs to be both translating and editing events. The unquestioning celebration and love of heritage television for the passivity and relaxation it brings in representing the past in this way demonstrates a desire for a simpler history. 'Passivity' and 'escapism' become particular affective modes of communicating something historiographically conservative. They suggest a phenomenological epistemology: that is, a way of *knowing* the past or engaging with it that is simple and straightforward, nostalgic and comforting. As the contrast with misery television, discussed below, demonstrates, the cosy view of the past that mainstream costume drama tends to present is as much a historiographical position as one that figures the past as grim and unpleasant. Escapism, here, is an express desire to turn from 'reality' to a cosseted, hyped-up realism that uses the tropes of period drama to soothe and comfort the viewer in the contemporary moment. Yet this escapism is one of the most popular ways of engaging with a type of 'past' on television. It is insufficient to simply dismiss the text as conservative entertainment.

One way to understand the appeal and the work of period television is to focus on the physical. Costume drama is a genre that depends on visual excess – the *mis en scène* is fascinated with the costume, the superficial finery and otherness that mark out such work as distinct from other film or television. Part of the enjoyment of costume drama is this difference, whether it be the trappings of aristocratic dress or the detail realized in more recent historical renderings. Architecture and objects are also part of the excess of the costume drama, well articulated in the opening sequence of *Downton Abbey*, which luxuriates in the physical trappings of wealth. This opening montage emphasizes stability and order, loyalty and faithfulness. Designed by Hugo Moss, with music by John Lunn, the titles work through montage by focusing on parts of the whole of the house, before both music and image come to a resolution and conclusion with a still of the house and the title of the series. The title sequence thus has a narrative effect and communicates many elements of the text effectively.

The first and final images in the *Downton* sequence are of the house itself, emphasizing again the centrality of this structure that will be diegetically and aesthetically central to the show. From the beginning of the series, primogeniture, inheritance, and genealogy are central to the action. The traumatic moment of British history – that which nearly undermines the aristocracy who own Downton Abbey and momentarily threatens to leave a relative commoner, who has a profession (he is a lawyer) and lives in a city (Manchester), sole inheritor of the house – is here imagined, not as the First World War, which the important aristocrats happily survive (but not all their servants), but the sinking of *The Titanic* in 1912. This event leads to the death of the 'rightful' heirs of the estate. The series seeks to alleviate the anxiety of this loss narratively, and much of its impetus is in the drive to maintain the sanctity of the house and estate. This narrative drive to stability and order allows for otherness – particularly the elopement of the middle daughter with the Irish republican chauffeur, or the eldest daughter's fling with a handsome Turk – by bringing it back within the governing structures of family and property. The war comes into the house – it is used as a hospital for convalescing soldiers – and this temporarily threatens the structures of ownership, as the evil character Thomas, a former servant, maintains that he is in charge of the running of the place. However, this is a temporary shift, and the war concludes. Where a series such as *Brideshead Revisited* reflected in complex ways on the structure of the house and the emotions – nostalgia, desire, melancholy, anger, guilt – that it might engender, *Downton* is more simplistically concerned with emphasizing order through the wholeness of the estate. This is clearly historiographical in purpose, both series taking the physical and material (the house, the gardens) to stand as metaphor for various historical elements and modes of representation and comprehension. It is self-conscious articulation of the physical space of the past as something writable and interpretable.

The second image of the opening sequence is the opening of shutters, framing an entry into the house (and the series, imagined structurally or formally as something solid and precisely rendered, something with imaginative or aesthetic architectonics). The camera pans slowly over several objects that materially render the series' reification of class relationships, as unseen servants' hands dust chandeliers or arrange silver cutlery on a table. Some of the images are almost excessively symbolic – a dog walks loyally next to its owner, post is arranged for those with agency (the aristocrats) while, in the background, a servant is walking past literally out of focus (background noise, irrelevant, without identity), a bell rings to summon an unseen servant, a petal falls from a vase of freshly cut flowers. The sequence communicates the fragile beauty of a world now lost (cut flowers, the post), the virtues of blind loyalty, and the unseen work of the house. Above all, the sequence self-consciously points out the construction of the beauty of the house, the thing desired and wished for. If the series is imagined as the structure of the abbey itself, a space the audience is invited to enter, the opening sequence archly points out just how the effects of such beauty are actually the consequences of much hard work and unseen – but known, if mainly unacknowledged – labour. There is a striking similarity in the opening sequence to a cognate series, *Upstairs, Downstairs* (BBC, 2010–), which also explores the relationships in a house between aristocratic families and their servants, and which also imagines the loveliness of the setting – the costume – while demonstrating how this is something made and in need of much maintenance. Many period dramas of this kind deploy montage sequences in the opening credits, demonstrating proleptically a concern with the construction of a narrative. This concern with finery demonstrates a way that the tropes of 'realism' – the 'costume' of costume drama – are themselves signals of a kind of conservative historiography. The pleasure of the text is associated with its excesses of costume, which themselves are imbricated in the basic representational and epistemological building blocks of the genre. The kind of past that is presented here is not a coincidence, and the way of knowing through the excessive representation that is on-screen presents a pastness dependent on materiality. This is a material epistemology predicated upon finery and the pleasure taken in a kind of well-dressed passivity. The 'costume' in the phrase 'costume drama' demonstrates something self-reflective and engaging. Most costume drama, as a television genre, has a clear diegetic concern with 'costume' and performance. The technical details of dress are often obsessed over, and the rich excesses of costume are part of the texture of the shows. *Downton Abbey* is replete with scenes in the class interspace of the dressing room, where servants and masters come together to create the illusion that is 'costume'. The spaces serve as a contact between classes, but also as a reference to the artificiality inherent in the shows. Both *The Paradise* (discussed below) and *Downton Abbey* draw some of their dramatic impetus from roles relating to dress, as both have narrative strands relating to who dresses the lord (*Downton Abbey*) and who is in charge of ladies' wear (*The Paradise*). Furthermore, this abiding interest in the mechanics of performing a type of role through costume demonstrates the wrought aspect of identity and also that of historical rendering, as the actors are 'dressed' as much as the set is, for authenticity and for splendour.

In his polemic *Capitalist Realism*, Mark Fisher argues that post-2008 Western culture now resources only one way of imagining the world, predicated upon ideological ascendancy and a 'deeper, more pervasive sense of exhaustion, of cultural and political sterility'.[17] In contrast with postmodernism, which engaged with modernism in its flattening of historical awareness into a series of unattached presents,

'What we are dealing with now is not the incorporation of materials that previously seemed to possess subversive potentials, but instead, the pre-emptive formatting and shaping of desires, aspirations and hopes by capitalist culture' (p. 9). 'Heritage' has often been seen to be part of this process. The debates between Raphael Samuel, Patrick Wright, Alison Light, David Lowenthal, Robert Hewison, and others, during the 1980s, revolved around the problematic development of 'heritage' as what Samuel termed, 'Thatcherism in period dress'.[18] As Patrick Wright noted, 'the argument associating "heritage" with decline has certainly failed to thrive. It has been repeatedly dismissed on the grounds that conservation and heritage values have actually proved to be good for the economy'.[19] Costume drama – 'period dress' – was part of this process. However, Samuel discerned something more radical in historicized practices from re-enactment to folk singing, and his sense of the potential for critique within historical modes of knowing the past demonstrates a utopic ideal that the past might allow the imagination of a new future. *Downton Abbey* and the cognate costume shows that are concerned with the establishment of particular capitalist models seem, on the one hand, to demonstrate Fisher's thesis – that, even in the past, it is impossible to conceive of an alternative way of living to capitalism – while at times, on the other hand, rendering a kind of critique akin to Samuel's model. Certainly, a new concern with the origins of recognizable financial models – with an inbuilt paternalism and a sweeping away of 'old' ideas for a new modern mode of existence – might be seen to be colonizing the historical imagination in aid of a contemporary ideological template. Capitalist *historical* realism, therefore, might suggest that the ways of imagining the past allow an audience only one particular present. This is the costume drama as something that manipulates the desires of the audience for a particular historiographical and political purpose.

Costume and the self-conscious pleasure of the text

To develop this model of period texts as proselytizing for a particular capitalist or historiographic normality, it is important to demonstrate how conservative costume dramas dramatize ephemeral commodities such as fashion and dress.[20] This is part of a self-consciousness on the part of the genre regarding consumption and heritage. The two shows discussed here demonstrate a diegetic concern with costume, display, and visual pleasure. As such, they illustrate the genre's self-conscious deployment of particular tropes of excess and beauty. *The Paradise* is a BBC adaptation of Émile Zola's *Au bonheur des dames* (1883) about the development of new retail models through the consolidating of practice in what is recognizably a department store. *Mr Selfridge* is an ITV drama about the establishment of Selfridge's great London shop, itself an innovative retail model. Both series, shown nearly concurrently (September–November 2012 and January–March 2013; scheduled on purpose so as not to overlap), provide a development of the normal obsessions of period drama: the physical space (normally a house), costume itself, inheritance and ownership, and class. In the department stores of these shows, viewers can see a social mobility often ignored by other, more aristocratically driven shows. The retail space – the market – is more democratic, providing a flexibility otherwise lacking, a possibility, which versions of the past in much costume drama do not afford their protagonists. In their interrogation of standard tropes, and in their overt celebration of costume, these two series show a characteristic self-consciousness about the way in which period drama works.

Both *The Paradise* and *Mr Selfridge* inflect the standard costume-drama concerns of inheritance and property by focusing the action on the development of department stores and retail models in London's high-imperial period (1870–1909). English literature that is adapted – and costume drama generally – is relatively obsessed with the physical space, from Brideshead Castle, revisited for a kind of involuntary Proustian memory moment by Charles Ryder, to the contested house at Robin Hill in *The Forsyte Saga*, to the self-conscious country house motifs of later versions by Alan Hollinghurst (*The Line of Beauty*) and Ian McEwan (*Atonement*). Similarly, property, inheritance, and genealogy are the provinces of most writers whose work is adapted (Dickens's *Bleak House* being the template to an extent here). In using a French source text (*The Paradise*) or an American protagonist (*Mr Selfridge*), these two series made a shift away from the spaces of aristocratic psychodrama to the conceptual legitimacy of the shop, the physical and imaginative locus of consumer capitalism. Class is replaced with the market, and the issues at stake become more about commodity and desire for things than the interrelationships between people.

Just as Zola's book marked a shift in the novel's predilection with aristocracy, a radical shift of direction to the metropolitan that would signal, eventually, the shift towards a particular type of modernism, so *The Paradise* is part of a series of costume dramas newly interested in the middle class, in capitalism and consumption, and in the development of a recognizable bourgeois class in something of a tension with the aristocracy. The penniless shop girl Denise finally wins the heart of Moray, highlighting a rather idealistic social mobility that is the consequence of her decision to leave her uncle's draper's shop (located opposite the glamorous Paradise store) and work in the more faceless department store. The aristocratic characters are marginalized and used for capital investment; indeed, in one episode, Lord Glendinning offers Moray more money to purchase leases on the shop (and so become a landowner). Moray's perpetual problems with Glendinning's loans demonstrate the problem of older feudal systems of property ownership and the way that they get in the way of commerce.

An exchange early in *The Paradise* demonstrates this move in a self-conscious way:

Lord Glendenning:	Does the world truly need more perfumes and petticoats?
John Moray:	Need is not the issue here – I deal in appetites. There is a weakness in women that we can exploit to the advantage of business.[21]

The question is asked in the context of Moray's engagement to Glendenning's daughter, so that the inheritance and property-right issue is still in the frame, and yet the seeming dismissal of costume marks this drama's application to be doing something new in presenting a narrative about retail. Glendenning's patrician sneer at the consumer capitalist model, which operates on the principle that necessity is pretty irrelevant, is countered by Moray's cynical precision. Business is driven by appetite, need, a weak desire for shiny things that might be exploited. Part of the point here is that Moray is hardly an evil manipulator – like Harry Selfridge, he simply understands (and makes money from) women's need to have nice things to wear. Indeed, both characters are lionized for their comprehension of the need for quality and their understanding of women's needs. In the late nineteenth century, the new woman is a consumer, seemingly, and she will be well served by these shops. The new middle class drives the expansion of the mercantile community through its need for clothes and accoutrements.

The exchange between Glendenning and Moray, purposefully or not, goes to the heart of the contemporary costume drama. Glendenning's words are diegetically authentic but also self-reflective on the part of the script, wondering out loud about the real need for another costume drama (a genre defined, linguistically, by the centrality of dress). Period drama is both material (petticoats), in its concern with the physical and the authentic, and ephemeral (perfume), a confection, indistinct, appealing to the senses and the emotions. Moray's riposte suggests that the product is actually a commodity, something without utility, produced to fill a gap and slake a thirst or satisfy an appetite, but with little substance or actual purpose. In the same way that *Mad Men* reflects upon the creation by advertising men of dreamed – unreal – product, not least of which is *itself*, *The Paradise* suggests that the boom in costume drama might have something to do with weakness, appetite, and the exploitation of needless desire in order to make profit. The show demonstrates the way that things are sold, in the same way that *Mad Men* celebrates the way that objects are made into commodities, in part through the intervention of the advertising industry. Similarly to that series, both *The Paradise* and *Mr Selfridge* emphasize creativity within the consumer experience, harking back to a time when shopping was personal (rather than mass) and creating a kind of nostalgia for a type of elegant retail. They have key characters who have a particular knack for decoration, or promotional ideas, and, as with *Mad Men*, this is celebrated as flair and creative insight (even, in the character of Henri Leclair, the French window-dresser in *Mr Selfridge*, as *art*). On the one hand, this celebrates work in a way that has been hitherto unusual in period drama; on the other, it demonstrates that the shows are concerned with the construction of the artificial, the precise, fictional arrangement of objects to create narratives of consumption. This is a self-consciousness on the part of the texts themselves, a reflection upon their own fictiveness *and* their own figuration as historical fictional commodity (desired, marketed, performed, sold).

Many critics have pointed out how costume drama works on a model of consumption and is particularly related to the commodification of the past through discourses of heritage and to tourism.[22] Hence, the phenomenon of the popular costume drama fundamentally works in relation to an imaginative (and real) economy of desire and demand. Amy Sargeant argues that costume drama should be related to the 'marketing and consumption of Britain's cultural heritage as a tourist attraction'.[2] Interviewed in 2013 while in China on a trade mission, the Chancellor of the Exchequer George Osborne emphasized the importance of heritage and costume drama to British export figures:

> What we want to see is Chinese tourists, just as a generation ago we had a whole wave of Japanese tourists, the new phenomenon in the world is Chinese tourism. That's fantastic for the British hospitality and tourist industry [. . .] One hundred and sixty million Chinese are watching *Downton Abbey*, which is more than double the number of people who live in the UK.[24]

Here, *Downton Abbey*'s transnational status as a cultural product with extensive reach and influence becomes the basis for an entire tourist industry, a calling card for UK PLC. The key sense of the costume drama as part of an international economic nexus articulates a desire for it – a demand – from a global marketplace. Costume drama itself is a commodity. Post-*Downton Abbey*, it is clear that this type of show has an audience around the world and is, therefore, very profitable.[25] The BBC has always made costume drama with an eye to the American market, but now the interest in British period television is huge and global. Series 3 of *Downton Abbey* sold hugely as a DVD before Christmas 2012, and *The Paradise* was released as a BBC DVD immediately after the end of its run, to capitalize on the Christmas market. The shows are material commodities, clearly, things and artefacts that are made for a particular need, product, with all associated marketing. They are made to be consumed passively. Yet the workings of their commodification are such that the enaction of capitalist drives found in *The Paradise* may be read back on to the action of the texts themselves. Costume dramas are desired as a commodity. They satisfy appetites, provide a material, affective salve for a particular heritage–need–desire. Hence, the engagement of the audience with the costume drama might be figured, following Moray's words, as transactional, part of the commodity process; heritage is fetishized, made attractive, desired in the same way that things and possessions might be. Moray's words, though, also signal a pleasure in the costume, and it is important to comprehend the desire for the period text in this context, too. They allow the postulation of a historiography of desire for the commodified past, articulating this transactional moment as something that can be accounted for, a kind of commercial heritagolatory. The commodity is desired because of its various 'values'. The enjoyment of the text, here, is shot through with the pleasures of consumption. The texts themselves, in their self-conscious meditation upon display, performance, desire, and commodity, are both complicit and explicit about this process.

Misery programming

One way of conceptualizing the affective relationship with the fiction of the past is to think of it as commodity, then, and to reflect upon its self-consciousness regarding its own monetization. A recent contrasting strand of programming has begun to provide an alternative to the rarefied heritagolatory of *Downton Abbey* and mainstream costume drama. If *Downton* and its like are concerned with pleasure that is predicated in part on passive enjoyment, the shows analysed here seek to correct that view of the past. Indeed, their very existence is partly a riposte to a particular conservative genre predicated upon a historiography associated with passivity and escapism. The new type of series provides a different model of dramatic engagement with pastness, one that is concerned with authenticity, dirt, and misery. This might create a problematic binary, as misery is represented as working class and realistic, splendour as aristocratic and pleasurable. It also suggests a desire to present a 'proper' narrative, in the face of conservative costume drama's excess. If such costume drama works on a version of passive pleasure, desire, and a wanting-to-be-watched in the splendour of the historical imaginary presented, misery drama's *mis en scène* is bleached austerity, dark greys, and shadows. These series are social realist in purpose, and their entire palette and vocabulary, from incidental music to costume to the accents of the characters, are intended to provide an alternative to costume drama's 'mainstream' version of a bourgeois history. They include illness, casual violence, child labour, dirt and mud, cruelty, rape, disfigurement, death, hardship of all kinds, and terrible poverty. The programmes are social-history documents that strive to show a more authentic life, particularly revising idealized versions of the nineteenth century. They provide an alternative to the pleasures of the pseudo-realist costume drama and, in this act, demonstrate the conservative historiographical impulse of such texts.

The Mill (Channel 4, 2013) elaborates the appalling working conditions of child labourers in cotton mills in 1833. It is intentionally bleak. In the first episode, an accident in the mill involving a child is intercut with the mill owner toying with his rich cooked breakfast. This latter character and his elegant dining-room setting are more familiar to a period-drama audience than the filthy orphaned children working in the mill. Their richness is clearly contrasted with the children receiving a ladle of porridge into their hands while another of their number has his arm amputated. *The Mill* is a clear corrective to idealized versions of the past, attempting to engender interest in working conditions, the law, the development of industry through technology, and the ways in which ideologies of oppression might work within a society. It is particularly interested, as a series, in the idea of indentured labour, foregrounding how apprentices were considered the property of 'paternal employers': 'They own you until you're twenty-one'.[26] The testimony of a freed slave at a civic meeting is contrasted with the conditions the labourers have to work under. This, then, leads to social disunity and discord. The violent overseer argues, 'I've never done anything that wasn't done to me', and the series is clear about the way that horror distributes itself from within a cruel and corrupt system. Any political agitation or sense of collective action is punished severely. Channel 4 prefaced Episode 2 with the warning that it includes, 'scenes some viewers may find upsetting and language of the time considered offensive today'. This includes references to child prostitution and an exhortation to 'cough all of the city shit out of your lungs'. The warning emphasizes the sense found in these misery dramas that the otherness of the past is untranslatable and, in fact, unspeakable today, violent and offensive.

Reviewers often found the series over-serious and bleak: 'Do I want to watch a miserable, starkly realistic depiction of Britain's journey to wage-slavery, involving a good long think on a Sunday night about the millions of Britons who spent their lifetime in dour laborious woe?'.[27] The point here is the clear contrast with the feel-good Sunday costume drama and posits a passive viewer who would rather not have 'a good long think'. Along with *The Paradise* and *Mr Selfridge*, this show demonstrates a trend for engaging with the development of capitalism through the Victorian period and into the twentieth century, from consumption and commodity to the horrific labour conditions in the factories. *The Mill* also demonstrates dissatisfaction with the cosy rendering of the past in mainstream costume drama and an intention to disrupt the nexus of desire and pleasure that such series demonstrate. It is a clear corrective, and part of this is the challenge it makes to the viewer regarding comfort and passivity.

In similar style, *The Village* covers the period 1912–20, and, over that time, the series covers war, sickness, domestic violence, depression, rape, alcoholism, sacrifice, hardship, religious fervour, and death. Peter Moffat, the creator of the series, explicitly contrasted it with *Downton Abbey*'s treatment of a similar time period:

> I think we need to re-calibrate the way we look at history . . . particularly this period [. . .] It's seen now as officer-class history. I don't think there are enough of John Simm-type characters [a farm labourer] who, after all, make up most of the population.[28]

This sense of restitution is key to this new strand of misery period drama, a feeling of gritty realism in contrast to the soapy product that is mainstream period drama. The show is explicitly compared to the 1980s German series *Heimat*, suggesting an interest in wide-sweeping versions of history as family and national epic, using the village as microcosm, rather than the country-house version of history that sees the development of events as they impact upon the fortunes of the aristocracy.

The Village demonstrates its commitment to social history through a framing device using the now-nonogenerian central character, Bert Middleton. He introduces himself and then recollects ('Where were we then?') events of the summer of 1914. Bert's recollection shapes the story as the narrative of memory, but also introduces the melancholic element of death to the series ('This will be the last thing that I do', he claims). He looks at images of his family and his playmates, of his brother and his teachers, and is the only person still alive. He is reverse-anachronistic, the past in the present, witness to the unknown things of the past. In the second episode, the following dialogue points out the distinction the series makes regarding its subjects:

What was your childhood like?
Short.

What made it short?
Being poor, being hungry all the time.[29]

Bert produces various bits of evidence – a postcard, some photographs – that testify to his veracity as a witness. In the first episode, a sepia photograph melts into the live-action arrival of the first bus in Bert's village, the arrival of modernity into the countryside of England. Middleton is a 'witness', and his story is given docudramatic impetus as his voice-over begins to narrate events (with the interruption of the interviewer emphasizing the archival-witness nexus that is being mimicked here). The arrival of the bus is immediately contrasted with the character of Joe pumping water. Bucolic scenes of the glorious countryside of the village are soon replaced by a vicious domesticity, as Simm's alcoholic, paternal character beats and humiliates his children. The neat novelty of the gaudy bus and the idealized countryside are explicitly undermined. The standard period motif of the 'house' as characterizing stability and order is challenged by this domestic and normalized violence. Simm at one point recounts the age of the house by pointing out bits of the kitchen floor that have been worn down by five generations of the family standing in front of the fire. The cleaving to the space of the farm is not positive here, though, but cloying and destructive.

Further scenes involve Bert being caned at school for not learning his numbers. Similarly, servants must face the wall when their masters approach, rather than engaging with them as they do in *Downton Abbey*. The paternal model of class relations and social ordering is disrupted here. The historiographical contrast between *Downton Abbey* and *The Village* is clear when we look at the way they treat the First World War. *Downton* concentrates on the relationship between the heir to the estate, Matthew, and his valet. Matthew goes missing – but is found – and his valet dies. The scenes at the front jar with the splendour of the house, but are quickly forgotten in the quest to discover whether the heir to the estate is alive or not. In contrast, *The Village* articulates the experiences of the conscript Joe, shell-shocked and angry that, 'You don't understand! None of you understand!'.[30] He recounts the death of a comrade: 'He drowned in his own blood . . . I held him and he stared at me, and he goes to put his hand to his throat to do what? To stop the blood? That's how he died. It is pathetic.'[31]

Yet again, critics found the series problematic. Recounting, 'A miserable start for *The Village*, the BBC's answer to *Downton Abbey*', reviewers in the *Daily Mail* argued, 'It was supposed to be a period drama to rival Downton Abbey. But viewers hoping for an upbeat Easter Sunday's viewing were presented with misery, depression and violence'.[32] The clear contrast is with *Downton Abbey* as a mainstream and escapist 'period drama', whereas *The Village* presents an alternative of misery and violence and purports to offer greater authenticity as a consequence. Writing of the conclusion of *The Village* in *The Daily Telegraph*, Ben Lawrence argued that:

Maybe the real problem lay with the scheduling. Viewers tend not to want challenging fare on Sunday nights. The costume dramas that have succeeded on Sundays – *Lark Rise to Candleford*, *Downton Abbey*, *Mr Selfridge* – have seduced audiences by rejecting any sort of reality and aiming for a cosy candlelit view of the past, or big, bold storylines with a soap-like quality. *The Village* could be unremittingly grim, and offered few moments of escapism.[33]

This review of Episode 6 of *The Village* directly contrasts the series with its peers and suggests a binary between 'easy' costume drama and more 'challenging' *realist* work. Costume drama on television has regularly been accused of this lightness, of avoiding 'big' ideas in order to generate pleasure for the viewers. Lawrence's words – 'seduced', 'cosy', 'rejecting any sort of reality' – suggest that this critical, commonplace binary has been internalized by those reviewing television.

These misery texts are actively anti-conservative. Their rejection of the enjoyment of the costume drama – in all its tropes, from costume to music to narrative clarity – is clear and heavily weighted. In some ways, they are as problematic as their inverses, insofar as their cleaving to an aggressively 'realist' mode fiercely suggests that they are somehow able to speak more accurately for a particular constituency. They explicitly work against passive models of 'pleasure' by making an audience suffer. In this, they reject a particular diegetic and generic conservativism. They force the audience to think about the ways in which costume drama works and the kinds of storytelling and narrative technique it generally deploys. In particular, these shows force an interrogation of the enjoyment of the text. They work against the desire for the text in order to subvert pleasurable genres. In this, their 'realism' is somehow more 'real' – material grittiness trumping the 'authentic' splendour of *Downton*. The 'real' is still subjective, but these shows suggest that they have a more honest impetus associated with their representational palette. Their historiographical intervention is associated directly with their content and modes of representation. Form is political, and clearly demonstrated to be so. They therefore seek to equip an audience with a means of critique. These texts provide a riposte to the capitalist historical realism of the paternalist costume drama. Their historiographical engagement seeks to disavow ways of rendering the past as something uninflected and to be nostalgically recalled. Yet the contrast between the two types of text is, to a degree, how the misery texts gain some of their traction. They are actively different to previous costume drama, defining themselves as the opposite of this kind of work. They force a kind of intellectual reading – one audiences might not wish for – in direct contrast to the passivity associated with other types of work. However, both are considered types of engagement.

Laughing at the past

There are other, material ways in which the pleasure of the text works in historical fictions of course. The concluding sections of the chapter look at two different types of 'pleasure': humour and desire. They seek to work out a more physical sense of how historical fictions might affect their audience, and how this might be conceptualized within a historiographical nexus. This present section considers how historical fictions have a pleasurable effect on a contemporary audience, that is, through laughter. Historical comedy demonstrates a concern with an affective response on the part of the viewer, in that it hopes to make them laugh. Laughter at the past is pleasurable because it confirms the audience in modernity, the present, and distinguishes carefully between then and now. In terms of pleasure in the text, comedy seems the obvious text to turn to, given that it wittingly provokes some kind of response, that is, laughter. The ways that it does this demonstrate both an epistemology (much historical comedy is predicated upon difference) and a historiography (much historical comedy seeks to postulate a particular way of thinking about the past).

Historical comedy tends to be parody, as might be found in movies such as *Robin Hood: Men in Tights* (Mel Brooks, 1993) or television such as *'Allo 'Allo* (BBC, 1982–92). The relative paucity of costume comedy series demonstrates again the overwhelming cultural currency of the mainstream costume drama. With the exception of the odd move into genre television, such as the crime series *Ripper Street* (BBC, 2012–13) or *Peaky Blinders* (BBC, 2013–14), television representations of fictional pasts are predominantly 'straight' costume drama rather than genre, and, hence, the orthodoxy of this type of show becomes the default way of representing that past. One of the reasons for this is that humour disrupts the passivity of response outlined above and so demonstrates the ways in which costume drama might move to shut down engagement. Yet historical comedy is clearly a place where a text expects a response on the part of the viewer. Analysis of costume comedy can, therefore, demonstrate key ways that a text might work to enact an affective response, and how this is intertwined with a reading of history and a particular historiographical imaginary.

Set in 1831, Julia Davis's macabre black comedy *Hunderby* (Sky Atlantic, 2012) is 'a peculiar creation that takes its many reference points into a disconcertingly unfamiliar place.'[34] This sense of being discomforted by the show is central to Davis's work, from *Nighty Night* (2004) onwards, and *Hunderby* is concerned with making the familiar odd and troubling. *Hunderby*'s plot takes elements from *Jane Eyre*, *Rebecca*, Thomas Hardy, and Gothic writing of the Victorian period. It involves an inheritance, a handsome doctor, a secret in a tower, and many familiar costume-drama locations, from the country house to the church. These clichés are impressed with a strangeness in their tone and language that makes them almost uncanny. It looks like something familiar, but is intentionally making the recognizable strange, in order to make a Gothic parody itself actually something troubling and Gothic. The palette is decidedly muted in terms of dress and art direction, and so the show again participates in the counter-argument regarding representing the past in period drama as splendid and sparkling. Hunderby is a cold, grim house in a windswept park, rather than a glorious building. The show, therefore, is a comedy as a parody of costume drama. As such, it demonstrates how much historical comedy works as a rereading of the past as seen through costume drama. It is a revision of the 'mainstream' view of the past, as presented in the realism of costume drama. Historiographically, the text counters the comforting versions of the past given in mainstream costume drama] Davis said that she wanted to mock the 'earnestness' of period dramas, 'finding them quite funny or seeing potential in them'.[35] By inviting an audience to laugh at the conventions of the genre, while also creating something new, the series presents a sophisticated rereading of the past. It also evidently seeks an affective response, laughter, and, hence, an engagement with the text that goes past the passive into something more active (if involuntary). It works in three dimensions, as it were, provoking discomfort, horror, disgust, and laughter in the body of the viewer.

Davis's script ironizes the perceived cadences, vocabulary, and tone of 'period' speech: 'It's all played admirably straight, much of the comedy stemming from the juxtaposition of the ornate language and what the characters are actually saying'.[36] The script is replete with a kind of irony and modern double meanings or puns. There are constant jokes about – and just simple references to – penises and defecation. *Hunderby* demonstrates the pompous quality of much costume drama and presents a different kind of version of the past, one that is much closer to the body in many ways. The script is scatological and filthy, combining diegetic straight talking about the functions of the body with *double entendre* to create a soundscape that is constantly disjointed. Jokes in the text are about the shifting of meaning from then to now, so that laughter at the lines invokes a historical irony or distancing:

> *Edmund:*   Do not smear me with the stench of your wrongs.
> *Dorothy:*   Her lungs have ballooned by twice.
> *Doctor:*   Nay, only by once, but her belly hath barreled by twinfold.[37]

The script clearly distances the viewer from the characters and their godly, tortured idiom and convoluted syntax:

> We do humbly ask our Father God that myself and my wife be blessed with a child before the year is through. We pray for the guidance of our Lord's gentle fist. Every child is born a filthy savage, smeared in Satan's faeces.[38]

There is, however, a clear political point being made here, as the 'filthy savage' comment picks out a number of references to racism and empire. There are visual jokes about the homoeroticism of missionary publications and the monstrosity of the seemingly civilized men who would happily live off the profits of plantations. The show is damning of various institutions – the church, science, medicine, patriarchal social organization – and the mocking of the language of such organizations demonstrates a historiographical desire to reply to them and speak for the marginalized.[39] However, at the same time, history itself is made funny, through mockery of attitudes. The series is full of jokes about terminology and the perceived unpolished elements of the eighteenth century: 'There we go ma'am. Biddy's battered bone buns to toughen your nipples for suckling. With a marrowfat ointment to grease your chute'.[40] Advice given to a couple looking to have a child consists of: 'Baby should sleep for 14 hours straight through. If he is heard it is because Satan has clambered into his cot and he's best left to fight it out'.[41] These are lyrical jokes about the peculiarities of language and a presumed strange Englishness, but they also create, as with the ironizing levels of the language, a power relationship of now–then, modern–historical. They connect the viewers to the series (through laughter) while distancing them.

To laugh at the past is to control it in some way and to attempt to be able to, hence, demonstrate an understanding of its difference from the now. The absurdity of the language renders the past something to mock and recoil from. The laughter here, then, is from a pleasure rooted in a clear sense of historical difference. The audience laughs with and at the past, regarding its foolishness. A similar effect is found in the character of Edmund Blackadder in *Blackadder* (BBC 1983–9), one of the few other costume comedies made for television. Blackadder regularly sighs with frustration at the stupidity of those around him, and his intellectual agency is ahistorical (although it never really helps him). However, the Gothic qualities of *Hunderby* ensure that the misrecognition that occurs and, hence, the laughter are never comfortable. The jokes are complex as, in demonstrating presumed historical difference, they place the viewer, as much as the characters, within historicity. The parody is recognizable and strange, real and not real (as all costume drama plays this uncanny game), fictional and authentic. The thing in the tower is regularly presented by a point-of-view camera shot, as if the monstrous, vile, helpless, tortured thing in the series is associated with the viewer. The audience is the Gothic monstrosity in the corner, the thing out of civilization. The reference is to Bertha Mason in *Jane Eyre*, Rochester's insane first wife, famously creole; Mason was locked in the attic and eventually burns down Thornfield Hall (a fire and a problematic first wife also occur in Daphne du Maurier's *Rebecca*, which Davis also echoes).

The puns and double meanings are jokes that also condemn the contemporary audience, who will see filth in everything and whose language is much less stable than that of previous times. The nostalgia invoked here might be for a time where meaning was fixed. The viewer is made uncomfortable in their relation to the past that is represented here. Pleasure is qualified by distress or the burden of misrecognition. The absurdity of the past makes it unreal and, hence, apart from the now, while audiences still kind of see that it is part of them. By challenging the costume-drama genre and, in particular, its language and visual tropes, *Hunderby* asks the viewer about how they imagine the past and what decisions are made in that recognition. The past is an odd place, and laughable insofar as it is alien and strange and other. By making the viewer think about what is wrong here, or why it feels odd or strange, and, moreover, by making the viewer uncomfortable and engaged, the series articulates a way of comprehending representations of the past. The strangeness of the past is what makes it funny, and in its being told this way it allows an audience insight into historical difference. Enjoyment – laughter – is here clearly aligned with a historiographical insight, and the pleasure of the text is found both in its absurdity and its self-consciousness.

Lost in Austen, the gaze, and the pleasures of the text

In ITV's 2008 *Lost in Austen*, a reader of Jane Austen's *Pride and Prejudice* becomes caught up in the action of the fiction in a kind of narrative time-slip. The heroine, Amanda Price, becomes magically enmeshed in the world of *Pride and Prejudice* through an interface in her bathroom, swapping places with Elizabeth Bennett, who enters modernity (and becomes 'real') with relish. At one point, Price returns to the contemporary world and is confronted with this new, 'modern' Bennett: 'Elizabeth Bennett is lending me her mobile', she wonders, awestruck at the reverse anachronism as much as at Bennett's translation into a truly 'new' woman. Price has to negotiate various aspects of the novel, relying on her knowledge of Austen to ensure a happy ending in reality and fiction. Price eventually stays in the fictional world to be with Darcy, with whom she falls in love, leaving Elizabeth Bennett in the contemporary, 'real' world. Amanda physically embodies the desire to 'live' in a text, falling in love within it and, ultimately, deciding to stay. As such, the series performs an affective need to connect to an imagined historical space, but, similarly, reflects upon the strangeness of this. This section, then, considers the way that pleasure in the text and pleasure in viewing the text are part of the experience and the diegesis of costume drama.

Lost in Austen is part of a suite of dynamic reimaginations of Austen's work, texts that consider the fiction of the past as something that might be easily disrupted, rewritten, rejigged, or improved with the addition of zombies and sea-monsters.[42] Price's experience satirically points out the way in which *Pride and Prejudice* has become a set of tropes to be played with and detached from their original, giving rise in recent years to film (*Bride and Prejudice*, Gurinder Chadha, 2004), advertising, novels (*Pride and Prejudice and Zombies*, 2009), reality television (*Georgian House Party*, Channel 4, 2002), and newspaper columns (Helen Fielding's 'Bridget Jones' series, *The Independent*, 1995–6). Austen, together with the fictional 'past' that she represents, opens up a visual and textual palette that allows film-makers, novelists, and television writers incredible latitude to reinvent and rework.[43] The fictional past becomes a repository of themes, ideas, images, and discourses to fuel new and dynamic work (and this is in addition to the numerous continuations, sequels, and prequels of Austen's novels that have been written since the mid nineteenth century).[44]

Quite apart from playing with the conventions of costume drama and challenging the ways that reader–viewers engage with the idealized past that Austen in particular represents, *Lost in Austen* dramatically represents the motif of encountering the past through reading about it and anticipates various ways in which reading–engaging–empathizing might be construed. The past is a place that has a strongly delimited narrative, where things happen that are correct; yet, at the same time, the local, the domestic, the particular might be interrupted, fragmented, spliced, or confused. Price is aware that she is imagining, dreaming, inhabiting another's world, but her very manifestation in that world changes it subtly and turns it into a story about *her*; it is a physical iteration of a central theory of romance fiction, that is, that it allows the fantastical projection of the reader's self into the story.[45] In this case, the desire is for what Jessica Cox calls a 'pre-feminist' past, 'in which gender roles were (seemingly) more clearly defined'.[46] Fiction in *Lost in Austen* allows a space of possibility, ensuring that the reader can hold a – physical and imaginative – place in then *and* now. This imaginative simultaneity demonstrates once again the interesting demands that historical fiction makes of the reader, and the implications for a model of the historical imagination are clear. The ways in which readers of historical novels engage with the past are sophisticated and thoughtful. Within these ways, readers need to deal with their own affective, empathic relationship to the past and the narratives they read. *Lost in Austen* posits that the imaginative, aesthetic engagement with a famous historical/literary event/text might provoke an affective, physical, emotional response. As a fantasy of reading, it illustrates a way to think about romance fiction and wish-fulfilment. It suggests that an affective, imaginative engagement with a text – the ultimate 'romance' text – need not be dismissed totally as passive or escapist. Indeed, the need for fiction to have effect forces an aesthetic and imaginative historiographical shift to happen. Literally, the bored, unfulfilled female reader can escape into the text of the past, wear gorgeous costumes, and be wooed by a ravishing gentleman.

At one point, late in the narrative, Price asks her Darcy to climb into a man-made lake, visually quoting the most famous scene from the seminal 1995 BBC *Pride and Prejudice*, in which Colin Firth, playing Darcy, swims in a pond and then encounters Elizabeth Bennett. Price's response is affective (she gasps), as well as amused and perplexed:

> Price: I'm having a bit of a strange postmodern moment here.
> Darcy: Is that agreeable to you?
> Price: Oh yes, very.[47]

Price's 'strange' and uncanny experience with the re-rendering of a scene from a fictional past in her 'present' figures well the complexity of the text's relationship to historical experience and reading. It is unclear what her 'postmodern moment' is – whether history itself has evaporated, or whether she is articulating a sense of metatextual self-consciousness. This latter is something that the viewer is assumed to share, so that those watching are automatically removed from the narrative, their subjective engagement with the text revealed; this is why the scene is funny (which it is). Clearly, she is also engaging with the past from a postmodern point of view, somehow abstracted from an emotional contact while also aware of the seductions of a totalizing, explanatory narrative of events (the metanarratives of story, history, love, and romance that are being pressurized here).

The scene also uses language to emphasize contrast: Darcy's word 'agreeable', assumed to be an understatement, is unable to express the complex emotions that

Price is feeling. The men of the past cannot understand the desire of contemporary women. The pleasure of this scene, in some ways, lies in the recognition of its quotation and the absurd quality that it attains, the intertextual playfulness. Yet Price's desire for Darcy is 'real' ('Stay where you are; if you touch me again I will never be able to say the words I must say'). The representation of the past here acknowledges both that it is 'false', insofar as it is a re-rendering of something that is itself an adaptation and a fiction, and also that the desire engendered by the historical body might affect and effect the response of the reader/audience to it. In order to articulate what she thinks, her rationalization of the situation, Price must keep the figure at arm's length. Yet her response to him is rational and textual, physical and fictive. In this scene, she figures the situation of the reader of historical fiction, distanced and desiring, aware of the unreality of the situation but entranced by its possibility. Her historiographical and aesthetic engagement with the text is emotional, bodily, sensual, and rational all at the same time, and her desire mingles with her intellectual awareness to create a unique response to the events of the text. Her pleasure in the text is both cerebral and affective, and both contribute to her comprehension of reading and engaging with a historical text and moment.

[margin note: This reminds me of the historiographical engagement in Possession]

Firth's emergence from the pond in 1995 has been regularly cited as the moment that costume drama became 'sexy', shifting from a genre interested in commodified heritage to one with a more affective, emotionally charged mode. Certainly, this iconic scene, which is not in the original novel, figures a crucial moment in the genre's development. Darcy is to a certain extent vulnerable, the male body becoming the subject of the female gaze. He is performing an act of athleticism, swimming in the lake, and so there is a performative quality; his actions have an agency, despite his fragile status and obvious embarrassment. The sequence also historicizes the desire that both Elizabeth and the audience are supposed to feel at this point. Darcy wears an undershirt, still costumed during his swim, and it is the clinging nature of his clothing that makes the scene so important. Desire here is about the dissolving of social barriers – the lack of 'formal' clothing – but also, more importantly, about a speculation, an imaginative leap, a dream of what is hidden but kind of in sight. Simultaneously, this desire is framed within a nexus of 'authenticity' and realist tropes – costume (or the lack of), architectural solidity, and a linguistic fidelity to an imagined Georgian idiom. The pleasure of the televisual text here is displaced on to the body of Firth/Darcy, emblematic of an engagement that is emotional, imaginative, aesthetic, and rational at the same time. It is a physical relationship, predicated upon the relationship with the body of Firth/Darcy, and an aesthetic and affective response to this.

The scene reflects upon the structures of social nicety. Darcy and Elizabeth make awkward conversation, and he repeatedly asks after the health of her family. The falseness of their dialogue demonstrates the wroughtness of most social interaction. Like the costume that Darcy is not really wearing at this point, conversation is a way of not saying anything real, of avoiding and covering up the truth. Darcy's uncostumed status, together with the sudden vulnerability that it brings, figures him as someone controlled by the viewer. Rather than his magnificent portrait, haughty (and, importantly, hung above Elizabeth's height, so that she must look up at it in an earlier scene), he is wet and alone. Furthermore, the 1995 scene cannily works through ideas relating to tourism, heritage, and inheritance. Elizabeth Bennett is visiting Pemberley, Darcy's home, on an open day – she is being a tourist, looking around the house and wandering the grounds. She looks intently at Darcy's portrait – her viewing intercut with his preparations to swim – and in general enjoys the house as an extension of his character. When he emerges, having rushed to put 'more formal attire' on, the conversation revolves around the house:

Darcy:	I hope you're not displeased with Pemberley?
Elizabeth:	Oh not at all.
Darcy:	Then you approve of it?[48]

The house, here, is obviously a motif for its owner, something that the novel emphasizes (Bennett falls in love with Darcy essentially by wandering around his property). Elizabeth's interest in Darcy in the series is intertwined with her love for his house and estate; he is both powerful and an object of fascination, his interior spaces penetrated by unknown visitors for the purposes of heritage titillation and education. The visitors wander and look at his possessions and, as Elizabeth does, stare at his portrait. As Amy Sargeant has argued about the costume film more generally, the nexus of desire, heritage, and consumption that the genre is bound up within encourages a sense of historical engagement that assumes a wish to consume and visit – and she points out that visits to the houses that stood in for Pemberley gained a huge increase in visitors subsequent to the series.[49] Possession and the tourist gaze are bound up within the scene diegetically and are part of its working outwards in relation to the viewer. Tourism is a voyeuristic activity, and Darcy's personification as man and estate allows the series to reflect upon the various ways that this works and is bound up with a type of desire.

The encounter between Elizabeth and Darcy when he is dripping wet is rendered through a sequence of quarter-length shot reverse shots. Darcy cannot look at her; she struggles not to look at him. It thus reverses, to an extent, the controlling male gaze discussed at length in film criticism since Laura Mulvey's seminal article.[50] Mulvey highlights 'how film has depended on voyeuristic active/passive mechanisms' (p. 18). Here, Darcy is unmanned by his lack of clothing and, hence, struggles to escape; Elizabeth is intrigued and attracted, but attempts to control this. Shot reverse shot is a staple of realist construction, the building blocks of linearity in editing and narrative cinema. The sequence, therefore, demonstrates Mulvey's point about narrative cinema being predicated upon desire and scopophilic impetus to surveillance and control. However, it undermines this via its content, instead articulating something more interesting about the role of a female gaze – not as controlling, but still full of desire – in disrupting standard gender and social dynamics, in challenging male wholeness and self-conception. As such, it also communicates a shift in the viewing power dynamics.[51]

The multiplicity of visual and intellectual engagement inherent in this particular scene exemplifies the way in which the gaze and the affective engagement with the 'past' work in costume drama. These examples, and those that are discussed below, render a kind of surveillance and desire as part of the diegesis of historical or adaptive texts. They are also qualities that are modelled as part of the experience of viewing, suggestive of an audience that has a kind of scopophilic relationship, not simply with the texts of the cinema or the television, but also with the historical mode. It might be termed the historical gaze. This is a kind of viewing that is predicated upon a contemporary/historical binary, allowing the comfort of control on the part of the viewer as they watch the grimness of the past from the easy present. This historical gaze is inextricably linked to realism and, hence, it is dependent on the tropes of narrative control inherent in this aesthetic approach – linearity, the acknowledged fiction of editing, order, comprehension, authenticity. The historicized body is disciplined and ordered by this gaze, and, hence, the past becomes comprehensible and almost comforting – certainly something to desire and enjoy. The historical gaze in these instances is imprinted with a desire for the physical body of the past. Equally, the body of the past is displayed to be looked at, part of the entire, pleasurable experience of enjoying the costume drama itself. Embedded within a discourse of realism through the tropes of authenticity, the historical gaze is assumed on the part of the viewer (as was discussed regarding *Downton Abbey*, above). The pleasure of the text is in part the attraction to it, but also the understanding that the text is there to be looked at, to be controlled, and to be enjoyed. This is entirely of a part with its address to realism and, through that, a way of knowing that is somehow authentic: 'The historical film thus deploys visual style to create a sense of historical verisimilitude'.[52]

Rather than always controlling, however, the historical gaze might be subverted, in the same way that Darcy's wholeness and the physical sanctity of his house and the ordering systems it represents are undermined by Elizabeth's chance encounter with him. It might, therefore, be considered something that achieves a certain distance, or an irony of a kind, or that disrupts the standard male–female gaze relationship. Indeed, in the case of *Spartacus*, below, it is distinctly queer. The historicized subject knows it is being gazed at and desired and knowingly performs itself as 'historical'. This will be discussed further in relation to dragging history in Chapter 6. The body on display is engaged with and observed, but this viewing is not the dispassionate objectivity of 'scientific' history, but a clearly conflicted, subjective, compromised relationship that entails desire, a type of shame, a kind of understanding, and a way of thinking and feeling the past that is outside a mainstream understanding.

Historical exploitation

A key text in this discussion of historical fiction and visual pleasure is the TV series *The Tudors* (Showtime, 2007–10). The series covers the reign of Henry VIII in a sensationalist fashion, preferring to emphasize sex and violence and splendour rather than authenticity of action. *The Tudors* is clearly interested in undressing the costume drama, frankly and deliberately seeking to make the past more sexualized. As the show's creator pointed out, 'Showtime commissioned me to write an entertainment, a soap opera, and not history [. . .] And we wanted people to watch it'.[53] Making the past something trashy, sensational, excessive, exploitative, flashy – aesthetically part of modernity, rather than a discourse of 'history' – renders explicit the action of representing the past. It demonstrates the clichés inherent in this representation, while upsetting them. The series challenges certain conventions related to action and behaviour in the past, mainly to do with commonplaces such as sex, swearing, and violence. Costume drama and period fictions on television generally present a well-behaved, orderly vision of the past, whereas *The Tudors* suggests a more brutal and excessive sense of history: 'Challenging the construction that it is only the academic historian who has the right to speak, *The Tudors* works in partnership with a transnational mass media to suggest that no one version of history can be privileged'.[54] The series is excessive entertainment that uses the past merely as backdrop, but, as Wray argues, it still has historiographic purpose. It asks the audience to consider why and how they remember within contemporary television culture. It demands that they understand what kind of history they are wishing for, and enjoying. This self-consciousness on the part of the audience – understanding that this 'history' is for pleasure – suggests that they are aware of how knowledge structures and imaginative locale are being constructed for them, and how this might be challenged.

The Tudors is excessive in its approach to the past, and this has led critics to argue that, '*The Tudors* has always struggled to calibrate a tone, both aural and visual, that might feel true to its period without seeming absurdly anachronistic'.[55] This sense that there is a true historical 'tone' that obviates anachronism suggests a well-defined set of imaginative spaces that period fiction might inhabit. Transgressing the boundaries of these spaces leads to an ahistorical mess. Yet these acceptable norms are themselves clearly unhistorical, and the contract that the standard costume drama makes with the audience is that they will not notice this. *The Tudors* and other shows that challenge this normality strive, in their deployment of anachronistic behaviour, to undermine the structures of authenticity and realism. Anachronism is something that ensures that, 'discourse is exposed as outside of temporality', and it is that which disorders and reorders time.[56] Obviously, all historical fictionalizing on television and film is anachronistic – the modern actor in the period setting and story – and this estranging quality, the telescoping of the then and now, is both seen and disavowed by the viewer. As Jeremy Tambling argues, 'If history is what happened, and what we say happened, the first only knowable through the second, history can only be anachronistic' (pp. 5–6). This constant self-referentiality on the part of historical discourse is exacerbated in historical fictions, clearly anachronistic renderings of a presumed past. By demonstrating the limits of these representations, this show – and others like it – draws attention to the niceties and conventions of fictionalizing about the past. The recognition and simultaneous disavowal of anachronism (the 'then/now' dichotomy that is both seen and ignored) demonstrate that engagement with historical fictions is a complex and sophisticated undertaking.

The gaze of the spectator is paramount to the workings of *The Tudors*. In particular, the body of the actor is key to the pleasure of the audience. Famously, the producers of the series decided against representing Henry VIII, played by Jonathan Rhys Meyer, as anything other than an athletic young man: 'We don't want to destroy his good looks. An exact portrayal of Henry is not a factor that we think is important'.[57] Rhys Meyer's Henry directly contradicts the popular image of the corpulent, bearded king, and again this challenge to representational historical commonplace offers a different reading of the purpose of period entertainment. It also emphasizes the embodied aspect of this representation, as the body of the actor occludes that of the historical figure. The star is to be looked at, admired, and desired (his next role was to play the vampire *Dracula* (2013), a character who literally has to be seen by others, as his undead status means he has no reflection in a mirror).

After the global success of *The Tudors*, there came a run of shows interested in historical events as means for telling lurid stories about power, sex, and corruption, including *The Borgias* (2011–13), *Da Vinci's Demons* (2013–), *Vikings* (2014), and the various series of *Spartacus* (2010–13). These shows construct a new genre of titillation that might be called historical exploitation ('histploitation'?), using outrageous storylines from the past to present material that is sexually explicit, gory, visually excessive, and often extremely violent. These shows are interested in excess and performance, concentrating on how power and display are intertwined in the papal, royal, and ancient Roman courts. The historical setting allows for a justification of the extreme material, with a clear sense that this is transgressing a normative sense of the past. The shows trash the more 'tasteful' versions of the past rendered in mainstream costume drama, shows that have a certain cultural capital. They resist the legitimate forms of historical representation found elsewhere and, as such, contribute to a wider paracinematic 'negation and refusal of "elite" culture'.[58] Certainly, the unhappy response from both critics and historians to shows such as *The Tudors* demonstrates an anxiety about correctness and authenticity. The television historian David Starkey articulates this clearly: 'terrible history with no point. It's wrong for no purpose'.[59] In response, it would seem clear that *The Tudors* is wrong just to be wrong, and to demonstrate that historical fiction does not need to have a point, and, indeed, epistemologically this pointlessness is key. Television is not necessarily about dogma or purpose, or, indeed, even education. The pleasure of the historical text allows a different kind of experience to be had. Whether this is rationally historiographical or not is unclear. The kind of historiographical position that these shows outline is yet to be written, because their gesture is dismissed. It does not present itself in the right way and so, therefore, is deemed irrelevant. However, the exploitation, or the trash history that these series present, allows their audiences a kind of engagement with a kind of pastness that may or

FIGURE 5.1 *The Tudors* publicity shot
Source: Showtime/The Kobal Collection

may not be 'real' or 'authentic', but is still an engagement of a kind. Furthermore, historical exploitation points, through the deployment of tropes of excess, bad taste, violence, gore, and sex, the ways that mainstream period drama presents a polite, disciplined, controlled past.

The poor-taste version of Rome that *Spartacus* reveals provides a cartoonish montage of muscles, sex, gore, and combat. This is demonstrated particularly in its hyperreal visual style during the fight sequences, with blood spattering prettily in slow motion. *Spartacus* retells the story of the slave who became a gladiator, and the series follows the brutal existence of fighting men in Rome. One of the characteristics of exploitation is the high incidence of sex and nudity, and *Spartacus* has multiple graphic polysexual sex scenes, in addition to regular fights between extremely muscular, oiled up, semi-naked men. The show is self-conscious in this representation of fighting. The gladiators fight for the enjoyment of a venal and aggressive society, and this sense of being tested physically and watched while doing it ensures that the series is aware of the multiple ways that the gaze might work to construct or to control. It knows the audience is watching and plays on its desire for blood and muscular flesh that is both diegetic and part of the pleasure of viewing. The series is concerned with the spectacle of violence and the combination of flesh

FIGURE 5.2 Fighting and muscles in *Spartacus*

Source: USA-TV/The Kobal Collection/Griffen, Kristy

and fighting that excites the audience. Indeed, in a key sequence that has the gladiators fighting in a household for the pleasure of an aristocratic family, one member happily talks of her excitement when watching the violence. The self-reflexivity here is overt, as the audience is forced to see its own complicity in the spectacle and its desire for the excitement – which is clearly intended to mean both dramatic and sexual excitement. Performance is never attended by neutral spectatorship, and the self-consciousness of *Spartacus* allows this to be revealed.

The 'mutability' of texts relating to Rome in popular culture has been the subject of much debate in recent years, sparked by the global success of the film *Gladiator* (Ridley Scott, 2000):

> Representations of the Roman past should not be judged by the ways in which they successfully represent a 'real' text or past events; rather, they should be seen as complex and rich dialogues with the past whose value resides precisely in how the past is reformulated in the light of the present.[60]

Scholars of classical reception, as much as those who work on medievalism, recognize the protean nature of the afterlife of the period.[61] The ways in which the past is used are uppermost in this kind of analysis. Romanticizing the past is bad 'history' as it is presently understood. However, it is also something that bespeaks a desire for a *kind* of past (and, it follows, a way of thinking about contemporary identity). These shows demonstrate a wish for a type of past. They show an understanding of the past that, at base, works on a physical, affective level. Enjoying the past, taking pleasure in its representation, and becoming affectively involved in versions of it (even within an escapist nexus) are all constituent parts of the wish for a particular kind of pastness. They are demonstrative of an affective epistemology that posits understanding of something that is 'pastness' through a bodily and emotional engagement. *Spartacus* is the logical conclusion of these overly excessive shows, staging its violent conflict simply for the titillation of the viewing public.

Historical exploitation, moreover, can be deadly serious in its engagement with the oppressive and ethically problematic effects of 'realism'. The intertwining of visual pleasure, violence, and historical representation opens up a set of ethical issues that need to be explored. Historical exploitation is radical in two ways. First, it asks questions of how the historical imagination has been supported by an aesthetic discourse of realism that occludes violence, historical difference, sex, class, death, and disease. Second, it also makes oblique commentary about contemporary culture and its obsession with violence – an obsession that has led to the historical imaginary itself being infected. There is also something deconstructive about the historical exploitation – undermining and attacking hegemonic systems of representation – and it certainly challenges rational models of history. Finally, this work is defiantly populist, reaching an audience demographic uncatered-for by 'traditional' period drama and, hence, marginalized. Historical exploitation gives the viewer pause, because it enforces an understanding of the problems of representing the past and the ethical discussions inherent in doing such a thing.

These concerns are brought into focus by *Inglourious Basterds* (2009), Quentin Tarantino's meditation on screen violence and historical representation. It is also a film that has divided critics and generated a huge amount of vitriol, in the main owing to the trashy aesthetic and loose handling of historical information.[62] The violence and controversial retributive narrative in both this film and *Django Unchained* (2012) are evidently historical exploitation, and this aesthetic is clearly part of Tarantino's approach to the past (his 2007 film *Death Proof* is an attempt at making a contemporary exploitation film). Both films argue for an aesthetic of the past that does not ignore the horrors of that past and that, through excess, might achieve a better communication of the grimness of events than can be achieved by a discourse – costume drama – that is somehow now a compromised mode. Tarantino's film has been described as 'parodistic irreverence', and it certainly pushes the historical film into particularly problematic ethical territory in its mixture of violence, gore, excess, metacinematic reference, and vengeance fantasy.[63] However, as Colón Semenza argues, 'One of the major goals of *Inglourious Basterds*, perhaps its *major* goal, is to encourage viewers to ask themselves what the ethical obligations of the filmmaker happen to be'.[64]

Inglourious Basterds relates two separate narratives of vengeance. In one, Shosanna Dreyfus plans to destroy the Nazi who murdered her family by burning down a cinema showing a new propaganda film. The other concerns the activities of the 'basterds', a commando band operating in France. At the end of the film, the movie theatre burns, killing all, including Adolf Hitler, in a counterfactual vengeance moment. Hence, the film reflects upon what it is to watch a violent film, as the final sequence in a burning cinema enacts a fantastical Jewish vengeance on a compromised audience. The film is exceptionally ambivalent about the ways that violence might be rendered on-screen and the effects of film as propaganda, while simultaneously revelling in cinematic violence. It therefore works fundamentally to provoke and dismiss cinematic pleasure, articulating a stern warning to an audience about enjoying historical representation and, particularly, war. It also engages seriously with discussions of memory, appropriateness, witnessing, and the Holocaust; similarly to *Django Unchained*, a film that attempts to understand and represent something of the horror of slavery, the film uses the tools of popular media (that is, cinema) to reflect upon both the horrific events of the past and the strange ways that they have been remembered. It also challenges an audience to understand the ways that pleasure and violence are intertwined in the cinema, and in historical recollection.

There is a link between mundanity and excess that is well worked out as both a historical experience and also as something that might create some kind of dramatic tension. The central scene of the film is a 20-minute sequence in a tavern, spoken nearly entirely in German, in which a very long drinking game is played. Several Allied agents are undercover in the tavern and are engaged in conversation with a group of drunk German soldiers and an officer. The sequence is a kind of hyperreal historical representation, attempting to communicate through its length a kind of understanding of the experience of the 'real' of the past. However, dramatically, it is extremely tense as a sequence, and the audience experiences a kind of *longeur* at the same time as being anxious about possible outcomes. It both wants and does not want the sequence to end, as the end might lead to death or violence for the protagonists. Eventually, it ends in a bloody and excessive shoot-out. Tarantino thus uses length here to highlight severally. The sequence briefly catches the audience in the double anxiety mentioned above. It is made uncomfortable by this set of moments – not only because of the tension of the scene (which is communicated mainly through glances between characters), but also through its unfamiliarity, length, and language. Tarantino's engagement with the audience is well attested; Alexander Ornella demonstrates his manipulation of the audience, using 'various forms of violence to brilliantly orchestrate (or manipulate) the viewers' emotions and bodily senses'.[65]

The film points out, through this sequence and other set pieces, how unused an audience is to extended scenes in historical film, demonstrating how 'reality' in costume aesthetics is underpinned by very modern editing techniques. As Chris Fujiwara argues in relation to the film's use of repetition and excess: 'The lack of movement by either the character or the camera calls attention to the redundancy that is the principle [. . .] the redundancy of the camerawork and editing'.[66] This principle of redundancy is primarily related to the film's meditation upon form and aesthetics: 'excessive information is not merely an ordinary hazard of storytelling but a thematic preoccupation, even a principle of the narration' (p. 38). This 'redundancy' is part of the film's aesthetic investment, ironically exposing the inherent problems in realist cinematic vocabulary by deploying them to such an extreme effect. In particular, the use of German throughout (with subtitles) has the effect of highlighting the aesthetic compromises generally made in making war films. 'Realism' is demonstrated, by inference and comparison, to be a set of accepted aesthetic rules. Similarly, gore and ultraviolence in the film (and its ignoring of the 'facts' of history through its counterfactual narrative) are used to bend the realist-period aesthetic out of shape, as happens at the conclusion of this sequence. The film points out the way that realist narrative dramatizes the past. Historical discourse here is constructed and made to mean dramatically, and the aesthetic of realism contributes to this falsification of a sense of the past.

Inglourious Basterds is an exploitation/histploitation film that asks its audience a series of ethical questions about the representation of the past – on the one hand, revelling in excess and gore; on the other, exploring how our versions of the past are fictive even when disguised as authentic. The historical exploitation, therefore, is engaged in revealing the problematic 'realism' of period drama. This can be made clear when two self-conscious elements of the sequence are explored. First, spoken German is foregrounded, as the accent of Michael Fassbender's undercover British agent is questioned. Despite his speaking the language authentically, he is not the 'real' thing. The sequence therefore comments upon the performance of authenticity. Second, the games – 20 questions, with a name on a card on the forehead of the player – highlight the ethical dubiousness of American exceptionalist narratives of the war. One character is an Apache Indian, and another, who is actually King Kong, works out through clues ('Did I come to America in chains from the jungle?') that he is the 'negro experience in America'. Although the horror of the Nazis is clear in the sequence (with flashbacks of torture and a toast to the '1,000-year Reich'), any sense of superiority is leavened by the reminder of 'equivalent' American atrocity. This is a strategy throughout the film and, as Hake argues, demonstrates Tarantino's 'artistic resistance both to the fantasies of universal humanism that buttress the postpolitical in the contemporary world and to the conventions of emotional realism that still dominate'.[67] For Hake, Tarantino's film demonstrates the problems inherent in passive aesthetics that appeal to uninflected versions of the past. The film, then, although heavily exploitative, reflects upon the ways in which historical representations work to themselves exploit the understanding of the viewer. Historical realist film does its own violence to an audience, interpellating them ideologically and rendering a historiographical discourse, while attempting to disavow this. The authentic tropes of costume- or period-drama film, then, are here critiqued as agents of a kind of historiographical passivity. Much as the proto-capitalist realism of costume drama is to a certain extent interrogated by 'misery' period shows, historical exploitation critiques the establishment, through realism, of a set of aesthetic discourses for rendering the past uninflected. It also highlights the ways in which the pleasure of the text is often created in historical films through ethically dubious means that disavow historical witnessing and reality. In this reading, such tropes as narrative speed, editing, violence, and non-diegetic music are critiqued as part of a process of deadening, seeking to turn the engagement with the horror of the past as something neutral and even enjoyable. Historical exploitation, then, might through its criticisms of realism provide a way of reading mainstream costume drama and, particularly, its gestures to pleasure.

Costume drama, in its very definition and essence, is a realist aesthetic – the point, surely, being the authenticity in the imagination of the 'costume'. Yet, even in the description of the genre, there is a sense of an inherent performance, a dressing-up. So, 'costume drama' articulates in its very nomenclature a tension between fiction and fact, between the real and the imagined, between something fake and something inherently, physically, proper. This cleaving (in both senses of the word) to and of reality while disavowing the truth-value of the text is something described by Jacques Derrida when discussing mime:

> He represents nothing, imitates nothing, does not have to conform to any prior referent with the aim of achieving adequation or verisimilitude. One can here foresee an objection: since the mime imitates nothing, reproduces nothing, opens up in its origin the very thing he is tracing out, presenting or producing, he must be the very movement of truth. Not, of course, truth in the form of adequation between the representation and the present of the thing itself, or between imitator and imitated, but truth as the present unveiling of the present.[68]

The mime highlights a lacuna in representation, something that hints at the possibility of truth. Yet this 'truth' is associated with nothingness, as it comes from 'nothing'. Somehow, it seems more authentic, despite its evident emptiness. However, Derrida continues:

> But this is not the case [. . .] We are faced then with mimicry imitating nothing; faced, so to speak, with the double that doubles no simple, a double that nothing anticipates, nothing at least, that is not itself already double. There is no simple reference [. . .] This speculum reflects no reality: it produces mere 'reality-effects' [. . .] In this speculum with no reality, in this mirror of a mirror, a difference or dyad does exist, since there are mimes and phantoms. But it is a difference without reference, or rather reference without a referent, without any first or last unit, a ghost that is the phantom of no flesh, wandering about without a past, without any death, birth, or presence.
> (p. 206)

This forms the basis of a doubling deconstructive historiography based on the idea of narrative–mimesis: 'everything in the story space creation process is a simulation based on the notion of *mimesis*, where art imitates (note: not corresponds to) reality'.[69] Historical fictions in general work in the realist mode, attempting mimetic reproduction while, at the same time, aware that this gesture is self-undermining. They produce 'reality-effects' of a kind, gesture towards something that does not and cannot exist. They are the double of something and, therefore, attain a ghostly quality. As this chapter has argued (and the next will too), there are many historical fictions that actively seek to challenge the orthodoxy of realism in their diegesis or content. What Derrida points out is that the mime artist's seemingly mimetic gesture is to something that does not exist; similarly, the impetus of costume drama and popular history is to represent something that never happened, even in the midst of suggesting its truthful authenticity. What is produced is a simulacrum or performance of pastness, a deployment of a series of realist tropes that attempt to construct a believable narrative while clearly undermining the very possibility of that 'realism' through their very ontology. This notion of the mime is central as a way of thinking about the ways in which the past is represented in historical fictive texts. Costume drama performs this doubleness, 'mimicry imitating nothing', undermining the realism of the realist mode and subverting mimetic tropes in a way that interrogates the entire process of historical fictive representation. The instances covered so far have multiple consequences for the way in which the past might be conceptualized, consumed, and interrogated by a popular audience.

The pleasure of the 'historical' text lies in the engagement with it – the intermingling of self and fiction as experienced by Amanda Price – rather than the creation of a distance. This is the 'complicity' suggested by Haneen. Historical fictions allow for an encounter with a kind of past that is predicated upon enjoyment, because, if they are not pleasant to an extent, they will not sell or achieve popularity. Even their escapist tendencies reveal a way of ordering the past that is innately historiographical, as the critique of such work demonstrated in the 1980s. The fundamental impetus of a historical fiction, then, be it film or novel or TV series, is an encounter with pastness via a kind of pleasurable encounter.[70] Historical fictions are texts that combine entertainment with education, instructing and delighting in equal measure. The model of historiographical engagement that they presume, then, is inextricably bound to this enjoyment. They present an epistemology insofar as they suggest an encounter with pastness and an ordering of knowledge about that past around certain tropes: viewing, desire, display, excess, realism. The shows that critique these tropes, either through misery, humour, or transgressive excess, demonstrate the ways in which passive costume drama works. They are themselves revisionist, challenging particular models of narrative historical representation. Yet the passivity and escapist aesthetic demanded in mainstream costume drama suggest an engagement of a kind – even in seeming disengagement. The need for a nostalgic, easy past is a kind of historical understanding. Furthermore, there is an epistemology associated with pleasure and linked to a kind of desire of the type that is described by the fictions themselves for the bodies in and of the past. The final chapter will consider something that has been in the background all along: the notion of performance. It will consider how, through this, discomfort, misrecognition, and horror work in relation to the affective economy of historiographical engagement already briefly outlined.

Notes

1 See the discussion of film as 'escapism' in Marnie Hughes-Warrington, *History Goes to the Movies* (London and New York: Routledge, 2006), pp. 2–4.

2 Hughes-Warrington, *History Goes to the Movies*, p. 3. A notable exception is Claire Monk, *Heritage Film Audiences: Period Films and Contemporary Audiences in the UK* (Edinburgh, UK: Edinburgh University Press, 2011).

3 See, for instance, Roland Barthes, *The Pleasure of the Text*, trans. Richard Miller (New York: Hill & Wang, 1980).

4 See Emily Robinson, 'Touching the Void: Affective History and the Impossible', *Rethinking History*, 14:4 (2010), 503–20, and even Eric Ketelaar, 'Archives as Spaces of Memory', *Journal of the Society of Archivists*, 29:1 (2008), 9–27. More widely, see Ann Cvetkovich, *An Archive of Feeling: Trauma, Sexuality, and Lesbian Public Cultures* (Durham, NC: Duke University Press, 2003).

5 'Paris Green', *Boardwalk Empire*, Series 1, Episode 11 (2010).

6 'The Heritage Film and Gendered Spectatorship', *Close Up: The Electronic Journal of British Cinema*; available online at: www.shu.ac.uk/services/lc/closeup/monk.htm (accessed 8 December 2014).

7 For general discussions of the costume drama, see Andrew Higson, *English Heritage, English Cinema* (Oxford, UK: Oxford University Press, 2003), particularly 'Mapping the Field', pp. 9–46, and Claire Monk and Amy Sargeant, eds, *British Historical Cinema* (New York and London: Routledge, 2002).

8 See Andrew Higson, 'Re-presenting the National Past: Nostalgia and Pastiche in the Heritage Film', in Lester Friedman, ed., *Fires Were Started* (London: Wallflower, 2006), pp. 91–109.

9 'Englishness' (letter), *Sight and Sound*, July 1991, p. 63.

10 Higson, *English Heritage, English Cinema*, p. 72.

11 See Janice Radway, *Reading the Romance* (Chapel Hill, NC: University of North Carolina Press, 1984), for a discussion of 'oppositional' readings of romance fiction.

12 Katherine Byrne, 'Adapting Heritage: Class and Conservatism in *Downton Abbey*', *Rethinking History*, 18:3 (2014), 311–27.

13 'Downton Abbey Second Series', *The Daily Telegraph*, 30 July 2011; available online at: www.telegraph.co.uk/culture/tvandradio/8670941/Downton-Abbey-second-series-first-review.html (accessed 25 October 2013).

14 Ibid.

15 'TV Review', *The Guardian*, 4 November 2012; available at: www.theguardian.com/tv-and-radio/2012/nov/04/tv-review-downton-abbey (accessed 25 October 2013).

16 'Dear Old Downton Abbey's No Place for Shock Tactics Like Playing the Rape Card', *The Mirror*, 8 October 2013; available online at: www.mirror.co.uk/tv/tv-reviews/downton-abbey-rape-scenes-not-2348806 (Accessed 25 October 2013).

17 Mark Fisher, *Capitalist Realism* (Ropley, UK: 0 Books, 2009), p. 7.

18 Raphael Samuel, *Theatres of Memory* (London: Verso, 1994), p. 290.

19 Patrick Wright, *On Living in an Old Country* (London: Verso, 1985), p. xiv.

20 This section is reprinted from 'Invitation to Historians', *Rethinking History: The Journal of Theory and Practice*, 18:4 (2014), 599–612.

21 *The Paradise*, Series 1, Episode 1 (2012).

22 See, for instance, the essays in John Corner and Sylvia Harvey, eds, *Enterprise and Heritage: Crosscurrents of National Culture* (London and New York: Routledge, 1991).

23 'Making and Selling Heritage Culture: Style and Authenticity in Historical Fictions on Film and Television' in Justine Ashby and Andrew Higson, eds, *British Cinema, Past and Present* (London: Routledge, 2000), pp. 301–15 (p. 301).

24 *Today*, Radio 4, 14 October 2013, 6–9 a.m. These figures were later contested as erroneous.

25 NBC estimates 120 million people have watched *Downton Abbey*; Jeremy Egner, 'A Bit of Britain Where the Sun Still Never Sets', *New York Times*, 3 January 2013; available online at: www.nytimes.com/2013/01/06/arts/television/downton-abbey-reaches-around-the-world.html?_r=1& (accessed 15 February 2013).

26 *The Mill*, Series 1, Episode 1 (2013).

27 Grace Dent, 'Grace Dent on TV', *Independent*, 2 August 2013; available online at: www.independent.co.uk/arts-entertainment/tv/features/grace-dent-on-tv-the-mill-channel-4-8742342.html (accessed 8 November 2013).

28 Gerard Gilbert, 'A Very British *Heimat*', *Independent*, 14 March 2013; available online at: www.independent.co.uk/arts-entertainment/tv/features/a-very-british-heimat-will-bbc-drama-the-village-be-as-epic-as-the-german-saga-8533200.html (accessed 8 November 2013).

29 *The Village*, Series 1, Episode 2 (2013).

30 *The Village*, Series 1, Episode 3 (2013).

31 *The Village*, op. cit.

32 Francesca Infante and Luke Salkeld, 'A Miserable Start for the Village', *The Daily Mail*, 1 April 2013; available online at: www.dailymail.co.uk/tvshowbiz/article-2302163/A-miserable-start-The-Village-BBCs-answer-Downton-Abbey.html (accessed 9 December 2014).

33 'The Village: Episode Six', *The Telegraph*, 5 May 2013; available online at: www.telegraph.co.uk/culture/tvandradio/10036702/The-Village-episode-six-BBC-One-review.html (accessed 8 November 2013).

34 Rebecca Nicholson, 'Hunderby', *The Guardian*, 14 January 2013; available online at: www.theguardian.com/tv-and-radio/tvandradioblog/2013/jan/14/hunderby-julia-davis-comedy-worth-watching (accessed 15 November 2013).

35 Alex Fletcher, '*Hunderby* Q&A', *Digital Spy*, 31 August 2012; available online at: www.digitalspy.co.uk/tv/interviews/a403093/julia-davis-hunderby-qa-i-dont-always-see-the-darkness.html (accessed 15 November 2013).

36 Gerard Gilbert, 'Julia Davis: Profile', *The Independent*, People section, 25 August 2012; available online at www.independent.co.uk/news/people/profiles/julia-davis-i-dont-want-to-offend-anyone-8073418.html (accessed 15 November 2012).

37 *Hunderby*, Series 1, Episode 2 (2012).

38 *Hunderby* Series 1, Episode 3 (2012).

39 *Hunderby*, op. cit.

40 *Hunderby*, op. cit.

41 *Hunderby*, op. cit.

42 See Gina Macdonald and Andrew F. Macdonald, eds, *Jane Austen on Screen* (Cambridge, UK: Cambridge University Press, 2003), and Suzanne R. Pucci and James Thompson, eds, *Jane Austen and Co.: Remaking the Past in Contemporary Culture* (Albany, NY: State University of New York Press, 2003).

43 See Julie Sanders, *Adaptation and Appropriation* (London and New York: Routledge, 2005), and Linda Hutcheon, *A Theory of Adaptation* (London and New York: Routledge, 2012).

44 Jerome de Groot, *The Historical Novel* (London and New York: Routledge), pp. 64–7.

45 Scott McCracken, *Pulp* (Manchester, UK: Manchester University Press, 1998), p. 75. See also Pamela Regis, *A Natural History of the Romance Novel* (Philadelphia, PA: University of Pennsylvania Press, 2003).

46 Jessica Cox, ' "A Strange Post(Feminist) Moment"? Conflicting Constructions of Femininity in ITV's *Lost in Austen*', *Critical Studies in Television*, 8:1 (2013), 36–51 (p. 36).

47 *Lost in Austen*, Series 1, Episode 4 (2009).

48 *Pride and Prejudice*, Series 1, Episode 6 (1995).

49 'Making and Selling Heritage Culture', in Ashby and Higson, *British Cinema, Past and Present*.

50 'Visual Pleasure and Narrative Cinema', *Screen*, 16:3 (1975), 6–18.

51 Claire Monk discusses the importance of the female gaze in viewing costume drama, *Heritage Film Audiences*, pp. 165–83.

52 James Chapman, *Past and Present: National Identity and the British Historical Film* (London: I.B. Tauris, 2004), p. 4.

53 'The Royal Life (Some Facts Altered)', *New York Times*, 23 March 2008; available online at: www.nytimes.com/2008/03/23/arts/television/23gate.html (accessed 22 April 2015).

54 Ramona Wray, 'Henry's Desperate Housewives: *The Tudors*, the Politics of Historiography and the Beautiful Body of Jonathan Rhys Meyers' in Gregory M. Semenza, ed., *The English Renaissance in Popular Culture* (Basingstoke, UK: Palgrave Macmillan, 2010), pp. 25–42 (p. 25).

55 Ginia Bellafante, 'Nasty, but Not So Brutish and Short', *New York Times*, 28 March 2008; available online at: www.nytimes.com/2008/03/28/arts/television/28tudo.html?_r=2& oref=slogin (accessed 27 November 2008).

56 Jeremy Tambling, *On Anachronism* (Manchester, UK: Manchester University Press, 2010), p. 15.

57 Chris Irvine, 'Henry VIII Will Not Get Fat', *The Daily Telegraph*, 31 August 2008; available online at: www.telegraph.co.uk/news/celebritynews/2655240/Henry-VIII-will-not-get-fat-in-historically-inaccurate-The-Tudors.html (accessed 22 April 2015).

58 Jeffrey Sconce, '"Trashing" the Academy: Taste, Excess, and an Emerging Politics of Cinematic Style', *Screen*, 36:4 (1995), 371–93 (p. 372).

59 'David Starkey's Blast for the Past', *Daily Mail*, 16 October 2008; available online at: www.dailymail.co.uk/tvshowbiz/article-1078114/David-Starkeys-blast-past-slates-BBCs-The-Tudors-terrible-history.html (accessed 27 November 2008).

60 Sandra R. Joshel, Margaret Malamud, and Maria Wyke, 'Introduction' in Sandra R. Joshel, Margaret Malamud, and Maria Wyke, eds, *Imperial Projections: Ancient Rome in Modern Popular Culture* (Baltimore, MD: Johns Hopkins University Press, 2005), pp. 1–23 (p. 2).

61 See Monica Cyrino, *Big Screen Rome* (Oxford, UK: Wiley-Blackwell, 2005); Maria Wyke, *Projecting the Past: Ancient Rome, Cinema and History* (London and New York: Routledge, 1997); Kathleen Biddick, *The Shock of Medievalism* (Durham, NC: Duke University Press, 1998).

62 For a discussion of the critical reception and contemporary cinema of revenge, see John Rieder, 'Race and Revenge Fantasies in *Avatar*, *District 9*, and *Inglourious Basterds*', *Science Fiction Film and Television*, 4 (2011), 41–56. See also Matthew Boswell, *Holocaust Impiety in Literature, Popular Music and Film* (Basingstoke, UK: Palgrave Macmillan, 2011).

63 Sabine Hake, *Screen Nazis: Cinema, History, and Democracy* (Madison, WI: University of Wisconsin Press, 2012), p. 160.

64 Greg M. Colón Semenza, 'The Ethics of Appropriation: *Samson Agonistes*, *Inglourious Basterds*, and the Biblical Samson Tale', *Adaptation*, 7:1 (2014), 62–81 (p. 62).

65 'Disruptive Violence as Means to Create a Space for Reflection: Thoughts on Tarntino's Attempts at Audience Irritation', in Robert von Dassanowsky, ed., *Quentin Tarantino's Inglourious Basterds: A Manipulation of Metacinema* (London: Continuum, 2012), pp. 215–45 (p. 216).

66 '"A Slight Duplication of Efforts": Redundancy and the Excessive Camera in *Inglourious Basterds*' in von Dassanowsky, *Quentin Tarantino's Inglourious Basterds*, pp. 37–55 (p. 39).

67 Hake, *Screen Nazis*, p. 162.

68 *Dissemination*, trans. Barbara Johnson (Chicago, IL: University of Chicago Press, 1981), p. 206. This section also appears in a slightly different form in *Acts of Literature*, trans. Derek Attridge (London and New York: Routledge, 1992), p. 157. This moment in Derrida's thought is key to the arguments of Judith Butler when conceptualizing

imitation and inversion; see 'Imitation and Gender Subordination' in Henry Abelove, ed., *The Lesbian and Gay Studies Reader* (London and New York: Routledge, 1993) pp. 307–20 (p. 319, n. 12) and discussion in Chapter 6.

69 Alun Munslow, *Narrative and History* (London and New York: Routledge, 2007), p. 24.

70 For the commercial and industrial context of the costume drama/heritage film, see Higson, *English Heritage, English Cinema*, pp. 86–119.

6

PERFORMANCE AND AFFECT

Towards the end of the first series of the American thriller *Homeland* (Showtime, 2011–), a pivotal scene happens on the site of Gettysburg. The central character, Brodie, has taken his family there as a prelude to a treasonous act (the assassination of a politician). While on the battlefield, Brodie recounts the story of Joshua Chamberlain to his son Chris, to make him both sense the import of the physical place to the event and also grasp the lesson to be learned from history:

> They charged down the side of the hill against the enemy. And it was so unexpected, it was so crazy, that the line was held that day. All because of a schoolteacher from Maine who was willing to do what was necessary for a cause that he believed in.[1]

Later, he asks his son to recall the story of Gettysburg and to remember to be brave and courageous. This is an attempt to give him some kind of emotional buffer for the time to come, after Brodie has been denounced as a suicide bomber. The Gettysburg scene demonstrates how historical experience – particularly that which might make one act differently in the future – is often imagined to be fundamentally physical. Brodie asserts the import of the place and the experiential engagement with history through the material. Yet he is a character whom the audience suspects, and his drawing of a contemporary reading from his version of what happened in the incredibly symbolic place where they stand gives a viewer pause. Brodie's version of the past, and the future, is ethically compromised; he seeks to use it to salve his own conscience, and to influence how things might turn out in the days ahead. This is all wrapped up within evidently problematic discourses of nationhood, achievement, tourism (and, hence, consumerism), sacrifice, and the suggestion, in Brodie's story, of some kind of truthful, central experience that leads directly from then to now.

Popular texts conceptualize the past – and our relationship to it – in this complex fashion. The past is rarely straightforward, generally compromised, and ethically dubious. The lessons from history, if any, are to be suspected, and any parallels that might be drawn are inevitably in thrall to the desires of the present. Similarly, an engagement with that past might be anything from awe-inspiring (normally unflappable children are moved), terrifying, to amusing or simply boring. The material, the bodily, the physical are paramount and, hence, ensure an obvious partiality of experience while they enact an affective engagement. Finally, the representation of this experience of the historical suggests how narratives of the past might have the (in this case problematic) ability to reach into the present and future. Yet, in this moment, the audience must reflect that this is inherently tragic. Chris's recollection of, and possible lesson from, history will be deployed in an attempt at reanimating his dead father in his imagination. History has a power in the present, seeming to enable a configuration of identity (around ideals, here, of sacrifice and bravery) through this affective appeal to the emotive, the physical, and the material.

This final chapter reflects upon the physical body in *Hunger* (Steve McQueen, 2009), the films of the *Red Riding Trilogy* (Channel 4, various directors, 2009), and Howard Brenton's play *Anne Boleyn* (2010). These three very different texts show the ways in which the body works in historical fictions (in multiple ways) and enable the chapter to make certain assertions about the relationship between ethics and performance. Hence, the final arguments return to those of the opening chapter regarding ethics, reading, self-consciousness, and historiographical integrity. The chapter does this in order to consider the status of the 'historical' text and the ethical positions of the audience/film-maker/'historian' that seem to be brokered by it. The texts considered here point out the distance between knowledge and feeling. They reflect upon the problematic rendering of the past within a leisure space, remaking the past for viewing pleasure. In these texts' meditations upon performance, archive, re-enactment, and witnessing/authenticity can be seen again the ways in which popular texts enable a new way of thinking about pastness. The texts suggest that the past must shock by its obscenity and otherness, and anything that attempts to obviate this horror (by making 'history') is constructing a phantasmagorical dream world of commodified pastness. It would be blowing smoke in the eyes of the audience, rather than allowing it to see the ashen remains and to mourn what is past. Each text also plays with the idea of affect in historical representation, asking the audience how it is able to empathize and understand – and recognize – the historical other. In particular, the affect of the text is provoked by the body, and the relationship between the two and epistemology is demonstrated and interrogated. In all three of these texts, the ethical discussion relating to representation results in an urgent disavowal of the standard tools of historical documentation. In their place is suggested a broken, but possibly more useful, historiography of the material. As Carolyn Dinshaw argues, 'a history that reckons in the most expansive way possible with how people exist in time, with what it feels like to be a body in time, or in multiple times, or out of time, is a *queer* history'.[2] A strange and dislocating interrelation of the physical and the temporal, something that might be considered *perverse* in its challenge to rationality, is the central historiographical move of historical fictions, as has been argued throughout this book. These texts demonstrate powerfully this important epistemological shift, replacing the rational with an idealized empathy that itself is to be suspected.[3] They interrogate what it is to respond emotionally and physically to events in the past, or to fictive events that are situated in that past. Similarly to those texts considered in Chapter 5, they ask what it is to react intellectually–emotionally–physically to a representation of the past, and what effects such a hybrid understanding has on the historiography of the text.

The opening section here on the *Red Riding Trilogy* considers how a text might focus all manner of meditations upon historicity through a central motif of performance. This performance allows for a heightened emotional and affective response on the part of the viewer – an empathy – while simultaneously denying any semblance of a *real* connection between then and now brokered by a fictional construct. The use of affect to effect connection is held up to be a suspect technique, part of a suite of narrative tropes that must be interrogated. Affect is not something transhistorical, and the connections it seems to make must be considered very carefully.[4] These texts show this affective work and also how it might be questioned, and why. Howard Brenton's *Anne Boleyn* continually rehearses tropes of performance and dissidence to reflect upon the historical contingency of any action (both real and performed). Both *Anne Boleyn* and Steve McQueen's *Hunger* emphasize the importance of the body in rendering a seeming connection between then and now: the body as historiographic tool, physically 'writing' a kind of history, an epistemological resource. *Hunger* meditates on the ways in which the 'real' can be expressed on film, forcing the viewer into a visceral and affective reaction with events in order to ensure a consideration of the ways in which historical film works. All three texts engage with the ethical problematic of representing the real, and the realist mode, particularly through their complicated relationships with, and renderings of, 'real' historical figures. In these meditations on the ethics of representation, then, they enact the key debate that popular history provokes: what does it mean to deliberately *lie* (or create fiction) about the past? Furthermore, what does this explicit fictionalizing reveal about 'real' history? How does the body work here? As in *Homeland*, it is clear from a consideration of these texts that the ways in which the past is rendered are highly performative, ethically problematic, narrative (and embedded in a realist–materialist discourse, demonstrated by Brodie's inspiring storytelling on the physical site of Gettysburg), often with a skewed or biased attempt at education or ownership of a memory. The conceiving of performance in historical fictions demonstrates both the unfixed nature of identity and the ways in which history is constructed. The affective in these texts interrogates historical essentialism, allows a reflection upon historical agency, and, in particular, provokes the audience to conceptualize its relationship to the historical other.

The *Red Riding Trilogy*, smoke, ethics, and performance

Exploration of the past through the consideration of particularly horrific crimes or occasions is common in recent British culture. Gordon Burn's books about the Ripper case, *Somebody's Husband, Somebody's Son* (1990) and the Wests (*Happy Like Murderers*, 1998), and his fiction that involves the Moors murders (*Alma Cogan*, 1991), are influential explorations of the traumatic quality of these crimes. Traumatic past moments have been considered in the television films *Bloody Sunday* (Paul Greengrass, 2002) and *Omagh* (Pete Travis, 2004). Such films have also looked into the horrific crimes of Rosemary and Fred West (*Appropriate Adult*, ITV, 2011), the investigation of the Yorkshire Ripper murders (*This Is Personal*, Granada, 2000), and other events of great trauma, such as *Hillsborough* (Granada, 1996).[5] Crimes such as those of the murderer Malcolm Webster (*The Widower*, ITV 2014) and Ronnie Biggs (*Mrs Biggs*, ITV 2012) have been made into television drama. The ethical and political decisions involved in these accounts of near-contemporary history suggest that TV films are prepared to combine elements of fiction with violent and traumatic events in order to explore, as much as possible, the implications, challenges, and causes of modern sensibilities. So, it might be argued that there is a fascination with comprehending through televisual representation, of returning through docudrama or fiction to scenes of great social sadness and horror. In many ways, this owes everything to the key work in the genre, Truman Capote's *In Cold Blood*, with its combination of reportage and consciously engaged subjectivity on the part of the writer.[6] The combination of reportage and fiction is key in the ethical consideration of how to represent the past event to the present audience. In particular, these programmes navigate a problematic path between sensation and narrative, striving to account for horrors while presenting an always compromised story of events.

David Peace's *Red Riding* novels reflect upon horrific crimes throughout the 1970s and the 1980s and are themselves an impassioned political and historiographical intervention, arguing throughout for a complex engagement with the way that the past is rendered.[7] Peace's novels consider police corruption, murder, and child abuse in Yorkshire, finding in this grim material a way of rendering the violence inflicted upon the UK by the right-wing policies of the Thatcher government and the inherent inequalities and aggressive nature of British society in general.[8] The constant presence of trauma from the past in the present that is figured by child abuse in his novels suggests that revenants from history work without pause to fragment and destroy contemporary identity. Memory, in his novels, is insubstantial and frightening, something to be avoided. Peace's novels were filmed by Channel 4 in 2009, as a trilogy (*1974*, *1980*, *1983*). They were screened on television, although they are films and received a limited festival release. The project was experimental, as each individual film had a different director while maintaining the same cast. This leads to textual complexity and, built into the renderings, a sense of partiality. The films' concern with ethics, performance, and revealing the political and historiographic problems inherent in realist tropes – as well as their

A circling around the trauma—

constant reflection upon memory, violence, haunting, and trauma – means that they clearly demonstrate the contentions of this book. The following discussion looks at key elements of certain of the films in order to make some key assertions.

The films present a layered self-consciousness as part of their formal rendering. *Red Riding 1983* opens with a sur-credit or paratextual sequence, a flashback set-piece wedding shot in slow motion, soundtracked by Marion Newman singing '*Eia Mater, fons amoris*' from Vivaldi's *Stabat Mater*. It surely means to recall the epic and baroque wedding opening to *The Godfather* (Francis Ford Coppola, 1972). *Red Riding* presents the English North ('Where we do what we want') as a bleak, grim rejoinder to Hollywoodized crime – this land of rain, vice, sleaze, and shadow. Intercut with the slow-motion wedding segments, senior policeman Maurice Jobson stares at himself in the mirror (itself a standard cinematic and televisual trope of self-recollection, comprehension, or revelation) and poses for group photographs. He is both in the crowd and not of it, seeing as a memory. From the outset, then, the film is concerned with foregrounding the ways in which its diegesis is constructed, pointing out its wroughtness. This is historical, yes, but a version of the past that is obviously a *version*, formally foregrounding the fact of its fictive quality, pointing out the ways in which the visual evidence has been arranged to construct a narrative (by Jobson, by the audience, by the director, Anand Tucker). The film is a piece of art representing an imagined or constructed (and, given the source material, *written*) past. As such, it renders itself suspect through its own fictiveness, while deploying tropes of realism. The self-conscious artistry of the scenes – slow motion, music and soundscape, choreography – is held in tension with the props of pastness – costume, hair, cars – that gesture to a desire for authenticity, the heft of the 'real'. The precise relationship between these two things – fiction and 'fact' – open up a space for conceptualization of the ethics of representation (and, hence, of the audience's comprehension and understanding of the past through the discourse that we call 'history'). The viewer is invited (but not explicitly, although also *explicitly*; not asked, but *shown* by techniques that are hiding in plain sight) to reflect upon the ways in which the fictions of the past perform themselves, comport as fact. An audience is given the means to a critique, enabled to see how 'fact' is actualized. Holding in tension an awareness of fictionality with a manifest interest in authenticity, the viewer is a precise and astute reader of the text as it contributes to the historical imaginary (what they think the past looked like). But further, the viewer might perceive something less concrete, a sense of an engagement with the past, something like a historiographical sense of the shifting and complex nexus point where representations become 'history'.

This formal elaboration of pastness continues throughout the film. After the wedding photographs, the corrupt policemen gather upstairs to discuss their deal, toasting themselves and looking forward to greater profits. The scene of this conversation plays with visual tropes of pastness. It uses bright light in the same way that 'remembered' sequences mimic overexposed photographs and the bright sunshine of supposed childhood innocence (this technique is used later in the film when it presents BJ's memories of the beach). The sharp light is cut through with smoke to create a clear sense of something part remembered, half-heard (or misheard). This technique allows a shift between sharp and indistinct. The sequence is constructed as something overheard or seen from a distance. This formal effect is linked to the 'occulted' nature of the content of the scene, as both contribute to a sense of something unknown being brought to (half-) light, something indistinctly remembered once again surfacing in the contemporary consciousness. From the beginning, then, the texture of the film is interested in playing with perception and memory, with foregrounding, at a material level, issues of clarity, recollection, and comprehension.

The men are smoking cigars, creating a fug that renders the room impressionistic. History, or the visual representation of the past (which might be argued to be the same thing in this instance), is smoke-filled, something both sharp and indistinct at the same time, overexposed by light but with something floating about that cannot be pinned down. The *Red Riding* films make formal use of this effect, lingering on characters smoking as well as lighting rooms (mainly pubs) so as to emphasize the fug that seems to surround the figures (which they, diegetically and/or historically, don't see as sharply as the viewer). This effect is referred to at the conclusion of the film, when John Piggot (Mark Addy) emerges from the underground area with the missing girl while pigeon feathers fill the air around them (Figure 6.1). The effect is both magical and unsettling, lending an unreal aura to the images. The girl, who had been taken by a murderer, is a ghost (but alive) reclaimed from (presumed) death. She has already been played by another girl in a re-enactment of her disappearance (discussed below), and so she is presented as a solid echo, a miracle. Her return is the revelation that prompts the *end* of traumatic history for others (her saving is intercut with the killing of an abusive priest), a death that is seen to allow those he abused to find a kind of peace. There is something self-consciously spiritual about this linkage, as the child attains a halo (although the audience will also remember the way that the paedophile John Dawson would make his child victims into angels by sewing swans' wings on to their bodies).

FIGURE 6.1 *Red Riding: 1983* (Anand Tucker, 2009)

The cigar smoke in this opening scene is something that makes things indistinct, as vague as a dream (see Chapter 3 for a discussion of smoke in historical fictions). 'John has his own dreams', says chief policeman Bill 'Badger' Molly (Warren Clarke), as the paedophile property magnate John Dawson accepts a cigar, which he is then given a light for. This linking of dream and smoke – the camera lingers on his accepting the object and it being lit – emphasizes the ghostly, echoey, uncanny quality of the scene. This is augmented by the fact that the viewer who has seen the first two films (i.e. a viewer with a sense of the 'past' of the film's diegetic world) knows that Dawson will be shot and killed 'soon' after this meeting. So, Dawson is a 'ghost' or an echo in the chronological grammar of the trilogy. The credit sequence is from 1974, setting up a 'past' for the diegetic 'present' the film presents (but is also a new version of a scene from the film *Red Riding: 1974*, creating a history of signification). This internal time is such a feature of popular cultural texts, it is nearly unnoticeable, but *Red Riding: 1983* skilfully combines its realistic *mis en scène* and tone with the phantasmagoric effect of light, film speed, and smoke to comment upon such representations of memory and pastness.

The sur-credit sequence dissolves into still photographs of young girls, the ones that will be (or have been, diegetically–chronologically) taken and killed. Yet one lives (saved by Piggott among the pigeons). The audience is invited to assume death, signified by the school photographs that become staples of news coverage of disappearances. The film performs Barthes' death of time enshrined within the actual deaths of these girls (within the diegetic world of the film), but reflects upon the facile fictiveness of this performance. This is not in the real world, and the deaths that the images imply are those of actors, fictional creations. This opens up Gayatri Spivak's 'ethical aporia', the sense that consequential upon the fundamental misrecognition between self and other ethics is an imaginative act attempting (and failing) to comprehend the other within the alterity of pastness.[9] Such an ethic is always doomed to failure. Drawing the attention of audiences to the fictiveness of representation of the past allows an absence that implies their desired ethical position to the other. They are asked to reflect upon death that did not occur, to make the empathic leap to recognize horror and trauma, while still acknowledging the distance between this and *actual* horror and trauma. This distance allows them to reflect upon the ethical implications of articulating a version of the past through images – both as evidence (historical and criminal) and as a way of constructing narrative. The performance of the 'real' here – the tropes of realism – is contested and undermined. The narrative apparatus of mainstream history is pulled apart.

One of the key ways that the film forces this is through its own internal reflection upon performance. *Red Riding: 1983* properly begins with a post-credit opening sequence that turns out to be a police reconstruction, foregrounding to begin with the intersection between pastness, criminal investigation, and a public, even performative, memorialization of the prelude to a presumed traumatic event (the disappearance and probable murder of a child). After the still shots of girls in school uniform, the camera moves on to a young girl leaving a school. A newsreader

FIGURE 6.2 *Red Riding: 1983* (Anand Tucker, 2009)

voice-over describes her disappearance: 'At approximately 4 p.m. yesterday evening, Hazel Atkins disappeared on her way home from Morley Grange Junior and Infants. Hazel is 10 years old'. The film allows the viewer to expect the worst before the girl walks in front of a television camera, evidently participating in a re-enactment of the crime, walking up a lane in front of multiple witnesses before being embraced by her mother (Figure 6.3).

The voice-over combines the exact (Hazel Atkins's age) with the horribly imprecise ('approximately'). The absence here of hard, precise knowledge about when, where, and what happened the day before is the reason for the re-enactment – the events that are being performed are what is assumed to have happened, but has actually (evidentially) *not*. Hazel did not walk into the arms of her mother at

FIGURE 6.3 *Red Riding: 1983* (Anand Tucker, 2009)

the end, but rather was taken by someone. The girl walking up the alleyway who is being described by the voice-over is not the girl who disappeared but a performance of her, the reconstruction an attempt at jogging the obviously imperfect memories of any potential witnesses. The reconstruction is itself an echo of the first film, as the school is the same one that Clare Kemplay attended, setting up a sense of internal, diegetic pastness (or even, given that it is being narrativized for an audience, 'history'). This is explicitly referred to by one character to emphasize the link.

The film's metafictional re-enactment of Hazel Atkins' disappearance here provides an instance of re-enactment and 'historical' performance as an uncanny doubling. The child (who is a child actress acting an acting child) who is–isn't Hazel (who herself is a child actress) walks down the street performing the other, while obviously being filmed and recorded. In this self-conscious moment, the film concentrates on the strange quality of performing the past in the present (or a presumed past: no one knows actually what happened to Hazel Atkins; no one, it seems, has *witnessed* this event). The section reflects upon the strangeness inherent in filming the past, reperforming and, hence, intentionally creating a double (but a false double, a fictional echo). The rendering of the past on film hence re-enacts something presumed to have happened, while being structurally or formally ghostly (it is de facto spectral), insofar as it presents itself as a fictional after-effect. *Red Riding: 1983* portrays the filming of the past as participating in a narrativizing of an unknown, but ultimately a rendering that has a false ending (the happy reunion of 'Hazel' with her mother). The creation of a narrative (literally a journey, that of the child) of past events on film, then, renders that which is absent present, potentially obviates the (presumed) horror of the 'real' events, strives to weld a happy ending on to a neatly ordered sequence of moments. Such a film would have revelatory power, insofar as it would attest to something that happened without witnesses; it would become something that would have testimonial force itself. Furthermore, the film that is being made is observed by the 'real' viewer through the 'real' camera, through playground railings. The viewer becomes a hidden observer in another moment of self-consciousness. Tracking the girl up the alleyway, the viewer/camera becomes complicit in events, while understanding their doubly fictive quality.

The verisimilitude of most film, and in particular that of the 'realist' historical mode (largely all historical drama and film), seduces a viewer to, subconsciously or otherwise, imagine the past in a particular fashion. This sequence points out the falsity inherent in this authentic fallacy: what might look real is not; it is other; recognizable, but recognizably wrought and (for those who wish to catch the killer) desired. The use of re-enactment forces the viewer to think about the ways in which such an action is-but-isn't a real embodiment of the past, is a performance of pastness.[10] Hazel's disappearance creates an absence. The re-enactment is a self-conscious exercise in constructing a narrative in order to fill this gap, to make sense of time, to fill the missing moments with something comprehensible. The re-enactment is an aftershock, a ghostly image of what did happen. Crime creates these revenants; it is an event known and not-seen, discovered, but not disclosed. Crime fiction undertakes this constantly – the backwards tug of a murder investigation being, as Todorov argued, to fill in gaps:

> The first, that of the crime, is in fact the story of an absence: its most accurate characteristic is that it cannot be immediately present in the book . . . The status of the second story is, as we have seen, just as excessive; it is a story which has no importance in itself, which serves only as a mediator between the reader and the story of the crime.[11]

The detective story, then, forces an awareness of the epistemological gaps inherent in comprehending the 'story' of the past. Even a story in which the viewer or reader has been witness to the crime itself enables a reflection upon the ways in which that event is rendered into contemporary comprehension (and significance). Historical film similarly re-enacts moments that may or may not have happened, imposing a contemporary, performative, mimetic visual truth upon a chaotic past. *Red Riding*, in its focus on the horrific after-effects of crime (the grieving mother, the broken lives), suggests that, even in cases where the perpetrator has come to trial, there is no coherence or closure. What happened in the past keeps the present fragmenting. What this moment of re-enactment enables the viewer to do, though, is reflect upon the ways in which visual historical narratives are constructed in order to fill in epistemological gaps.

Throughout, the question of epistemology is at the forefront. In particular, the trilogy foregrounds the ways in which knowledge is constructed, performed, and, most importantly, controlled. *Red Riding: 1983* has its own sense, in particular, of the archive. Scenes from other films in the trilogy are reused in this final text, again constructing an internal history. They are deployed to communicate and elaborate upon the trilogy's interest in non-linearity, fragmentation; they proffer a model of memory that is not linear. Piggott uses microfilm, echoing Edward Dunford's trawl through the archives in *Red Riding: 1974*. This enaction of the detective–journalistic–legal investigation figures historical research as part of the search for truth, compromised as it is. Indeed, the journalist working the archive is a cinematic cliché, part of the way in which the 'truth' is uncovered. The information is there, but only to the seeker who looks in the right way. The archive – print and image – might contain (despite its chaotic nature) a thread that can be traced forward to now, somehow, that can give an insight into the contemporary. There is a clear self-referentiality about the popular text representing the archive. This is the 'real' locale of pastness, whereas the film is simply a version, a 'history'. Both Dunford and Piggott believe that the archive contains 'truth', given their investment in, on the one hand, participating in its creation (as a journalist) and, on the other, considering the collective archive of the law to be something that has iteration in contemporary identity (as a solicitor, even a drunk one). Dunford's colleague, Barry Gannon (Anthony Flanagan), further argues for a faith in the archive: 'You're ignorant Dunford. Try carrying a history book along with that

In death, too – not just crime/murder

Reminds me of Girl with the Dragon Tattoo

notebook of yours'.[12] The combination of journalistic nowness (the notebook that records instantaneously) and the pedagogic textbook of history might lead to an understanding in the contemporary moment.

At the same time, the action of the films (and the source novels) mitigates against the 'truth' of the archive – the truth has been buried in the past and will remain there. What Dunford discovers never sees the light of day. He becomes part of the official archive (Piggott looks at the newspaper story of his death). Quite what his actions meant as he met his end can only be explained by an occulted history, something outside the archive (that is, the film that is *Red Riding: 1974*). The archive tempts the user to think there might be an alternative future, but this is an illusion. The slippage between then and now is not along a timeline, but geographical and anthropological. Jacques Derrida, articulating the archive in *Archive Fever*, points out the geographically specific physicality of the past/present:

> It is thus, in this *domiciliation*, in this house arrest, that archives take place. The dwelling, this place where they dwell permanently, marks this institutional passage from the private to the public, which does not always mean from the secret to the nonsecret [. . .] With such a status, the documents, which are not always discursive readings, are only kept and classified under the title of the archive by virtue of a privileged *topology*.[13]

The archive is a space, something that becomes and is physical in its appropriation of the discourse of the past. The archive is a place of transformation, where the private becomes subsumed into the public. As Derrida defines it, the archive is 'the principle according to the law, *there* where men and gods *command*, *there* where authority, social order are exercised, *in this place* from which *order* is given' (p. 1). It is constructive, something that closes down identity and ignores difference. The archive affects the past and the future; it warps and changes and perverts. Piggott and Dunford cannot gainsay this, and what they find in their investigations is never spoken of; it cannot be used to interrogate or fragment that which happened, that which is recorded.

The past has place, and that situation is in contrast to the dynamics of nowness – for Derrida, the binary is false, but the chaos of now and the chaos of then are disciplined and organized in different ways, for similar ends. The archive takes on physical constitution and, thence, authority, the objects and artefacts that are the past in the present forcefully and materially marking out their field of combat and dominance. The archive brings the past into the present, or locates it within the present, inflecting the now from within the now. Derrida recognizes the power of this embeddedness, the fact that the archive is constantly in the now, it is not history or past, despite the fact that it represents or creates or orders cultural imaginations of other times. The archive is memory, is signification, is 'at once *institutive* and *conservative*. Revolutionary and traditional [. . .] It has the force of a law, of a law which is the law of the house (*oikos*), of the house as place, domicile, family, lineage, or institution' (p. 7).[14] Whereas the popular historical text translates the past into the present, the danger of the archive is its material manifestation in the now and, thence, its constitutive power of the contemporary, its construction of what might be said or thought. In many ways, the popular historical text, whether it be film or television or book, is the other of the archive, the dissident, illegitimate reflection, with playful inversion and misrecognition inherent in its being. Where the archive is memory, the popular text is misremembered, misquoted, it points to the play in the structure that Derrida first outlined in his 1966 *Writing and Difference*.

There is another archive, though; a carrier bag full of papers that rent boy and marginal figure BJ keeps close to him. These documents contain the 'real', unofficial truth, are the key to understanding what actually happened. These papers stand for the 'occulted' history that David Peace invoked when writing the source novels for the films. Peace argues that his works elucidate an unseen, antagonistic past that dwells in the shadows and avoids 'history'; in order to understand the trace of what happened, it is imperative to investigate these occulted moments.[15] Peace suggests his is a secret history, an alternative, othered history to that official, ordered taxonomy that infects the present and interpolates modes of behaviour and identity in the now. This occult history is jarring and strange because it is uncanny, the viewing of something seemingly known revealed as horrific. This is the 'strange familiarity' that Nicholas Royle claims is an inherent effect of various reading strategies (psychoanalysis and deconstruction) that at base mimic or are at least invested in comprehending the uncanny.[16] Peace would seemingly add his mode of reading the past (or of translating that past into 'history') to these techniques that strive for 'strange familiarity', ways in which challenging and undermining the official stories might open up new ways of being and behaving, might subvert or invert social norms and dominant discourses. Yet all historical fiction might have or attain the status of such 'occult history', telling a story anew, constructing a fictional other in order to reflect upon the ways in which the 'real' has been attained, mimicking History; in short, undermining the ways in which the past is narrativized and controlled through strategies designed to point out the indeterminablity of epistemology.

The papers BJ holds are mainly those that Dunford collected and pinned on a wall in a motel room in *Red Riding: 1974* – mimicking the police procedure for collecting together a 'story' of a crime. They are reduced to marginalized, occulted status by the actions of the 'state' (the corrupt police officials) and toted around by the most othered character in the film, BJ, who lives on the sidelines of society. In his first appearance with the archive, he actually disappears by sliding down an alleyway along the side of a house, actualizing his alienation from 'real' mainstream society. He is the curator of the alternative archive, the repository that may or may not allow for a new insight, the destruction of the dwelling of history, and, hence, the revelation of a new type of identity in the contemporary. The fact that his archive never sees the light of day suggests that the occulted story may in itself still be inert, still lack iterative historiographical power in the now. His archive is never domiciled, never housed – BJ is rarely (if ever) seen inside, and there is no repository or holding place for the textual memories he keeps.

The ethical implications and contradictions of the trilogy come to the fore towards the end of *Red Riding: 1980*. This is an extract from the Yorkshire Ripper's, Peter Sutcliffe's, confession scene: 'She was drunk. She was laughing at me and she said "Get it over with". I said "don't worry, I will". And I hit her with the hammer. She made a lot of noise, so I hit her again.'[17] Sutcliffe continues, talking about what happened while he killed the woman and what he did to her body post-mortem. The account is graphic, explicit, and absolutely horrifying, and nearly impossible to watch. The scene is a performance in multiple ways, and one that forces particular affective responses in its various audiences. Sutcliffe knows he is being watched, by viewers inside and outside the interrogation room. The camera moves between them. There is even, within the testimony of the horror of the past, a self-consciousness imbued in the fictional enactment. The actor playing Sutcliffe is a version of the 'real' figure, channelling his words, appearance, and accent. Sutcliffe's words resonate, and the scene cuts to DCI Hunter driving, with Sutcliffe heard in voice-over, as the words Hunter has heard and cannot now *not* remember haunt him in his contemporary moment (demonstrated by the linearity of the narrative, what happened in a previous scene is diegetically *past*). Every image, story, text, film is a revenant of the past, an iteration of the haunting of the present in this film. Sutcliffe's words and his story from out of the past change the present and open up again the trauma of the initial moment of horror and violence. How is it possible to re-represent this moment, these testimonies? The scene and the speech are based, in part, on the recorded testimony and evidence Sutcliffe gave when he was first arrested. This is a replaying of an event the audience presumes happened, a reversioning of the past, a channelling, and an imitation of something from history.

The film has already fetishized the recorded voice, both through referring to the various recordings and phone messages that the case featured and by having a fictional character found dead with a cassette stuffed in his mouth. The replaying of the recorded (in analogue or text) past demands an ethical mediation and an awareness of the aesthetic, cultural, and authorial work of the representation of the horrific, violent otherness that the past represents. The film reifies the recording (it is used by the police to 'identify' the Ripper, for instance) as a kind of evidence that cannot be gainsaid. There is a deal of metatextual referentiality at play during this sequence: intercut shots of reel-to-reel recorders, shot-reverse-shot dialogue, tracking, the use of reflection to comment upon identity (as with Jobson in the first scene of *Red Riding: 1983*) and surveillance/witnessing (see Figure 6.4), and the move to voice-over. This makes it demonstrably wrought, theatrical, performed, an enactment of an event, but one that points out its own artificiality. At the same time, these tropes are clichés of procedural crime television and film, possibly reanimated by their self-conscious deployment here.

The scene demands that the viewer consider how they relate to this testimony, and the inherent fictionalization of this narrative. Is it reasonable for a drama to perform these words? Is it reasonable for an audience to watch this testimony (as the police do) unfold as part of the filling in of a puzzle, the rendering of a

FIGURE 6.4 *Red Riding: 1980* (James Marsh, 2009)

convenient 'truth' into the narrative formula of the film? What might be gained from staring into this emotional abyss? At base, the sequence forces a reconsideration of ethical and moral decisions in the present and, hence, an underlining of identity. This is the past as affectively, empathically other – so far from the contemporary as to ensure a visceral reaction in the viewer. It is crucially performative, insofar as the words rendered on-screen live/'live' and gain increased power by being embodied, played, performed. Yet this power is similarly, simultaneously undermined by the acknowledgement of the performance. This is–isn't Peter Sutcliffe, yet if it isn't (it isn't), then what, really, is the audience doing watching him? What is their motivation for an interest in this? Does the 'real' crime make the imaginative ones less or more problematic? What kind of sensationalist desire for horror has led an audience to this moment? Or is it an attempt at understanding, comprehension of something in the past never grasped? The moment is comprehensible, but out of understanding, a useful motif of 'history' as translator of horror into neutered record. However, just as it is artificial, at the centre of the scene is the horrific testimony. Whether 'real' or not, the words that 'Sutcliffe' uses are so grimly descriptive, delivered in an unemotional monotone, that the viewer (as his diegetic auditors do) *must* react and feel visceral, affective horror at what he is speaking of. Irrespective of the viewer's intellectual detachment, there is an imaginative and affective response. The historical text discloses the disjunct between then and now/time travel/relativity, opens up the gap while attempting to close it. This scene reveals the ethical problems of authenticity and 'realism'.

This sequence with Sutcliffe is an extraordinary moment that urges the viewer to reflect upon their own relationship to the violent past and to think on the traumatic rupturing of then from now. Sutcliffe challenges the scopic power of those watching him to control and comprehend, and the sequence fetishizes their anguished faces as they discover that the past is violent and horrific and it will haunt them if they gaze upon it. *Red Riding: 1983*, in this sequence, but also more widely, presents the past as something nasty and horrific, to be avoided. In the diegesis of the film, investigation of the past leads only to more pain and less truth. Using the mimetic quality of film – although subtly undermining this with the constant referents to the fictiveness of the sequence by considering props, recording devices, and other elements that demonstrate the way that even seemingly direct testimony can be appropriated, narrativized, controlled – the scene forces an awareness of itself and the fictive claims to 'truth' it is undertaking. In doing so, it puts the entire process of historical representation into flux, particulary through its ethically problematic affective quality. Using the tropes of realism, the film can impute the ways in which 'truth' is narrativized in historical drama and, hence, undermine the ways in which such a thread of authentic, coherent truth might be presented to an audience.

The intervention of the past in the present in this instance fractures identity in the now, replaying the encounter with the ghost of the past as a traumatic sundering of the self from normality. The listening officers move from being a team to a set of individuals alienated from the modern world, sucked by the past into a kind of fugue state. In this sequence, the jag of the real hits the viewer. This is the violent horror of the past, framed as testimony (witnessing), an uninflected, monotone account of the incomprehensible actions of the insane. This makes the past unknowable, at the same time as it renders it textually – the words describing events cannot be reconciled with bodily action, experience, or ontological comprehension of what is being described. In this instance, the past is othered violently, disconnected, while it is, unambiguously, most viscerally and empathically meaningful and affective to the viewer. This quality of being at once other and simultaneously experienced in the self, of uncanny connection to something that is evidently not real or true, is a fundamental experience of historical fictions (and, one might argue further, of all 'history'). The audience is forced to affectively respond and 'understand' the other of the past and engage with it, while intellectually comprehending its fictive quality.

Affect is deployed here in order to problematize narrativizing in historical representation. Similarly, the performative here demonstrates the constructedness of testimonies of the past. Towards the end of *Red Riding: 1983*, a medium claims kinship (like the novelist, like the film-maker) with the dead, speaking a version of the past (and literally putting on voices). She claims to hear the missing girls speak and renders their words. Yet it is a trick, a bit of conjuring that provides comfort in the now, such is the desire to understand, to gain a seemingly comprehensible truth. 'Sometimes the dead speak through me', she says, presenting herself as a mere conduit. She resurrects them vocally, an echo of their reality. Yet she is a fake, despite being consulted by the police. Her version of their past is untrue, a performance, smoke and mirrors. The film encourages the viewer to situate themselves in relation to the representation, to reflect upon the ethics of representation. Throughout, the film is pointing to its fictive ventriloquizing and replaying/re-enacting of the past. It is not quite self-conscious or obviously a historiographic metafiction of the kind that Linda Hutcheon, Kate Mitchell, or Amy Elias describe.[18] Indeed, those kinds of work might be considered red herrings, insofar as their excesses prevent analysis of the historiographic work that *all* fictional versions of the past undertake. Historical drama relies upon dramatizing the state of flux that exists in a text that at once cleaves to authenticity (and is textually accurate, insofar as it has a novel as its basis), while revelling in its own fictiveness. In this, the text undertakes historiographical work, communicating an undecidability about the tools of communication. The films of this trilogy meditate upon their own fictive quality and mourn their own inability to reconcile or communicate the past in anything other than a conflicted, broken way. They ventriloquize badly, attempting to mimic something lost, and, hence, present a conflicted ethics of representation, their ghostly echoing something that will be taken up in the next section.

Anne Boleyn, drag history, and the body of the past[19]

Howard Brenton's play *Anne Boleyn* was performed at Shakespeare's Globe Theatre in London (itself an ersatz reperformance of a 'real' space), in conjunction with Shakespeare's *Henry VIII*, in the summer of 2011.[20] It was thus put in dialogue with a 'contemporary' historical/history play, albeit one that itself renders the recent past in very careful terms.[21] *Henry VIII* is a play about spectacle and dynasty, concluding with the birth of the child that will become Elizabeth I. Brenton's text interacts with this key play to reflect upon the way that memory is constructed, the performances that make meaning (particularly on-stage), ghostliness, and reputation.[22] Brenton plays with genealogy, ghosts, memory/revenants, haunting, and all within a narrative that dramatizes a theological debate about, among other things, limbo – a debate that itself influenced the writing of *Hamlet*.[23] Echoes of *Hamlet* abound in the way that the play conceptualizes inheritance, governance, and memory; as an intertext, it exemplifies and enacts the play's themes, embodying the past and haunting the present. The play also reflects upon the unique effability of the performance moment itself, asking how such flickerings of action in time and space might be recorded or archived, and what significance they might have accorded to them. The relationship between affect and performance here is key, and Brenton's text considers both in the frame of historiography to seek to understand how popular history might work.

Brenton's Preface to the printed edition of the play pinpoints some 'unease' in attitudes to Boleyn: 'We love her story but feel guilty toward her'.[24] His argument about Boleyn pinpoints her complexity in popular culture, as well as outlining his particular approach. Recounting the ways her story has been told by historians and fiction writers, he suggests, 'There are many Anne Boleyns [. . .] There is some truth, no doubt, in all these perceptions of her' (p. 6). He points out the drama of her story and the reason for its long popularity: 'It is a tragic and highly dramatic scenario and, as far as it goes, true' (p. 7). Yet this, he continues, 'is a modern reading' (p. 7), eliding or missing Boleyn's key contribution to theological change. Although this has been a staple of historians' version of Boleyn for decades, her importance as a promoter of religious reform has not trickled down to popular accounts. Brenton calls her interest in reform being 'in love with the most dangerous ideas of her day' (p. 8). She is 'ahead of her time' in her thinking (p. 8). His play thus has a definite historiographical impetus – to reinsert this theologically astute Anne into the story – and, hence, presents a challenge (implicit on-stage; made explicit in this Preface) to other accounts of Boleyn. It therefore points out, fundamentally, the multiple ways that Boleyn has been made to mean. He argues that, 'I wrote the play to celebrate her life and legacy as a great English woman who helped change the course of our history' (p. 8), clearly outlining the historiographical intervention being made by the text, as well as a keen sense of history as a matter of progress and development (and something shared, 'our' English history). He shares this revisionist position on Tudor figures (Boleyn and Cromwell) with Hilary Mantel, and the sense in both writers' work on the period of needing to undermine, or challenge, what a reviewer of *Anne Boleyn* called the 'pop image of Anne as the doomed siren', demonstrates the clear intervention they are attempting.[25]

Brenton similarly points out the ways in which an epistemological position can be underpinned by physical elements: 'The cruelty of the past can be thrown into sharp relief by present-day knowledge', he writes, discussing Boleyn's several miscarriages.[26] The secular, rationalist present recoils in the face of the 'cruelty' of then. Those in modernity judge those in the dark chaos of then. The fact that this medical element is the nub of the historical point – the physical condition of this historical figure – demonstrates once again why this case is so attractive to fiction writers. It allows a clear consideration of that which is seemingly shared, the body, but also articulates a clear modern–past difference. The tension between the transhistorical body and the 'past' opens up an ethical dilemma – how is it possible to judge, or articulate, or represent Boleyn, with this 'secret' knowledge she herself was not privy to? Is such a judgement not simply undertaking an annexing of her body similar to that by those historical personages who attempted to control her (and whom she is celebrated for defying)?

When he first meets her, Brenton's Henry asks Boleyn, in response to some evasive flirtatiousness, 'Your history! Give me that, if nothing else!' (p. 22). Although he is asking for her life story, the punning conjunction of 'history' means that, to an audience at least (with the benefit of historical hindsight), he is asking to control the way that Boleyn is remembered – as he surely has. The real Boleyn did give him her history, and the inflection of her story by the relationship with Henry and his treatment of her means that she is nearly impossible to see independently. Furthermore, the play reminds us constantly that the site of historical debate and the moment of connection are physical. The actual and historiographical conflict over Boleyn is about her body (sexually, as a physical Queen, maternally, even her spiritual physicality). The play presents us with her rejection of various 'courtly' contraceptive devices, and she rejects them all: 'I am not going to be a mistress! No fiddling with womanly devices. No bathing in scents and rose water' (p. 32). What is at stake here is distinctly physical, resolutely about the actuality of two bodies. In order to circumvent the patriarchal versioning of Boleyn, Brenton's play seeks to render her 'real', or materially *present* in the past.

Anne Boleyn opens with a very corporeal rendering of a relationship between ghost, memory, and audience. Boleyn (played at the production for the Globe by Miranda Raison) takes to the stage in '*her bloodstained execution dress*' carrying a large bag (p. 11). '*Working the audience*', she goads them: 'Do you want to see it? Who wants to see it?' (p. 11). The implication is that she has 'her' severed head in the bag; after all, she is wearing the last costume she wore alive, showing us her blood, and her execution is one of the key elements of her myth. She then pulls out a Bible, and claims, 'This killed me! This book! This put me in the Tower, this made the sword' (p. 11). The play initially, then, wrongfoots the audience by pointing them towards textual (the book) and material (the sword) elements of her story. She then pulls out 'her' severed head, joking, 'What did you think I was going to show you? This?' (p. 11). The actor's body here is a ghost and a time traveller, as well as being a solid, material thing performing. The empathic connection made in historical fictions through the body is rejected here – Boleyn's 'real' body is dead, and she carries a reminder of this (the head). Yet her ghostly self still exists, and this is what speaks to us – a memory, rather than the thing itself. If nothing else, the scene dramatizes some of the most peculiar elements of historical fictions – the relationship between the physical and the textual, the strange and even uncanny (given the clear doubling) effect of being addressed by someone who is evidently dead, violently sundered from being in your present. The objects

FIGURE 6.5 Miranda Raison in *Anne Boleyn* (2010)

on stage – body, head, Bible – ensure that, from the beginning, chronology is unfolded and challenged. The tension in this opening scene between all three objects on stage – the physicality of the head, the textuality (but godly materiality) of the Bible, and the ghostly revenant of the embodied Boleyn – is what the play explores throughout.

Boleyn haunts the production – at points literally spooking James VI and I in scenes set during his reign. For Brenton, it seems she similarly haunts English history, like Hamlet's father, asking for revenge (or at least a reckoning) and pointing out the flaws in our remembering: as James says, 'She will not have the country rest' (p. 21). The play enacts this, as James discovers both her coronation dress and her Bible (and spends the last section of the action searching drunkenly for her buried body, or her ghost). James's opinion of Boleyn as the Great Whore of history is undermined by his encounter with these ghostly objects that somehow incorporate her in his diegetic now. The play makes regular references to the way in which Boleyn is thought of in the country, and how she is imagined by those outside the court – one such leading Cardinal Wolsey to acknowledge, 'Terrifying thing, the popular imagination' (p. 36). This acknowledgement of the distinction between collective imagination and active reality – and the deeply problematic nature of a broad popular acceptance of certain clichéd caricatures – is something the play works hard to expose. An arch moment between Cromwell and Boleyn articulates this (p. 62):

Anne: They see you as a vicious man on the make.
Cromwell: They see you as a hussy who planned to get your claws into the
             King from the moment you came to Court.

The complex difference between image and 'reality' suggested by this exchange suggests that Brenton is challenging the 'popular imagination' and the ways that it has set in cliché these two extraordinary figures. They are already ghosts of themselves, false renderings.

In addition to his haunting by Boleyn, or even somehow in response, James spends some time wearing her coronation dress, which is found in the opening scene. The costume, text, and ghost/body provide a trinity of memory; importantly, they suggest that historical connection is made affectively (through objects), and that this might challenge 'accepted' historical fact. James is initially inspired by the dress to make a bawdy, affective connection:

James: She was crowned in this? That witch's body, folded within these
             very creases? (*Laughs*) Think . . . (*Lifting the hem up his leg*) The
             hem slid up to the thigh by the hand of the great Henry himself.
             There could even be . . . (*Lifts the dress right up, looking on the
             underside*) interesting stains.
(*James ruffles through the underside of the skirt, intent on what he is doing*) (p. 15)

James 'performs' Boleyn here and also Henry, moving her hem and becoming abstracted by his relationship with the physical entity of the past. He performs a strangely sexualized re-enactment (or, at least, imagined enactment, the physical action being as much part of his dream of the past – his own desire for the lascivious version of the past – as any actual event). Boleyn's relationship to the King is defined through her costume and Henry's abjected, almost involuntary sexual response to her body (and her dress). What is James looking for exactly? Evidence of some physical kind, brought into his present through being preserved in fabric? Some proof of the materiality of the body that inhabited the dress? He certainly demonstrates the difference between the living, 'contemporary' body and the textual echo of it, manifested here in the object that is the dress.

The play thus reflects upon modes of recollection and historical connection that are enacted through physical performance and possibly contained within the material artefact. James also finds Boleyn's Bible and a book by Thomas Cranmer in a box, and the disquieting combination of dress and texts makes him concerned. Act 2 of the play opens with James wearing the dress and dancing with George Villiers, '*who is not in drag*' (p. 48). They '*dance as man and woman, beautifully, arms extended, whirling figures. The music stops, they embrace and kiss passionately*' (p. 48). Although the reference to 'drag' is a stage direction, it makes it clear that the context of this scene is cross-dressing (familiar to most of the Globe's audience as a key motif in Shakespeare's drama). James's relatively well-known homosexuality is evident here, but the drag element is more about his encounter with Boleyn's memory/ghost.[27] He, like Miranda Raison, is performing Boleyn; he is echoing the past, but also enacting it. Yet, at the same time, the enactment of the past is entwined with avowedly complex sexual and gender configurations (not simply homosexual, but somehow involving desire encountered from history – the 'stains' – and, hence, confusing heteronormative linearity and even temporality).

Judith Butler's theory of performance and gender in relation to drag has been key to much contemporary queer theory. Her insight that 'gender is a kind of persistent impersonation that passes as the real' seeks to destabilize those binary relationships that falsely fix gender relations and definitions of sexuality.[28] Her key argument relates to the way in which drag performance articulates a conscious/ unconscious insight within performance that points to a central ambivalence of definition:

> If the anatomy of the performer is already distinct from the gender of the performer, and both of those are distinct from the gender of the performance, then the performance suggests a dissonance not only between sex and performance, but sex and gender, and gender and performance.[29]

This 'dissonance' provides a moment of fragmentation that challenges the binary definitions of identity, a troubling of immanence that has also been taken up in performance studies.[30] As she articulates elsewhere, Butler's purpose is to use drag as a self-conscious 'performance' of reality, as opposed to an imitation or mimetic rendering:

Drag constitutes the mundane way in which genders are appropriated, theatricalized, worn, and done; it implies that all gendering is a kind of impersonation and approximation. If this is true, it seems, there is no original or primary gender that drag imitates, but gender is a kind of imitation for which there is no original.[31]

Drag renders the binary of gender moot, purposefully pointing out that the 'real' does not exist in identity. With James's wearing of Anne's dress, *Anne Boleyn* achieves a moment of interruption, dissonance, and rupture. The audience is forced to recognize that the whole play is itself a drag version of history, a reperformance of something that does not exist. The disjunct between performance and 'reality' obviates the original. The relationship between then and now is syncopated, rather than binary, in a state of flux; renderings of the past as 'history', then, attempt to close down meaning, disavow this fundamental chaos. The dragging of history enables an audience to perceive that renderings of the past do not present any 'reality', and, further, that such an 'original' moment is unclaimable, unknowable, unpresentable. Yet there is a complicity inherent in these renderings. The audience members participate in this interruption of normativity, desire it even (insofar as they wish to be part of the audience and voluntarily turn up to watch the play). Elizabeth Freeman discusses the way that certain dissident or 'forms of interruption' that might be challenge the 'temporal order': 'Queer temporalities [. . .] are points of resistance to this temporal order that, in turn, propose other possibilities for living in relation to indeterminately past, present, and future others: that is, of living historically'.[32] Queer time is that which interrupts and offers alternative possibilities for then, now, and the future. Drag history – historical fictions – render the past queerly unknowable, but, in that, enables a more complex and hopeful future. It disavows the binary controls of originality and reality. Furthermore, as Butler argues, the very *drag* of the performance has to be acknowledged by an audience at some level (or it is transvestism). What makes it drag is the recognition of the mimicking of something considered fixed and stable.

Similarly, Boleyn's performance of herself (holding her head) and the affective connection between James and Boleyn made through the material of her dress (and possibly some physical emissions) invoke Rebecca Schneider's argument about the importance of 'stickiness' in describing emotional responses to pastness.[33] Affect is tactile, somehow physical, and this makes for uncomfortable but new relationships:

> The stickiness of emotion is evident in the residue of generational time, reminding us that histories of events and historical effects of identity fixing, *stick* to any mobility, *dragging* (in Elizabeth Freeman's sense) the temporal past into the sticky substance of any present. To be sticky with the past and the future is not to be autonomous, but to be engaged in a freighted, cross-temporal mobility.

(pp. 36–7)

The syncopated lag of performance of the past forces this into effect, confusing the linear and the real. Affective effects (bodily and physical) complicate and challenge identity in the now. Similarly, the authenticity of *Hunger*'s literal stickiness makes the connection unbearable, disgusting, horrifying, but still forces an affective connection that, in itself, brokers a non-authoritarian (and a defiantly non-*textual*) relationship between then and now.

Brenton's play is self-conscious in its proffering of motifs and metaphors for engagement with history – particularly historical cliché. Anne's haunting of the stage (particularly, given that this was written for the Globe Theatre, of a stage that itself is reconstructing or re-enacting a historical entity) and the play is one such. James's cross-dressing allows him to be both male and female, then and now, self and historical other. Another is the idea of the enemy within, working with the structure while undermining it. An exchange between Boleyn and Tyndale about his banned book is as follows:

> *Anne:* His Grace the Cardinal doesn't see everything. There are many copies of your Testament at Court, behind walls, in secret panels.
>
> *Tyndale:* So the True Word is worming in the woodwork of English palaces? I praise the Lord.[34]

The idea of a text sitting unseen within a physical structure and undermining it conceptually (as well as materially) pervades. It is a metaphor for the strength and power of the present text to challenge the outline of history, 'worming' the official English spaces by living in the imaginations of those who encounter it. This sense that historical fiction might have an insurrectionary motivation, might be intentionally, literally subversive, underlies Brenton's revisionist claims on Boleyn (after all, if it had no effect on the way an audience *actually* thought about her, what would be the point of writing the play?).

Anne's 'ghost' on-stage concludes the play by talking to the audience. 'The demons of the future', she calls them (p. 114), a vision she sees just before death. In this interspace, she glimpses a future that sits with her in mutual incomprehension:

> *Anne:* Dear demons of the future, what I can't tell . . . what I can't tell is what you believe. You're so strange to me, as I must be strange to you. [. . .] Goodbye, demons. God bless you all.
> *(She blows the audience a kiss)* (p. 115)

The audience members are 'demons' insofar as they are not of Boleyn's world, conceptually and materially. The ethics of representing her, the continual representational aporia they discover, the horrors that they might visit upon her make them demons. The audience obviously isn't diegetically in her 'world', but it also sits, unable to understand her (and she them). The play can translate a version of the past, but an audience will still comprehend, at the finale, that the ability to materially bridge the gap between Boleyn and themselves is impossible. The audience is uncanny, strange, and other to her – at this point, the play's formal self-consciousness points this out by reminding us that Miranda Raison is on a stage, divided from the audience. Boleyn's final act of affective, physical connection – a failed kiss, into the air and touching no one – is both performative and doomed, bespeaking connection while demonstrating emptiness. The strange, ghostly, uncanny thing on stage is itself a strange, ghostly, uncanny rendering of the past, a dream of a person.

Hunger: **Authenticity and abjection**

The final discussion of this chapter concerns the film *Hunger* and its meditations upon horror and the body in historical representation. *Hunger* was released by Film4 in 2008. It recounts the events of 1981 in the Maze prison in Northern Ireland, where Bobby Sands and his fellow republican prisoners are initially on no-wash, no-blanket strike. McQueen's film recounts the dirty protest and then hunger strike undertaken by the Irish prisoners in the Maze in the early 1980s, culminating in the death of Sands while he was on hunger strike. *Hunger* considers the ways in which the 'real' can be expressed on film, forcing the viewer into a visceral and affective reaction to events in order to ensure a consideration of the ways in which historical film works. Furthermore, the film uses its discourse of authenticity to reflect upon the role of commemoration and memory in the construction of political identity. It is a key text for considering the ideas relating to ethics, performance, affect, and historiography that have been raised so far. Like *Red Riding Trilogy: 1980* and its appropriation of a real-life murderer, and *Anne Boleyn*'s interrogative protagonist, the provocation of *Hunger* is for the audience to deal with the consquences of having a fictional text perform something problematic. In this case, it is rendering the body very explicitly and, furthermore, representing the conse-quences of starvation. It is also the account of violent actions. These texts point out the distance between epistemology and ontology and the ethically problematic rendering of the past. In particular, this final section explores the ways in which the body and, in particular, bodily substances and excretions (food, blood, smoke, excrement, semen, urine) work together with violence in *Hunger* to establish a sense of bodily authenticity. The film explores the idea of authenticity in several ways (bodily 'reality', violence, abjection). The film provokes connection and disgust, brokering a relationship with the past that is both empathic and defensive. Furthermore, as with that which is excreted from the body, the film seems to conceptualize the past as the abjected material of now, wasted, ejected, recognizable but othered, something that reconfigures our sense of our self in challenging and traumatic fashion: 'There, I am at the border of my condition as a living being'.[35]

In terms of its content, the 'authentic' action of *Hunger* is contrasted with the posturing bravado of political engagement. Bobby Sands sees his sacrifice as clarity itself, purposeful and pure: 'I have my belief. And in all its simplicity, that is the most powerful thing'.[36] The film renders a relationship with the past through sense and touch, suggesting new ways of thinking about historical comprehension. Yet this does not mean it uses the easy, conservative–realist strategies attacked by docudrama film-makers such as Peter Watkins.[37] *Hunger*'s formal qualities allow for a radically political film to emerge – not ideologically republican, but proferring a model of resistance and dissidence through its historiographical innovation. *Hunger* uses its discourse of authenticity to reflect upon the role of commemoration and memory in political identity. In *Hunger*, the abject body reaches beyond the limits of communication to create what might be termed the 'affective authentic', an effect that seeks to communicate through physical empathy, as well as alienate and distance in the same manner. A kinship is suggested, a genealogy even, that creates a taxonomic and possibly even hierarchical connection with the past that obviates (or eludes) intellectual engagement. To what extent is this one-way? Does the 'affective authentic' imply a relationship with the past? How does this then intersect with the text's evident fictive qualities? Does this inflect the evident political engagement of the text?

The opening sequence focuses on blood and pain. A man (Raymond Lohan) soaks his swollen hands in a bowl of water, wincing as the soap stings his bruised flesh. He does this several times in the film, and his bloody knuckles are focused upon (at times quite beautifully, in the snow in an early sequence, when he smokes outside in a sweat-stained shirt). The opening sequence focuses on aspects of the guard's preparation for duty that will echo in later scenes. He enters the locker-room, walking past half-naked, but healthy (and overweight) bodies. He puts on his uniform, changing from civilian to employee of the state. The dispute that Sands and his fellow strikers had with the British government was that it did not recognize them as soldiers as they fought without uniform; they go naked rather than wear the prison uniform that marks them. It becomes evident later that the guard's bruised knuckles are the consequence of his beating the prisoners. His loneliness in the early sequences mark out his unease with this role, with becoming the violent bodily expression of the state. His eventual murder demonstrates how he has become part of the political process rather than an individual, in the same way that Sands desires to lose his selfhood in order to force change. The guards are also often filmed in the snow and evident daylight, in contrast with the dark interiors of the prison.

The first lines of dialogue come 30 minutes into the film and are quite startling, coming after an intense moment of torture and violence. Mostly, the film is nearly silent, with only diegetic sound – the car radio, the creaking of hinges, footsteps, doors shutting. Scenes are often played in silence, with minor sounds, and this contributes a clear sense of authenticity to the film – an almost sensory precision that suggests that anything extra would be frippery and *unrealistic*. This clarity of purpose is formal and political. In an early scene, a prisoner is forced to strip naked, and the silence of the scene enhances the abject horror of what is happening. His vulnerabilty and his fear become something physically expressed through the paleness of his body. *Hunger* is, therefore, presented as serious, missing any wrought detail, even to the point of being eerie and strange. This seriousness of purpose is striking – seen in the lack of obvious effect in the framing of shots, for instance, or the minor dialogue throughout. The film is austere, quite clearly realistic (despite its cinematography, which is exceptionally clear and precise). Its ability to mix realist formal techniques with a sense of the performative is demonstrated in the central scene, a discussion between Father Dominic Moran and Bobby Sands. It is 17 minutes long, and the camera is in the same position for the entire scene. The conversation is, therefore, rendered realistically – the actors work very hard at this – while making an audience aware of how uncomfortable they are with this static camera. It points out how unusual this is, just how much 'unseen' technique there is in filmic rendering of dialogue. It is, therefore, both alienating and realistic, almost austerely realist in some ways, but able to point out the wroughtness in that realist move.

The seriousness of *Hunger* signals that it is interested in communicating something 'real' about the past, or experience of the past, but also suggests that to do anything else would be to compromise. However, the film is also about martyrdom, about creating a political storyline out of events, and so its clarity of purpose is at odds with these elements that focus upon the problems that representation might contribute to. It is not, though, shot in hand-held cinema *verité* or documentary style. *Hunger* therefore works through its formal qualities (or rather what is seemingly *not* happening) to persuade the viewer of its gravitas, its authenticity, its reality. It has the heft of reality, and this is communicated through its affective qualities. In fact, one of the things the film demands of the viewer is a response that both invests in the 'realism' of the film's rendering and simultaneously disavows that reality through an appreciation of the beauty of the way in which it is presented. This doubleness also permeates the film's political engagement, able happily to think about ambiguity in representation, in contrast with the clearly marked lines that Sands considers the world to contain. The film is both realistic and obviously impressionistic, enabling the viewer to comprehend the politicized ways in which the past is turned into a particular narrative in order for the present to 'understand' it. Sands does not necessarily want to be explained, but to be understood on his own terms; his body is the final thing that he 'owns' and that he can use to protest with. Similarly, the film suggests that, when the past is made into history, there are a number of abuses upon its independence and sanctity; it is construed, translated, re-rendered, understood for particular reasons, made to serve certain agendas.

The formal elements of the film are clearly intentional:

> What I wanted to do was to know what it felt like to be in the Maze at that time – to capture what is not written about in history books. I wanted the first part to be like walking into a room and turning off the lights so you feel your way through the room by touch; learning the architecture, the geography . . . Originally I didn't want to have any dialogue at all. Word can often just fill space and it is just noise after a while and this can take

away from what's actually going on. Instead I wanted to focus on the texture of what it was like being there at that time – the atmosphere. These are the things that don't get written in history books and I wanted to use a magnifying glass and put these things on a plinth in some ways – similar to black and white photography when you can sometimes better see the architecture, the shape of things.[38]

McQueen points out the effect of the defamiliarizing techniques he uses – lack of dialogue, slow shots, no ante-diegetic sound – by suggesting it polarizes the film but makes it clearer. As with black and white photography, it enables a clearer view of the subject. The viewer is immediately alienated and connected – placed in a position of discomfort (a darkened room) rather than a passive attitude, but encouraged to engage with a tactile past, a space with architecture, geography, texture. The past in this representation is something to be explored rather than comprehended.

Furthermore, McQueen here articulates a historiographical purpose, a desire to communicate physically ('what it felt like') rather than textually ('what is not written about in history books'). The viewer understands the past in a sensory way rather than an intellectual one. The idea of the 'texture' of the past, its 'atmosphere', rather than something more definable but less imaginatively 'real' – this sense that the past can somehow be engaged with on a sensory level – suggests that the film is attempting to articulate the idea of an affective or possibly empathic historiography. This 'connective' historical fiction would work to 'know what it felt like', to communicate 'what it was like being there at that time'. This is more important, or more effective, than 'actual' history, and McQueen posits an alternative way of knowing about what happened in the past (or a different way of accessing a version of that past, or another type of historiographic representation) predicated upon sense. To gain an impression of pastness, rather than an intellectual or rational comprehension of what has been turned into history, is his purpose. This empathic historiography, articulating something that might communicate sensually rather than intellectually, might be the impetus for almost all popular history. As here, it might be placed into a – patently false – binary with 'real' textualized historical work, or that 'written about in history books'. Historical fictions depend on this empathic move, a connection between audience/reader/viewer and 'text'. They work through emotion, affect, and an address to a connection between self and historicized other that is extremely complex. The historical other is alien, evidently at a remove from the now, indeed is that which defines now as *now*; yet it is also (in historical fictions) made recognizable, a distorted reflection.

This is why *Hunger's* concern with the body in history is not only diegetically compelling (it has political heft as a film) but also more widely important for conceptualizing or meditating upon the historical work that fictions might undertake. Early scenes have the prisoners smearing their excrement on the walls, or adding old food to a rotting pile of faeces and mulch in the corner of their cell. They pour urine on the floor and into the corridors. They live naked, their hair and beards growing unkempt until forcefully cut. At points, they are forcefully taken out of the cells and hosed down, and the walls are cleaned with an industrial cleaner. The early shots, mentioned already, of the guards showering in their locker room, are contrasted with the horrific filthiness of the prisoners. Communication with the outside world is bodily, too – messages are moved in mouths, concealed in various body orifices. The state is clean, aggressively so (considering the soaking of the fists that the film opens with), cleaning away the evidence of the prisoners' bodies. Sands argues that they suffer 'brutality, humiliation, our basic human rights ignored'. As Matthew Brown points out, '*Hunger* is fascinated by how prisoners turned their individual bodies into sites of protest'.[39] The politicized body is the abject body – filthy, naked, vulnerable. As David Inglis has argued, consideration of the 'faecal realm' might allow us to further see 'the role of the body [. . .] in the construction and operation of modes of political power'.[40] The film demonstrates how the prisoners consciously step out of the formal language of debate in order to attempt to render something new, to not be controlled by a state they feel they are at war with. The prisoners refuse to be disciplined, ordered, civilized. As a consequence, they (and the film) resist rational comprehension and attempt to evade being interpolated and controlled. Their bodies are governed – insofar as they are restrained – but the prisoners obviate this through reminding the state that the body is leaky, oozing, primal, not something easily held or controlled.

As a consequence of their resistance, the physical horror visited upon the inmates is particularly visceral. They are forcibly shorn and bathed and have forced cavity searches; they are beaten, punched, dragged, and thrown around. They are pushed through a gauntlet of riot shields and beaten with batons at one point, their naked bodies bloody and broken. Their pain, in contrast to the strength and power of the guards and riot police, is made clearly evident. Towards the end of the film comes a long scene (4–5 minutes) of clearing up the mess – a guard sweeping the corridors clear of urine, played into a static camera. The camera then pans across the blood and faeces and urine while, in voice-over, Margaret Thatcher describes the hunger strike: 'They seek to work on the most basic of human emotions, pity'. The fundamental affective reactions of the viewer – pity, empathy, physical disgust – are here reconfigured as political effect.

Smoke, too, is figured as part of the body's waste, something outside comprehensible signification and control. Sands rolls cigarettes using the pages of his Bible, immolating the 'word' and ingesting it (the only thing he takes into his body throughout the film). The priest and Sands joke about the uncleanliness of smoking ('a filthy habit') while sharing cigarettes. The conclusion of the scene lingers on Sands thoughtfully smoking (after refusing to be moved from his decision to go on hunger strike) and then purposefully grinding out his cigarette. Smoke here is aligned with the useless evacuations of the body, something indefinable and provoking, refusing regulation: 'what is *abject*, on the contrary, the jettisoned object, is radically excluded and draws me toward the place where meaning collapses'.[41] It is authentic but outside taxonomy, 'real' but obviously performed. Julie Kristeva considers that the abject material – rotting food, excrement, blood, pus – provokes:

a massive and sudden emergence of uncanniness, which, familiar as it might have been in an opaque and forgotten life, now harries me as radically separate, loathsome. Not me. Not that. But not nothing, either. A 'something' that I do not recognise as a thing [. . .] On the edge of non-existance and hallucination, of a reality that, if I acknowledge it, annihilates me.[42]

Kristeva's abject materials provoke a crisis of selfhood and of signification. Something, not nothing, physical and imaginary, something real that sits outside comprehension. Abject materials are at the border of our humanness, reminding the body of its indistinct edges. [The ways in which the abject is managed, controlled, ignored, or disciplined, then, is historically specific and a way of controlling the subject. This is because of the very transitoriness that Kristeva perceives.]

Similarly, the past is filthy, something other to us that is somehow connected but incomprehensible and disgusting – terrifying in its chaotic grotesqueness. It is ejected and ignored. The contemporary world strives to control it through organizing principles that obviate its horror. Its strange otherness – part of the individual, somehow, but marginalized and outside their bodies – makes it fascinating and terrifying. Discomfort with the abject past is due to its inherent strangeness, an uncanny physical quality (it happened, but it is no longer, it has no physical manifestation). Kristeva argues that abjection stands for the lack and the recognition of emptiness and desire for the other: 'There is nothing like the abjection of self to show that all abjection is in fact recognition of the *want* on which any being, meaning, language, or desire is founded' (p. 5). These systems of creation, of making, are predicated upon lack, and the abject demonstrates this, as the past, something uncanny, other, but indubitably there (whatever it is), creates contemporary identity while demonstrating its lack of solidity (as Butler argued).

The film undertakes in some ways what the hunger strikers are doing – reaching beyond signification into this affective realm, striving to resist the power of a controlling discourse (in the film's case, history) through the constitution of a new (old) language produced by the body. This is not to suggest that the film's purpose or effect is in any way the equal of their protest, but that the subversion of authoritative and controlling tyrannies – and the violences they visit upon the 'subject' – is something shared by both. *Hunger* establishes a resistance to the governing tropes of 'history' through an insistence on the historiographic significance (an iterative power) of the body (blood, organs, sweat), and, more than that, the waste materials ejected by that body (semen, urine, excrement, blood, smoke). The various bodily fluids that *Hunger* shows us are challenges to order, provocations to discern a new way of conceptualizing a relationship to the past. This is particularly demonstrated in the way that Sands's death is medically managed. The state strives to make him comprehensible by hospitalizing him, but his body refuses to be controlled, leaking and bleeding throughout. Again, the film refuses to let the viewer comprehend this action, indeed lingers over the fundamental insanity (i.e. that which is outside rationality) of what he is doing.

Sands's use of his own body as a way of expressing his political will ties flesh and commitment together clearly. The 'authenticity' of martyrdom and bodily engagement in political struggle is clearly being explored here. The strikers' protest is in many ways incomprehensible to the civilized outside world, the colonial force behind the walls of the Maze.[43] Sands comprehends that, in order to make their protest meaningful, it has to go beyond articulation, to be something that is both comprehensible (everyone has a body) but simultaneously incomprehensible (how could he do that to himself?).[44] This connection between viewer and film – made through the conduit of the suffering political body – is part of McQueen's purpose in making the film: '*Hunger* for me has contemporary resonance. The body as site of political warfare is becoming a more familiar phenomenon. It is the final act of desperation; your own body is your last resource'.[45] Rather than incomprehensible, McQueen considers that the hunger strikers are prescient; their bodies talk to our bodies across history, connected by political identity or even the possibility of protest. This provokes a doubling, a connection that is at once troubling and revelatory:

> *Hunger* is doubly uncanny in the sense that we have not only seen images of prisoner abuse in Northern Ireland on film before, in such films as *In the Name of the Father* (Jim Sheridan, 1993) and *H3* (Les Blair, 2001), but we are also startled into a recognition that these historicized visions of torture, in the wake of the Guantanamo prison abuse, are both contemporary and repressed.[46]

This uncanniness suggests something that an audience would desire not to see, a revenant of past violences visited upon them. It is doubled because what they might seek to control as 'historical' has an echo in the present, a double, a link to now. The past is not something other to rational modernity, but simply a foreshadowing of horror in the present. On this model, then, *Hunger* allows a consideration of the way that the violent iterative power of past events might actually be controlled by their representation in fiction, and, further, how *Hunger* attempts to elude that control and bring an audience to a recognition of something instead of simply a rendering of it. This is historical fiction as interactive, demanding, as presenting a historiographical account of how the past is made into history.

The film concludes with a long sequence of Sands undergoing the strike and dying. This begins with the prison doctor outlining to his parents the consequences of his decision in formal medical language. The camera lingers on the body of Sands – his painful thinness, his wasting, the sores and ulcers. It is utterly painful to watch, and the affective connection that the film consciously makes – Sands flinching from having lotion applied to sores on his back, for instance; Sands unable to stand having vomited blood – is extremely powerful. It is both connection – a recognition, a physical sense of shared horror at the pain involved – but obviously also a clear disconnect, insofar as the audience of this film will surely never undergo such a trial. At the same time, it is clear that this is acting. Fassbender's commitment to the cause – losing a great deal of weight in a crash diet that saw him finally ending up just over 9 stone – demonstrates a desire to method-act in as authentic a way as possible, and the film spends time concentrating on his shrunken abdomen, his weak movements. This physical commitment is somehow 'right': anything else would seem to lessen or trivialize the intense trial that Sands underwent. The audience knows, though, when they flinch, or look away, that this is a representation. The death sequence takes around 30 minutes (it took 66 days for Sands to die). It is not totally realistic – Sands experiences hallucinations of his younger self and birds flying – but in the main it is forensic in its detailing of the physical deterioration and failing of his body.

In a similar way to the instance of Peter Sutcliffe in *Red Riding Trilogy: 1980*, the audience has an emotive, physical response to the seemingly ungilded performance of authenticity. The body here is somehow transhistorical – something that connects an audience with a historical personage. The body somehow stands as an entity that is comprehensible now and then; it is a point of connection. Yet an audience is aware that both Sutcliffe and Sands are themselves performing. They are making themselves mean, attempting to control the way in which they are understood. Sands, particularly, sees his actions as politically purposeful and iterative: 'I will act, and I will not stand by and do nothing'. His strike is highly performative, an aggressive passivity that the film suggests might mean any number of things – martyrdom, murder, suicide. His body refuses to be inscribed and to have meaning imposed upon it, even as it disintegrates.

Sands's death at the conclusion of the film is followed by five pieces of information – facts regarding his death, his election as an MP during the strike, the deaths of prison guards at the hands of paramilitaries, the calling-off of the strike after the death of nine men, and concluding with, 'In the following days and months, the British Government effectively granted all the prisoners' demands but without any formal recognition of political status'. So, the film moves from the affective into the textual, contrasting the sensory, impressionistic elements that

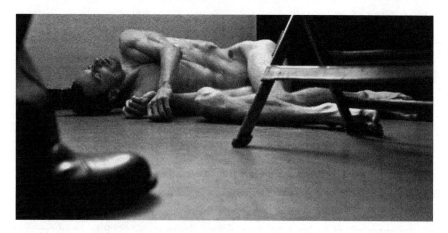

FIGURE 6.6 Sands collapses, *Hunger* (Steve McQueen, 2009)

made up the body of the work with 'actual' information and detail. Historical films about true events regularly conclude with this kind of textualized information that seemingly ties up the loose ends of the past into something comprehensible and allows the fictional representation dialogue with the 'real' account of history (discussed further in Chapter 1). It is a move to 'official' history, something more regularized and authoritative.

In the three texts considered here, the material is performed and presented in varying ways. Each text carefully considers the relationship between performance and representation within a set of 'historical' tropes. They then augment this relationship with affective moves that are designed to undermine the 'historical' and render the past something both foreign and completely recognizable. The historical empathy that is constructed asks the audience to understand their relationship to the past, and to conceptualize how that past is constructed. So, on the one hand, the texts render a new historiography through an affective connection with the past. As was argued in Chapter 5, this kind of affective response to the past is something unseen and unconsidered by mainstream historical work. On the other hand, the texts allow the viewer or audience to articulate a critique of the normative ways that the past is presented in the present. They encourage critique and questioning. The texts meditate upon the strange ways that contemporary culture remembers, not least through the ethically dubious activity of historical fictionalizing.

Notes

1 'The Vest', *Homeland*, Series 1, Episode 11 (2011).
2 Carolyn Dinshaw, 'Temporalities' in Paul Strohm, ed., *Twenty-first Century Approaches: Medieval* (Oxford, UK: Oxford University Press, 2007), pp. 107–23 (p. 109).
3 The interrelation between queer, affect, and the other is the theme of Judith Butler's chapter 'Critically Queer' in *Bodies That Matter* (London and New York: Routledge, 1993), pp. 223–42, itself a response to Eve Sedgwick's *Epistemology of the Closet* (Berkeley, CA: University of California Press, 1990).
4 Clare Hemmings, 'Invoking Affect', *Cultural Studies*, 19:5 (2005), 548–67.
5 See Derek Paget, *No Other Way to Tell It: Dramadoc/Docudrama on Television* (Manchester, UK: Manchester University Press, 1998).
6 Jack De Bellis, 'Visions and Revisions: Truman Capote's *In Cold Blood*', *Journal of Modern Literature*, 7:3 (1979), 519–36. The events of the murders and Capote's response to them are explored in the biopics *Capote* (Bennett Miller, 2006) and *Infamous* (Douglas McGrath, 2006).
7 See Katy Shaw, *David Peace: Texts and Contexts* (Eastbourne, UK: Sussex Academic Press, 2010).
8 See Shaw, *David Peace*, and also Matthew Hart, 'An Interview with David Peace', *Contemporary Literature*, 47:4 (2006), 546–69.
9 Gayatori Chakravorty Spivak, *A Critique of Postcolonial Reason* (Harvard, MA: Harvard University Press, 1999), p. 287, n. 135.
10 See Paul A. Pickering, '"No Witnesses. No Leads. No Problems": The Reenactment of Crime and Rebellion' in Iain McCalman and Paul A Pickering, eds, *Historical Reenactment: From Realism to the Affective Turn* (Basingstoke, UK: Palgrave Macmillan, 2010), pp. 109–34.

11 Tzvetan Todorov, *The Poetics of Prose*, trans. Richard Howard (Ithaca, NY: Cornell University Press, 1977), p. 46.

12 *Red Riding: 1974* (Julian Jarrold, 2009).

13 Jacques Derrida, *Archive Fever: A Freudian Impression*, trans. Eric Prenowitz (Chicago, IL, and London: University of Chicago Press, 1998), pp. 2–3.

14 Derrida, *Archive Fever*, p. 7.

15 See Shaw, *David Peace*, and Matthew Hart, 'The Third English Civil War: David Peace's "Occult History" of Thatcherism', *Contemporary Literature*, 49:4 (Winter 2008), 573–96.

16 *The Uncanny* (Manchester, UK: Manchester University Press, 2003), p. 24.

17 *Red Riding: 1980* (James Marsh, 2009).

18 Linda Hutcheon, *A Poetics of Postmodernism* (London and New York: Routledge, 1988); Kate Mitchell, *History and Cultural Memory in Neo-Victorian Fiction* (Basingstoke, UK: Palgrave, 2010); Amy Elias, 'Metahistorical Romance, the Historical Sublime, and Dialogic History', *Rethinking History*, 9:2/3 (2005), 159–72.

19 Excerpts from *Anne Boleyn*, copyright © Howard Brenton, 2010; published by Nick Hern Books (www.nickhernbooks.co.uk).

20 Jerome de Groot, *Consuming History* (London and New York: Routledge, 2008), p. 125.

21 On female lineage, collective memory, and Henry VIII, see Ruth Vanita, 'Mariological Memory in The Winter's Tale and Henry VIII', *Studies in English Literature*, 40:2 (2000), 311–37.

22 Brenton has been a key writer of iconoclastic and challenging historical plays for several decades; see Hersh Zeifinan, 'Making History: The Plays of Howard Brenton', in James Acheson, ed., *British and Irish Drama Since 1960* (Basingstoke, UK: Palgrave Macmillan, 1993), pp. 130–45, and Peter Middleton and Tim Woods, *Literatures of Memory* (Manchester, UK: Manchester University Press, 2000), pp. 147–87.

23 See Stephen Greenblatt, *Hamlet in Purgatory* (Princeton, NJ: Princeton University Press, 2001).

24 Howard Brenton, *Anne Boleyn* (London: Nick Hern Books, 2012), p. 5.

25 Michael Billington, 'Anne Boleyn', *The Guardian*, 29 July 2010; available online at: www.guardian.co.uk/stage/2010/jul/29/anne-boleyn-review (accessed 4 July 2012).

26 *Anne Boleyn*, p. 8.

27 See Michael B. Young, *King James and the History of Homosexuality* (New York: New York University Press, 2000).

28 *Gender Trouble* (London and New York: 1990), p. vii.

29 Ibid., p. 137.

30 For the central importance of the body in queer theory, see Elizabeth Grosz, *Volatile Bodies* (Bloomington, IN: Indiana University Press, 1994); Eve Kosofsky Sedgewick, *Touching Feeling* (Durham, NC: Duke University Press, 2002); and Judith Butler, *Bodies That Matter* (London and New York: Routledge, 1992).

31 Judith Butler, 'Imitation and Gender Insubordination', op. cit., p. 313.

32 Elizabeth Freeman, *Time Binds: Queer Temporalities, Queer Histories* (Raleigh, NC: Duke University Press, 2010), p. xxii.

33 Rebecca Schneider, *Performing Remains* (London and New York: Routledge, 2011), pp. 36–7.

34 *Anne Boleyn*, p. 48.

35 Julie Kristeva, *Powers of Horror: An Essay on Abjection*, trans. Louis-Ferdinand Céline (New York: Columbia University Press, 1982), p. 2.

36 *Hunger* (Steve McQueen, 2008).

37 See particularly his *La Commune (Paris, 1871)* (2000), which employs *verité* realism while using discursive techniques, addresses to camera, and non-professional actors.

38 Interview with Steve McQueen in Maple Pictures' press release for *Hunger*, 2008, p. 3.

39 Matthew Brown, 'Cities Under Watch: Urban Northern Ireland in Film', *Éire–Ireland*, 45:1 (2010): 56–88 (p. 72).

40 'Dirt and Denigration: The Faecal Imagery and Rhetorics of Abuse', *Postcolonial Studies*, 5:2 (2002): 207–21 (p. 207).

41 Kristeva, *Powers of Horror*, p. 2.
42 Kristeva, *Powers of Horror*, p. 2.
43 Brown, 'Cities Under Watch', p. 73.
44 See Chris Yuill, 'The Body as Weapon: Bobby Sands and the Republican Hunger Strikes', *Sociological Research Online*, 12:2 (2007); available online at: www.socresonline.org.uk/12/2/yuill.html (accessed 1 July 2015).
45 Interview with Steve McQueen, p. 2.
46 Brown, 'Cities Under Watch', p. 72.

CONCLUSIONS

A final example of the complexity and the strangeness of fictive historiography is Terrence Malick's *The New World* (2005), his much discussed film about the Jamestown colony and, in particular, the figure known as Pocahontas.[1] The film is important in its address to something ineffable, its self-consciousness about historicizing, and the range of ways that it meditates upon how the past might be understood. It is this range that *Remaking History* has been interested in, arguing that historical fictions open up a multiplicity of ways of comprehending, analysing, illustrating, narrativizing, and understanding the past. Some of these ways – desire, pleasure – are decidedly outside rational, mainstream models of knowledge. Concomitantly, some are more recognizable but peculiar to their particular formal, generic, textual, and fictive contexts. *The New World* brings together something of each aspect that has been discussed throughout this book, but in an individual and complex way that demonstrates the diversity of popular historical fictions and their historiographic engagement. In part, developing another individualized reading of a text as a conclusion demonstrates the point of the book: each historical fiction contributes something very particular to the historiographic and historical imaginary, to historical sensibility, and, hence, a much more subtle and nuanced sense of their workings is necessary.

The New World sees the first contact between Europeans and Native Americans and the subsequent building of the Jamestown colony as both a moment of potential and of destruction. It is a strange, elusive film that attempts to render the experience of watching the past elliptical, odd, and other. It is concerned overtly with the strangeness of attempting to represent the past, and the aesthetic and ethical challenges inherent in that rendering. The Native Americans are used as a motif to suggest occluded knowledge, something unseen by rational European eyes. The film attempts, aesthetically, to make an audience aware that things and experiences and knowledges outside a rational Western taxonomy might exist.[2]

This is demonstrated in the actual first moment of contact, where Native Americans and Europeans alike are lost in a kind of wonder, outside comprehension for what is occurring. The moment is loaded with a kind of significance, but also childlike, suggesting a marvel that will soon be destroyed. John Smith writes in his diary, 'They are gentle, loving, faithful, lacking in all guile . . . the words to lie . . . have never been heard. There is no jealousy'. Although this is standard noble-savage language, familiar in early-modern caricaturing of the Native American (and the film's echoing of these problematic stereotypes has been much criticized), Malick is attempting to communicate something beyond understanding. Similarly, when Pocahontas visits England, she herself encounters a new world, and this othering of the centre is part of the film's attempts at rendering familiar discourses strange.

Malick's attempt at discovering a new visual language for the past is the key. The impetus is to take the narrative form of the movie and to make it somehow richer and stranger as a phenomenon. This is a challenge to the rationalizing, controlling effect of some period realism and mainstream historical discourse. This demythologizing is something that his work throughout his career has attempted, particularly in relation to tropes of heroism, historical exceptionalism, and the West.[3] In *The New World*, Malick continues 'a conversation or debate between what he suggests is the dominant Western worldview and a competing perspective'.[4] This is particularly demonstrated by the film's elliptical temporality, moving elegantly back and forth within sequences – but even in seemingly straightforward sequences, cutting strangely and with a clear disregard for linear narrative logic. Even the mainstream material narrative of film is seen to be a suspect way of rendering experience and, therefore, representing the past. The film's critique of colonialism and its mapping, disciplining, organizing function is contrasted (naïvely, in many ways) with the less rigid, hierarchical modes of knowledge of the Native Americans. Rigid, linear, authentic film-making is itself part of a rational, realistic discourse of control that ignores other ways of knowing and is complicit, therefore, in the imposition of a particular colonial outlook. Film itself is a system of knowledge that must be critiqued and interrogated, its strategies and approaches consciously undermined.

Furthermore, Malick's general concern with the feel of film – its emotive resonance rather than its narrative – ensures that *The New World* demonstrates how the affective, experiential nature of historical fiction is key to its historiographic effect. The film invites the gaze of the spectator, but never allows that gaze to be disciplinary. Instead, an audience is moved around by a constantly shifting camera and brought to some kind of rhapsodic awareness of the possibility of the other. There are strange cuts and an evident lack of dialogue. Sound and light are used to enrich the spectacle, but also to suggest the ineffable and uncontained. Malick creates a narrative about unseen, unfilmed events and suggests through them types of knowledge, experience, and understanding that are marginalized by realist practice.

The film, although in many ways romanticizing the past, is keenly self-conscious about the ways that culture proleptically figures the past in the present, and also how the events of the past might haunt a future as yet unknown. The film's final sequence has John Rolfe (Christian Bale), the later husband of Pocahontas, reading in voice-over a letter to his son about her death written at the time of the event (the son being alive but too young to understand). The scene suggests Rolfe's European desire to rationally textualize memorial experience. He strives to understand and control events, even when they are happening, something that is contrasted throughout the film with the types of knowledge the Native Americans possess (particularly, their memory related to things in the natural world). Over a montage of shots of the green landscapes of both England and New England (although, in England, nature is bounded in controlled gardens and fenced forests), Pochahontas's energy and happiness are emphasized. She dances and prays to the Earth, as the prelude to Wagner's *Das Rheingold* rises in the background (this latter famously a retroactive mythologizing of Europe, and particularly the river Rhine). The sequence is, hence, naturalistic and entirely wrought, rhapsodic and ritualistic, suggesting something ineffably beyond rationality and attempting to attain (aurally and visually) a kind of aesthetic spirituality. This is something that Malick has repeatedly approached in his films, particularly in *The Tree of Life* (2011) and *To The Wonder* (2012).[5] It is intensely meditative and intended to move the audience in ways previously unattempted by historical film. It is a vision of the sublimity of the past. Yet here, this spiritual aesthetic is complemented by the film's mode of historical enquiry. The ineffable here is a set of knowledges and practices that are traceable – the past – but elusive. Finally, the effect of the final sequence is intensely pleasurable. The music and the gorgeous cinematography attempt to move the viewer to something that is incomprehensible but intensely cinematic. The 'new' historiographical experience it strives for is built on enjoyment. Yet this enjoyment is built on establishing a new way of rendering the past formally, as Malick rejects linearity and formal straightforwardness.

Malick proffers a set of ideas about how a culture might think about the ways that it remembers, and the relationship between artistic production and this memorializing. In his example might be seen the ways in which fictions offer a critique and a development of 'History', as well as a way of thinking differently about the past and its manifestations in the present. Historical fictions offer flexibility about thinking regarding narrative, time, linearity, and order. They suggest that something is unknown, and attempts to 'know' it are to be treated with suspicion. They meditate upon the relationship between authenticity and accuracy as modes of representation. *The New World* combines the various elements that have been discussed throughout the chapters of *Remaking History*: ethics, politics, and nationalism (Part I); haunting, ghostliness, and the undead (Part II); and pleasure, affect, and performance (Part III). Its diegesis and narrative style discuss the ethics of representation and the politics of historicizing; it reflects upon the consequences for the historical imaginary of particular *nationalistic* originary moments; it demonstrates the way in which epistemology is constructed for particular purposes through narrative and imaginative elements; it dramatizes the relationship between the real and the 'factual'; it is self-conscious about storytelling; it discusses new ways of conceptualizing time and knowledge itself; it renders the ghostly Pocahontas as *haunting* the present in various interesting ways, and her actual presence after death in the film's last sequence is a moment of uncanniness that resonates strangely with the attempt at 'textual' archiving of her life; it is concerned with wonder and awe, both on the part of the audience, and also in relation to ways of knowing; it is intensely *pleasurable*, and this is part of its texture as much as its historiographical sensibility; it attempts to communicate emotion, *affect*, and strangeness as part of its purpose and way of *performing* the historical. As such, *The New World* is both exemplar and metonym for historical fictions insofar as they might be codified. However, it also demonstrates the strangeness, naïveté, incoherence, diversity, fragmentation, and possible conservatism of such texts. It is maddening and indefinable and odd and beautiful, and, as has been argued throughout, this constellation of qualities all contribute fundamentally to the ways in which it presents the past.

Remaking History has argued that popular texts do historical work through their representations of various pasts and the relation of the contemporary to them. In particular, the book has sought to state more firmly the case for studying historical fictions in their own right as constituent parts of a culture that comprehends the past in a complex way. As a consequence, the book has looked at a range of media to illustrate the central point, considering them all to be 'historical fictions' of some kind, or at least concerned with the impact of the past and the way it is told and conceptualized in the present. The texts under analysis here represent a diversity of sources with many different intended audiences. They provide both a contribution to the historical imaginary *and* a reading-back moment, an instantiation of the popular historiography of which they are a minor part. This might be conservative, and certainly some of the texts under consideration seem to want to close down interpretation, to ensure a particularity of identity. Yet, in the main, popular historical texts are interested in communicating the complexity of communication, representing the past in such a way as to allow an insight into the strangeness of what is called 'history'.

Notes

1   See, for instance, Roger Ebert's discussion of the 'visionary' Malick, 'The New World', *Chicago Sun-Times*, 19 January 2006; available online at www.rogerebert.com/reviews/the-new-world-2006 (accessed 2 December 2014); and the more hostile analysis ('As an epic, it's monumentally slight') by J. Hoberman, 'Mr. and Mrs. Smith', *Village Voice*, 13 December 2005; available online at: www.villagevoice.com/2005-12-13/film/mr-and-mrs-smith/ (accessed 2 December 2014).

2   This is common in the accounts of the story, as is demonstrated by the song 'Colors of the Wind' in the Disney film *Pocahontas* (Mike Gabriel and Eric Goldberg, 1995), which includes the refrain, 'You'll learn things you never knew you knew'.

3   See Martin Flanagan, '"Everything a Lie": The Critical and Commercial Reception of Terrence Malick's *The Thin Red Line*' in Hannah Patterson, ed., *The Cinema Of Terrence Malick: Poetic Visions* (London: Wallflower Press, 2012), pp. 123–36. See also Stephen Rybin, *Terrence Malick and the Thought of Film* (Lanham, MD: Lexington Books, 2012).

4   Jon Baskin, 'The Perspective of Terrence Malick', *The Point* (2010), 2; available online at: www.thepointmag.com/2010/film/the-perspective-of-terrence-malick (accessed 8 May 2014).
5   See, for instance, the discussion in S. Brent Plate, 'Visualizing the Cosmos: Terence Malick's *Tree of Life* and Other Visions of Life in the Universe', *Journal of the American Academy of Religion*, 80:2 (2012), 527–36.

INDEX